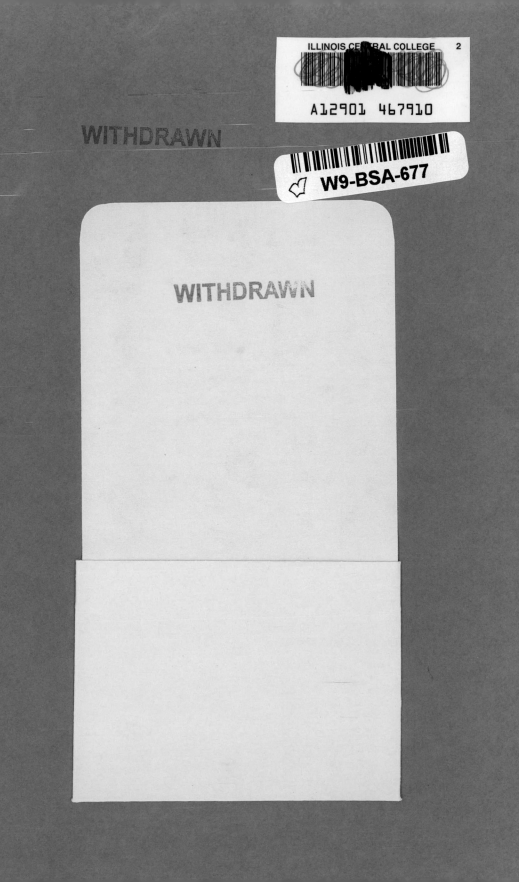

The GREAT BOOM

By the Same Author

The Pursuit of Wealth: The Incredible Story of Money Throughout the Ages
When Giants Stumble: Classic Business Blunders and How to Avoid Them
Coolidge: An American Enigma
Dangerous Dreamers: The Financial Innovators from Charles Merrill to Michael Milken
The New Game on Wall Street
RCA
Salomon Brothers 1910–1985
IBM vs. Japan: The Struggle for the Future
Car Wars: The Battle for Global Supremacy
The Rise and Fall of the Conglomerate Kings
ITT: The Management of Opportunity
IBM: Colossus in Transition
The Worldly Economists
The Last Bull Market: Wall Street in the 1960s
The Fallen Colossus: The Great Crash of the Penn Central
Inside Wall Street
The Manipulators: America in the Media Age
They Satisfy: The Cigarette in American Life
N.Y.S.E.: A History of the New York Stock Exchange
Herbert Hoover at the Onset of the Great Depression
The Entrepreneurs: Explorations Within the American Business Tradition
Money Manias: Eras of Great Speculation in American History
Machines and Morality: The 1850s
Amex: A History of the American Stock Exchange
The Age of Giant Corporations: A Microeconomic History of the United States
Conquest and Conscience: The 1840s
The Curbstone Brokers: Origins of the American Stock Exchange
Panic on Wall Street: A History of America's Financial Disasters
The Great Bull Market: Wall Street in the 1920s
The French Revolution
The American Revolution
The Big Board: A History of the New York Stock Market
The Origins of Interventionism

Co-Authored

The Quality of Earnings with Thornton O'Glove
The Entrepreneurs: The American Experience with David Sicilia
The Challenge of Freedom with Roger LaRous, Linda DeLeon, and Harry Morris
Our Changing World with Carl Oliver
The Auto Makers with Paul Sarnoff

The GREAT BOOM

1950–2000

HOW A GENERATION OF AMERICANS CREATED THE WORLD'S MOST PROSPEROUS SOCIETY

ROBERT SOBEL

TRUMAN TALLEY BOOKS
ST. MARTIN'S PRESS
NEW YORK

www.stmartins.com

Library of Congress Cataloging-in-Publication Data

Sobel, Robert
  The great boom, 1950–2000 : how a generation of Americans created the world's most prosperous society/by Robert Sobel.
      p. cm.
  Includes bibliographical references.
  ISBN 0-312-20890-1
    1. United States—Economic conditions—1945– 2. United States—Social conditions—1945– 3. Veterans—United States. I. Title.
  HC106.5 .S63 2000
  330.973'092—dc21

                                                                    00-025477

First Edition: July 2000

10 9 8 7 6 5 4 3 2 1

For Carole
With Love and Gratitude

CONTENTS

I do not mean that there is any lack of wealthy individuals in the United States; I know of no country, indeed, where the love of money has taken stronger hold on the affections of men and where a profounder contempt is expressed for the theory of the permanent equality of property. But wealth circulates with inconceivable rapidity and experience shows that it is rare to find two succeeding generations in the full enjoyment of it.

—Alexis de Tocqueville, 1835

Sixty years ago there were no great fortunes in America, few large fortunes, no poverty. Now there is some poverty (though only in a few places can it be called pauperism), many large fortunes, and a greater number of gigantic fortunes than any other country in the world. . . . One may surmise that the equality of material conditions, almost universal in the last century, still general sixty years ago, will more and more diminish by the growth of the very rich class at one end of the line, and of a very poor class at the other end.

—Lord James Bryce, 1894

Since the New Deal and the 1930s there has been a revolutionary development in the technology of industry and in the fiscal policy and social doctrine of governments. The assumption of reformers from Theodore Roosevelt through Woodrow Wilson to Franklin Roosevelt was that the poor could be raised up only by a redistribution of wealth. The basic assumption of the pre-war reformers is being dissolved. We have come into an era when the class struggle, as Marx described it a hundred years ago, has been overtaken by events.

—Walter Lippmann, 1964

The
GREAT
BOOM

PROLOGUE

The Great Boom opens by discussing how Americans came out of World War II with dreams, plans, and hopes, but few optimistic expectations. How did Americans who in 1945 imagined their futures might not be particularly bright come to accomplish so much during the ensuing fifty-plus years? Their children were able to build upon strong economic foundations, although some rejected their parents' goals; but in general, they too succeeded in realizing similar ambitions and, from their own experiences, learned not to attempt to dictate the scenarios for their children's lives. The grandchildren of the World War II GIs are now the junior managers and Internet entrepreneurs, and are starting to make headlines in the business and political press. They are not yet on the national scene—that is the role their parents still fill. After all, as these words are being written, George W. Bush, the son, not the grandson, of the former president, who is a World War II veteran, is being considered for the GOP presidential nomination. But their turns will arrive. And when they do come onto the national stage, their ambitions, goals, and styles are likely to differ from those of their parents. But not wholly.

It is important to remember that the world was not born *de novo* with the coming of peace in 1945; the GI generation had to make do with what they found when they returned home. Alterations in the social and economic fabric before and since took place, and there were many changes in their lives and the country. Often these arrived in unanticipated ways, and doubtless other changes will do so into the new millennium. The continuities in the lives of individuals and societies are as important as the shifts.

Americans did not enter a bright new world in 1945 or return to the tarnished one they recalled when World War II began, whether they dated back to the fighting in China in the 1930s, in Europe in 1939, or to the attack on Pearl Harbor on December 7, 1941. In many ways these new veterans and other survivors of the war retained the values that had proven useful during military service, while picking up where they left off when the war started to affect their lives. Nor did the shifts in their viewpoints and values that occurred in this period come to a discernable end decades later. The heritage of these people lives on in the influences they had on their offspring. So their legacy continues to affect all of us, as well as those to come.

The persistence of those experiences and the values they inculcated in the population became more obvious toward the end of the 1990s. The popularity of two recent World War II films, *Saving Private Ryan* and *The Thin Red Line*, the best-seller status of Tom Brokaw's *The Greatest Generation*, the revival of swing dancing, and re-enactments of World War II battles in various parts of the country, akin to those of Civil War encounters, indicate that this age continues to live in the imaginations of individuals born well after World War II had ended. And this has become even more evident in recent years, as President Clinton's impeachment "crisis" and the maxims that were drawn from it have become topics of wide national concern. Many have noted the differences between the moral tone of the Clinton presidency and most of those that preceded it.

For me, the planning, research, and writing of this book was a pilgrimage. *The Great Boom* is, in varying ways, an autobiographical work. I have vivid memories of the war and post–World War II period. I knew GIs who emerged from the war. I attended college with them, and shared their hopes, fears, and aspirations. Their children and grandchildren were in my classes at Hofstra University, and I have kept in touch with many of them over the years. I feel as though I know them very well indeed.

A few months after V-E Day, then a teenager playing stickball in the streets of the Bronx, I was approached by a young sailor on his way home. He had a duffel bag slung across his back and a wide smile on his face. That sailor—he seemed to be my age—beckoned. Would I do him a favor? Of course. We walked together to a nearby house, and he asked me to stand in front of the door and ring the bell. I did so, and in a minute a young woman appeared. She looked somewhat disappointed at seeing me. Clearly she had been expecting someone else. With this, the sailor popped out from behind a bush and the two of them grinned widely at one another, followed by the most angelic smiles I have ever seen. The sailor then thanked me and offered me a quarter, obviously to pay for the service I had performed. "I can't take anything from you," I blurted. I returned the coin and started to cry. From the look on his face I think he knew why. At least I hope he did. I owed him and millions of others like him so much. I have never lost that feeling. I walked away and went home. It was not the time for stickball.

One more story: In 1957, I was hired as an instructor at Hofstra College on Long Island, and my wife and I were ready to purchase a house. I insisted on looking at Levittown, and we bought what was advertised as a two-bedroom ranch home there for $10,500. We were the second owners. The people from whom we purchased the house had a GI mortgage, which we assumed; and the monthly payment, including taxes, came to less than $100. My wife and our parents were delighted. It was a good buy, they said. I felt the same, but for different reasons. We would be living in a house that had been occupied by a World War II veteran, and I would have an important connection with people to whom I and my generation owed so much.

As it happened, I was to remain at Hofstra until retirement forty-one years later, but in time we moved from Levittown. I occasionally drive past that house, to recall what it meant to me in the 1950s. Over this period I instructed former GIs and Korean War veterans (of whom I was one), followed by the baby boomers and then their children—three generations, from the 1950s to the end of the twentieth century. I have vivid memories of all of this, some of which have spilled over into the narrative you are about to read.

But despite such experiences, this is decidedly not a personal narrative, but rather what I hope is a serious and objective study of a protean period in the history of the United States and the world.

These words are being written at a time when the American economy has been performing well, the securities markets continue on to new highs on a regular basis, and the world marvels at the successes racked up by the American version of free-enterprise capitalism. The euro has now become the currency of much of continental Europe, but in real terms the dollar remains the preferred money for international dealings. Those fearing for their future squirrel dollars away, in the sure knowledge that while other currencies may decline in value, the dollar will always be accepted anywhere in the world. OPEC has long conducted its petroleum business in terms of dollars, and a wide band of countries have adopted currency boards, the closest thing possible to a dollar standard. At one time currencies were not trusted unless they were freely convertible into gold at a specific rate. Now the dollar fills the role once played by gold. And all this a half century after World War II and at the end of the first decade of victory in the Cold War.

Many Americans have benefited economically from the Great Boom. So has the nation as a whole. (For that matter, so has the world.) Problems remain today, but these are strikingly different from those of the immediate postwar period. Writing during the stock market boom of the late 1990s, *New York Times* reporter Peter Applebome noted that "until recently, true wealth for most Americans seemed as distant as Bombay." Applebome continued, writing that "almost half of American households now own stock either directly or through pension or retirement plans, compared to less than a third at the beginning of the decade and less than one in ten in the 1960s." Thus, Applebome indicates that his original comment was not quite accurate. But is this so? The effect of the bull market, he suggests, has made "millions wealthy and millions more think they should be." Even so, if we factor out homeownership, 2 out of 5 households have more debt than assets.

Author Robert Frank, in his *Luxury Fever* (1999), reports that half of the respondents to a questionnaire claimed to have savings of less than $3,000, and that another 40 percent thought it would be a "big problem" to pay an unexpected bill of $1,000. According to his calculations (the methodology and categorizations are not discussed in any meaningful detail), 1 out of 7 Americans falls into the category of "poverty." If this is actually so, how can one justify the theme of this book and the suggestions made by Applebome? This matter will be addressed in the pages that follow. The underlying thesis of this book, stated simply, is that few Americans of the mid-1940s expected to become wealthy enough to pay off the mortgage on a fairly modest home, take vacations overseas, send their offspring to private colleges, retire to a sunny spot in the South, or leave behind a meaningful financial package for their children and grandchildren.

What do those people see when they look back to that period and consider their accomplishments and those of the country? At the dawn of the new millennium, the American people face a central question born of the great boom of the postwar period: how to adjust to the fact that many have been quite successful economically and professionally over the past half century. This was due to their own innate qualities, their hard work, good fortune, and the nature of the economy. Others have not been so fortunate. Do the former owe a debt of any kind to the latter? Former Commerce Secretary Peter Peterson, in *Gray Dawn* (1999), and others have suggested that the wealthy should forgo government pension benefits since they really don't need them. Perhaps so economically, but the prospect of the government reneging on its contracts is not particularly pleasing. Also, why let it go at that? Why not confiscate private pensions, and private wealth? This is not about to happen, but this is where such thoughts logically lead.

The economically successful Americans have become accustomed to the reality that in a free society some will wind up ahead and others will fall behind. The price of success for the society as a whole may be the failure of some of its members. One response would be to ignore them, but that is not likely to happen given the American penchant for charity and philanthropy. Even so, this is a sensitive matter that sets off economic, social, racial, and generational conflicts.

Finally, it is not impossible to imagine that the problem may one day resolve itself, through the workings of the new Internet economy, alterations in value systems, demographic changes, and other, perhaps unimaginable, changes that await Western civilization in the years to come.

It has been a fascinating journey, from the end of World War II to the post–Cold War period, from the time when I was a high school student to my retirement from teaching and my granddaughters entering preschool. One can only imagine that the most interesting years are ahead.

Robert Sobel
May 1999

INTRODUCTION

All history can show no more portentous economic phenomenon than today's American market. It is colossal, soaking up half the world's steel and oil and three-fourths of its cars and appliances. The whole world fears it and is baffled by it. Let U.S. industry slip 5 percent, and waves of apprehension sweep through foreign chancelleries. Let U.S. consumer spending lag even half as much, and the most eminent economists anxiously read the omens. The whole world also marvels at and envies this market. It is enabling Americans to raise their standard of living every year while other countries have trouble in maintaining theirs. And of course the whole world wants to get in on it. For it still can punish the incompetent and inefficient, and still reward handsomely the skillful, efficient, and daring.

—Fortune, June 1953

In recent years, a great deal of attention has been paid to the disparity of incomes and wealth in the United States between the very rich and the abject poor. While some of the figures employed by the pundits are suspect, it would appear, from reading and observation, that a large gap between the economic winners and losers truly does exist. On the one hand, there is the class of Americans financially capable of enrolling their children in private schools, purchasing expensive automobiles, going on costly vacations, and investing in Internet stocks, while on the other are the homeless and others who are the failures in the race for economic security. There are insufficient estate planners who have the requisite credentials and records of success to satisfy the requirements of the wealthy, and there is a shortage of social workers who cater to the needs of the abjectly poor (and a lack of public funds to pay them). In between these extremes lies the majority of the population, which does not require the services of either social workers or estate planners.

As far as the man or woman in the street is concerned, there are many more wretchedly poor than financially comfortable Americans. They are seen on the streets of the cities, and they are the subjects of television specials. Politicians discuss programs geared to end the cycle of poverty, which is considered one of the most pressing problems facing the American people. But the experts are usually wrong in their estimates of just how many poor people exist in America, largely due to the matter of definition. They have an inflated impression because they assume all poor people are alike, and that all require assistance from government. We know about the homeless who gather at soup kitchens and who have attracted the attention of private and public institutions. The so-called working poor hadn't entered the public consciousness until fairly recently. What, if anything, should be done about them?

In recent years a body of opinion has appeared that holds that the persistence of poverty is partially a result of the well-meaning but misbegotten programs meant to alleviate poverty but that in effect actually do the opposite. In addition, there is the deeply felt conviction on the part of others that the poor have only themselves to blame for their circumstances, that if they would take advantage of opportunities offered by a friendly society and government, they could migrate into the middle class. As it is, their failure to do so is a source of regret and, more important, shame. As author Edward Luttwak suggests, "Living in a country that so greatly respects and admires high-earning winners, losers find it hard to preserve self-esteem."

Understandably, much less attention has been paid to wealthy Americans. How many of them are there? Start out by realizing that if one takes pension benefits and other income into account, there are many more than is imagined. A recent book by Thomas Stanley and William Danko, *The Millionaire Next Door* (1998), was a long-term best-seller. It was followed by Richard McKenzie and Dwight Lee's *Getting Rich in America: 8 Simple Rules for Building a Fortune and a Satisfying Life* (1999). The authors claim that one's background doesn't matter when it comes to amassing wealth, blithely saying, "In fact, it is relatively easy." The authors write, "Most people want to get rich so they can have a good life. But, if anything, things work the opposite. If you lead a good life—a responsible life—and put in productive effort, then you'll get rich." The methods are quite simple: study, work hard, be honest, forthright, faithful, and frugal. In addition, get and stay married and "resist temptation." The authors came up with some curious statistics. If at the age of eighteen a would-be millionaire cut back $1.50 per day on alcohol, soft drinks, and junk food, by the time he or she retired, the savings would amount to $290,363 (if the money were invested to return 8 percent over the years).

Perhaps this is the place to reiterate that most statistics of this nature, some of which will appear in this book, have to be taken with several grains of salt. But what about the observation by a *New York Times* reporter who in

December 1998 noted that "in 1998, 301 families bought houses in Westchester that cost $1 million or more. That's a 50 percent jump from 1997, and testimony to the American economy's capacity to churn out affluent people like so many assembly-line Cadillacs." For that $1 million, a broker noted, the buyer might expect a five-bedroom, three-bathroom, one-car-garage home in Bronxville on less than one-quarter of an acre, without a swimming pool. "If you want a mansion," she added, "you're looking at $2.5 million."

Who can afford such homes? "The recently enriched," was her reply. "The houses the new rich pine for are taken by the older rich. When one does become available, there are plenty of unabashedly young tycoons to put in bids, ratcheting up prices."

Who are those older rich? Often a husband and wife whose children fled the coop several years ago and who are now grandparents many times over. Where did their money come from? That million-dollar home might have set them back $125,000 in the late 1950s, and the down payment for it might have been obtained from the sale of a small tract house purchased ten years earlier, and savings from a job the husband obtained after graduating from college, which he attended by virtue of the GI Bill of Rights. With degree in hand, he found work or opened a professional practice, perhaps moved on to other jobs, saved when he could, and then invested part of his savings in the stock market.

Several scholars have claimed that the number of millionaires in America today, absent those pensions and other benefits, is in the neighborhood of 50,000 to 100,000. But in 1984 a Palo Alto investment firm, Thompson Tuckman Anderson, estimated that there were 15,280 millionaires living in the northern third of Silicon Valley alone. Apparently what that firm did was to calculate the value of the stocks and options owned by individuals who worked for the electronics firms in the area, and went on to note that "Silicon Valley represents the greatest concentration of new wealth in the United States." Probably true, but it is also the case that such individuals, had they attempted to sell their holdings and "go liquid," would realize less than that magic million-dollar level due to lack of liquidity and the bite of capital gains taxes.

In any case, the number must be much larger today, especially if one takes into account the value of education and training, which, in the nature of things, does not find its way onto balance sheets and into brokerage accounts. There must be many thousands of surgeons who already possess the training and professional relationships to earn close to a million dollars or so each year by plying their craft. The entrepreneur whose company issued stock in an initial public offering, which came out at $15 and within a couple of days was selling for $50, cannot judge his wealth by multiplying the number of shares he still owns by the current market price, yet this exercise is now performed regularly by financial journalists.

Students of such matters often present figures for wealth and incomes as though they are interchangeable. But the figures for wealth put together by government agencies and concocted by journalists are questionable. The reader might ask himself or herself how the government, or anyone else for that matter, knows how wealthy he or she is? And how does one tote up wealth? Placing a dollar value on salable skills, such as those of the surgeons, as has been noted, is quite difficult.

Income is another matter. In 1995 the Census Bureau estimated that 6.3 percent of the nation's families were in the $100,000-and-above bracket. Adjusting for inflation, this was approximately three times as many as there had been a quarter of a century ago. This does not mean, however, that the family remained the same as it was then. Indeed, 4 out of 5 of those families are comprised of multiple earners. Even so, the bureau disclosed that 2.4 million men and 300,000 women had received six-digit remuneration in 1995. These ranks include individuals not thought of as wealthy a generation or so ago. Managers of fast-food operations, airline pilots, and high school teachers about to retire fall into that category, along with the vast majority of doctors. Some 250,000 lawyers are in the $100,000-and-above category. Simply stated, $100,000 isn't what it used to be. Nor is $1 million. In 1994, more than 68,000 tax returns were for family units with more than $1 million in income.

There must be hundreds, perhaps thousands, of millionaires who are unaware of their status. They don't take the trouble to tote up their assets and subtract liabilities, to determine their net worth. One of these, a colleague of mine at Hofstra University, informed me a few years back that he intended to purchase an automobile, a used vehicle of course, since that had always been his style. When I replied that one as wealthy as he could certainly afford a new model, he protested. "I'm not wealthy," was his rejoinder. A few days later, after he had gathered all of his papers for my perusal, I demonstrated that, taking into account his forthcoming pension (to which he had been contributing for more than twenty years), along with the value of his home and investments, he was worth more than $1 million. He was both surprised and puzzled. "I had no idea," he said, "but I still lack the twenty thousand dollars or so in liquid assets to buy a new car for cash." There is one more factor to consider: My friend was a professor of economics. One must wonder what went on in his classes.

This book is written with that professor (now happily retired, driving a used Taurus) in mind. It begins with a study of Americans like him (perhaps his parents), who at the end of World War II expected to have lives of relative penury. Instead they became wealthy, wealthier in fact that any previous generation in history, and did so in an almost absentminded fashion. This was the generation, in the words of Franklin D. Roosevelt on taking office, that had "a rendezvous with destiny." Such was not what the President had in mind in 1933, of course, but that appointment was kept more than once; it is chronicled in the first few chapters of this book, and referred to throughout the subsequent chapters.

How did this come about? Those expecting to read here about the growth of the American economy in the past half century may be disappointed, although the subject is covered in an oblique fashion. Rather, I have chosen to concentrate on the entrepreneurial vehicles created and developed in this period that were employed in the creation of wealth for Americans whose horizons in the 1940s were quite limited. Later, some of them would apologize to their children and grandchildren about the kind of world they were leaving them. The litany they cite includes fears of atomic conflagrations followed by nuclear winters, environmental pollution, fallout shelters, racism, sexism, the Korean Conflict and Vietnam War, global warming, population growth, support of dictatorial regimes, insufficient health care, the devaluation of education, the list goes on, from people who apparently never tire of finding fault with what they have accomplished—and failed to achieve. Some members of that generation were surprised when in the 1960s they discovered that their progeny did not appreciate either their values or their accomplishments. In any case, this book represents an attempt to present the other side of the ledger.

Where did all of this wealth come from?

First of all, education. This was the best-educated generation in American history. More attended college than ever before, and did so at a time when college educations were far more rigorous than they are today. As one who has been involved with higher education, as student and professor, for more than half a century, I can attest to the verity that freshman courses of the 1950s were comparable to advanced ones today, and current freshman courses in such subjects as English and history are on the same level as high school courses of that earlier period. Nor is this conclusion based solely on my own experience, but rather on discussions with colleagues from all parts of the country, who teach or have taught in colleges ranging from the highly selective to those with virtually open admissions policies. The educations received by students in the 1950s and 1960s prepared them for a business and professional world in which they could succeed, and provided them with the analytical skills necessary to continue their educations long after they left the classrooms. This matter will be discussed in some detail later on.

Next in importance in creating their wealth was the investment that was at the time not perceived as such: their homes. Homeowning became more affordable during this period than ever before. Over time the purchasers came to look upon their homes as investments as well as abodes, but that derived from experience, not intent. At first they simply wanted affordable, decent homes, something many of them had not known before the war. Houses purchased for $12,000 in the early 1950s might have been sold for $120,000 or more two or three decades later. By the late 1990s, homeowners were being informed by realtors like the one in Westchester County or her counterpart in the Silicon Valley that the golden age had ended. One advertisement carried the baleful news: "For 1998 we can expect increases in home prices on the order of only 5 percent." Not bad for a couple purchasing a $150,000 home with a $110,000 mortgage, intending to remain there for a decade or more. Do the arithmetic and you'll see what I mean.

Those World War II veterans, armed with diplomas, found their places in an economy that was far more exuberant than they had been led to believe it would be. They soon became trainees at a time when the ailing corporations of the 1930s, energized during World War II and still converting from their wartime roles, had jobs to fill. In the 1950s, they would confront a teacher shortage in the burgeoning public schools, awash with babies born in the "Great Boom" of the late 1940s and early 1950s. So those who opted for teaching careers would enter the job market at the best time in history. The veterans and others in their cohort who attended graduate and professional schools, which soon would unleash waves of lawyers and doctors upon the nation, did so when demands for their services were high and remuneration excellent. Many became salesmen at a time when the consumer culture was making its mark, assisted along the way with credit cards. New industries were developing on a regular basis, and these required personnel. A goodly percentage of them came from the ranks of those veterans.

And a sizable number became involved with the securities markets. As recently as the late 1940s it appeared that most Americans intended to avoid investing in the stock market. Memories of the 1929 Crash and its aftermath did not die easily. Despite a now forgotten stock market boom in the 1933–1936 period, few Americans were drawn to stocks. The prosperity of wartime America had no impact on sales of securities. Nor did the failure of the nation to fall into a new depression after the war soften such attitudes.

By the early 1950s, however, the generalized prosperity could no longer be ignored, and the effects were felt in several ways. First of all, more middle-class Americans were becoming open to the idea of investments. Next, aware of the need for salesmen to service this new population, stock brokerage expanded, though in ways that would have astounded the brokers of the 1920s. Since a new generation of investors required a new approach, this was provided by such rising revolutionaries (a term not used lightly) as Charles Merrill at the brokerage firms and Keith Funston at the New York Stock Exchange.

As important as these "salesmen" were, in time another factor—mutual funds—would prove even more consequential. First came the "load funds" that were sold by armies of part-time salesmen who received commissions on each placement. Then the so-called no-load funds, offered by such companies as Fidelity, T. Rowe Price, Vanguard, Scudder, and others, became even more significant. Whatever their provenance, mutual funds emerged as compelling investment vehicles for a new generation prepared to enter the investment market. Thus, the new interest in securities affected several large groups of wealth-seekers: salesmen, analysts, managers, and traders at the funds and investment banks; investment bankers taking new companies to market as well as servicing the old ones to provide "product" for customers; the customers themselves; and a wide variety of support personnel.

At the same time, major changes were taking place in

the area of employee compensation. Onerous tax laws led company executives to seek remuneration that was "off the books." This included first-class expense-account treatment on business trips and the use of corporate assets such as vacation lodges and automobiles. More important were the granting of options to purchase corporate stock at preferred prices, retirement packages, employment buyouts, and other devices that imaginative accountants thought up in this period to attract and hold managements.

For their part, workers received their share of the pie in the form of retirement plans of their own, as the term coined in the 1950s by management consultant Peter Drucker, "pension plan socialism," took root in large and small companies alike. Through the vehicle of 401(k) plans, American workers were assured of comfortable if not lavish retirements, while self-employed workers might take out Keogh plans to accomplish similar objectives. The government made it possible for almost all to have individual retirement accounts (IRAs), which added to the mix. In 1945 the more prescient workers realized that Social Security checks would provide no more than a fraction of what would be needed for a comfortable life after retirement, and knew that they had to save for that stage of their lives. This awareness was the unspoken factor that motivated much of what Americans did in the way of wealth creation during the second half of the twentieth century.

Such was the case into the late 1960s, a period marked by political unrest related to the civil rights movement and the Vietnam War, but during which economic prosperity continued. Then, in 1973, the Organization of Petroleum Exporting Countries (OPEC) first started to raise the price of petroleum, then embargoed the United

States, and followed with further price increases. That set off a period of dislocation, which brought an end to some of the wealth-producing elements of the 1950s and 1960s, shook up the securities markets, and marked the beginning of the troubling era of "stagflation" (economic stagnation combined with high inflation). Americans who clung to the old ways of creating wealth suffered, but those capable of adjusting to the new dispensation profited greatly.

Two relatively small but significant groups did not overly concern themselves with the creation of wealth. One because of family inheritances, the other because their personal values did not place a premium on wealth. In the past, inherited wealth formed the bulk of the wealthy of the next generation. Such was not the case after World War II; many entrepreneurial newcomers were able to enter the ranks of the rich because the existence of new industries and buoyant real estate and securities markets now provided abundant opportunities.

The second group emerged out of what originally was known as the "New Left." Some became part of the "Beat Generation" and went through other incarnations in the 1960s and beyond. These dropouts dismissed America's "materialist culture," in favor of lifestyles that they considered more spiritual or communal.

As these words are being written, many pundits seem to believe that America—and perhaps the world—is on the edge of a social and economic change on the magnitude of the Industrial Revolution, involving electronics, computers, and telecommunications. Whether this is so or whether those sages are confusing a turn in the road with something entirely new remains to be seen. In any case, I have elected to treat this matter separately so the reader can trace the origins of electronics and computers, when both appeared at the very beginning of the post–World War II period and then seemed more like science fiction than the stirrings of a new society. The implications of these developments are considered toward the end of the book, as a prelude to a new way of living. The people involved are not entirely part of the "Great Boom" during which Americans finally cast off the doubts and fears inherited from the 1930s, but they do embody the shape of the new ways that have little reference to the old.

In July 1945, scientist Vannevar Bush, who had been instrumental in the creation of the atomic bomb, sent a long report to President Harry Truman urging him to plan for an aggressive governmental role in promoting scientific research after the war. "It has been basic United States policy that Government should foster the opening of new frontiers," said Bush. "It opened the seas to clipper ships and furnished land for pioneers. Although these frontiers have more or less disappeared, the frontier of science remains."

If the sages, including Bush, are correct in their analysis, the grandchildren of the servicemen and -women who had memories of massive unemployment, military service against the Germans and Japanese, and the dropping of the atomic bombs will create a new kind of civilization in which the past truly is a prelude, but perhaps nothing more than that, bearing as much relevance to the economy and possibilities of the twenty-first century as does the Homestead Act of more than a century ago to the present.

One final note: The path to success that existed half a century ago remains, but to it have been added other passages. Indeed, there are so many routes to wealth and success today that it is not possible to list them all. The securities markets, once ancillary to housing, represent one such route. Because of the successes of parents and grandparents, today's young people may one day inherit more than they realize. They very likely will live longer, and have more years to save and invest money—in their IRAs, Keoghs, and 401(k) plans, among others. Will their lives be better, or richer, or more satisfying? Who can measure such things? When I asked a World War II veteran about this, he spoke for a while about his grandchildren, whose lives were so much easier than his had been. And then he added, "I wouldn't trade my yesterdays for their tomorrows." After a moment, he smiled and said, "That isn't an original thought, you know. I read it somewhere." Original or not, I had no doubt of his sincerity. But it does provide something to ponder as you read about how a generation of enterprising Americans created and dealt with the "Great Boom" of the second half of the twentieth century.

1

COMING HOME:
A TIME OF DESPAIR AND HOPE

Turn from the war, to the postwar future. I think of the fearful men in the high places of economic power who are frightened at the thought of peace, and the cynical men who are starting to say that there is no right to full employment in any society. I think of the near certainty that our powerful industrial leaders will have learned nothing at the end of this war, and that like the fabulous lemmings of Norway they will march into the sea of economic chaos, moved as by some tropism to seek destruction; different, however, from the lemmings in that they carry with them the economic destiny of a whole people.

—Max Lerner, "The Human Condition: 1944," *PM*, August 1, 1944

One of the most articulate and popular journalists and academics of mid-twentieth-century America, Max Lerner was a passionate New Dealer who, when World War II broke out, was teaching at Williams College and writing articles for a wide variety of newspapers and magazines. Invited to become a columnist at the liberal New York newspaper *PM*, Lerner accepted the assignment, commenting on the war, home front, politics, and anything else that struck his fancy.

After the successful D-Day invasion of Europe on June 6, 1944, Lerner's thoughts turned to the peace that soon was to come. While welcoming the impending end of the war, Lerner was not optimistic at the prospect. The arithmetic of the situation was compelling. It indicated that the bad times of the late 1930s would soon return. Lerner wrote:

> Today there are some 65,000,000 Americans fighting and working—roughly 10,000,000 in the armed forces, roughly 55,000,000 in all forms of industry and agriculture. This compares with about 45,000,000 in 1939. The difference is 20,000,000. Take off 5,000,000 for the women who will not want jobs after the war and for a standing Army. That still leaves 15,000,000—a figure comparable with the unemployment at the depth of the depression.

The thought was neither new nor original.

Lerner's apprehensions echoed those of many New Dealers during the late 1930s, when talk of an end to federal programs that created jobs sparked rejoinders that discontinuing such a policy would return the country to the sorry state it had been in prior to the New Deal.

A Bleak Past and Bleaker Future

At the time there was a generalized lack of confidence in what passed for free enterprise, more particularly, in the economy's ability to right itself without programs inspired by intellectuals from New York and other centers of abstract thought, and then implemented by Washington bureaucrats. In advanced intellectual circles it was modish to believe that the country could be saved only by an American version of what once had been hailed as the "Mussolini Miracle" of Italy, before opinion turned against the Italian dictator following his alliance with Adolf Hitler.

This was understandable, given the severity of the Great Depression and the perceived successes of the New Deal, and to be anticipated, for during the 1930s the death knell for capitalism was being sounded throughout the world. In 1937 President Roosevelt spoke of a nation in which one-third of the population was ill-housed, ill-clad, and ill-nourished. The situation hadn't changed much at the time World War II erupted two years later, when the unemployment rate was more than 17 percent. According to the 1940 census, which calculated earnings on the basis of wages and salaries alone and excluded returns from investments, 70 percent of the American people fell into the Census Bureau's category of "earnings poverty."[1] In 1938 presidential adviser Adolf A. Berle, Jr.,

---

1. Defining poverty is a questionable pursuit. In 1986, economist Walter Heller thought the poverty rate in 1947 was "an estimated 33 percent," and it declined steadily, bottoming at 11 percent in 1973. But in 1990 several scholars determined that 40 percent of those classified as falling under the poverty lines owned their own homes (with mortgages) and automobiles (paying off the notes over time). Others noted that the homes of some of the recipients of government welfare checks were air-conditioned and equipped with swimming pools. In 1969 one of the government's "Great Society" programs planned to finance excursions to Europe for poor people, a project that was scuttled when some congressmen noted that the children of their constituents couldn't afford such vacations. They wanted to know whether it was right for those receiving government assistance to live better than middle-class taxpayers.

spoke of the "obvious financial and industrial crisis which is plainly indicated within the next few years." The following year another adviser, Harry Hopkins, said, "With twelve million unemployed we are socially bankrupt and politically unstable. This country cannot continue as a democracy with ten million or twelve million unemployed. It just can't be done." Then came the war and the end of unemployment, its replacement being widespread labor shortages. But the idea of capitalism's dead end had not died. Would those predictions come true once the war ended?

This is not to suggest—as it was later on—that the Roosevelt Administration welcomed entry into the war as a solution to the problems of unemployment and depression. Even so, the thought was not completely alien to some. At Princeton in 1936 a group of students organized what they called Veterans of Future Wars, which attempted to obtain a federal bonus of $1,000 for each of the 15 million Americans bound to serve during such a conflict. Lewis Gorin, Jr., a Princeton senior, its first national commander, later wrote *Prepaid Patriotism*, in which he said that the bonus should be paid before the World War veterans squeezed the country dry with their demands for bonuses. The movement gathered tens of thousands of members on campuses throughout the country, and soon there was an auxiliary organization, the Association of Future Gold Star Mothers, which demanded government-paid trips to Europe during the next war so they could visit the graves of their sons who would die in combat. Another student organization, Future Profiteers, demanded advances on war contracts. It was a short-lived movement, however, falling apart with the arrival of the 1936 presidential election. It should be noted that most members eventually did serve in the armed forces during World War II.[2]

There were other reasons to expect bad times ahead, and not only for the short run. Demography seemed to dictate decline. In a 1943 article dealing with postwar expectations, the editors of *Fortune* stated that "unless the economic, social, and cultural structure of the nation undergoes great postwar changes, the birth rate will recommence its downhill trend," which had begun in the nineteenth century and continued, with interruptions, into the 1930s. A 1938 poll indicated that 79 percent of American women were in favor of birth control, with 3 out of 4 giving the reason as "family income," or, to be more precise, the lack of same. The *Fortune* writer concluded that the American impulse to limit births, which would become permanent, would add to economic problems:

> It has always been assumed in this country that an increasing population was not only normal but desirable. Now that the U.S. is faced with the leveling off of the population and the possibility of numerical decline, we must look ahead to the social, political, and economic effects implicit in those changes, and try to decide how to meet them. If the population should become stationary, capital investments, industry, and business could no longer be founded on numerical growth: they would have to be based on conservation and improvement rather than expansion, on quality rather than quantity. A stationery population or a somewhat smaller population would not neces-

2. "Lewis J. Gorin Jr., Instigator of a 1930s Craze, Dies at 84," *The New York Times*, January 31, 1999.

sarily be dangerous to the country's economic and social life so long as we took cognizance of it and adjusted our life to it.

The writer suggested that because of the expected population decline, it would become necessary for aged workers to remain on the job longer than anticipated. Ewen Clague of the Social Security Board recommended retraining working men and women at around the age of forty-five for jobs they might hold in their old age. *Fortune* concluded that by 1980 more than half of American voters would be more than forty-five years old, and would demand additional benefits from Social Security, and perhaps even government-provided medical care. How could the anticipated stagnant postwar economy deal with such matters?

Max Lerner and *Fortune* were not alone in their forebodings. University of New Mexico president J. Philip Wernette, who had been trained in economics, predicted:

Immediately after the war there will be a brief restocking period, when business and employment will be fairly good. When the restocking stimulus has spent its force, however, the outlook for the decades ahead is for continuous, chronic world depression, broken by occasional periods of severe depression. That is what we may expect, unless something is done to prevent it.

Alvin Hansen, a leading Keynesian economist, was troubled by the same forces he perceived in the economy and society as a whole. In his popular book *After the War, Full Employment* (1943), Hanson argued:

When the war is over, the Government cannot just disband the Army, close down munitions factories, stop building ships, and remove all economic controls. We want an orderly program of demobilization and reconstruction. The government cannot escape responsibility.

Paul Samuelson, soon to become the country's best-known academic economist by virtue of his highly popular textbook, agreed, predicting a major depression unless the government acted to stimulate the economy, and other experts took up the cry. As with Lerner, Samuelson's reasoning was based on experiences following the end of World War I and then the coming of the Great Depression:

The final conclusion to be drawn from our experience at the end of the last war is inescapable. Were the war to end suddenly within the next six months, were we again planlessly to wind up our war effort in the greatest haste, to demobilize our armed forces, to liquidate price controls, to shift from astronomical deficits to even the larger deficits of the thirties—then there would be ushered in the greatest period of unemployment and industrial dislocation which any economy has ever faced.

The war was over within two years, not six months. The transition to a peacetime economy was both swift and chaotic; even before the Japanese surrendered, a large number of consumer items were freed from the price controls imposed during the war, and Washington canceled many contracts for ordnance, including 30 percent of those for aircraft. In mid-1945, with the war over, meat, butter, and tire rationing ended and additional products were freed from War Production Board controls. The armed forces were soon demobilized. On V-J Day there were more than 12 million men and women on active duty. Two years later, the number had been reduced to 1.5 million. Within the defense-oriented sectors of the economy, the job loss was 2.6 million. The GNP declined by 1.6 percent from 1945 to 1946. The government conducted the largest surplus property sale in history, as factories were disposed of at 20 percent of cost.

Economic decline was the gospel during the immediate postwar period. It even found its way into the college textbooks. One of the most popular of the time, *An American History* (1950) by the noted historians Merle Curti, Richard Shryock, Thomas Cochran, and Fred Harrington, informed freshman American history students that major economic problems were occurring as the servicemen were being discharged:

> Even at home, all was not well. Prosperity appeared to depend in substantial part on exports for which foreign countries could not pay; and on an armament program which increased an already staggering tax burden. The individualism and the opportunity of an earlier America seemed to have faded; and some felt that the United States had suddenly grown old. Predictions of disaster were common, and despair became fashionable in intellectual circles. No longer did Americans speak of the inevitability of progress. Rather they talked of a confused and uncertain future.

Almost half a century later, former *Economist* analyst and Englishman-turned-American Michael Elliot wrote what by then had become the standard view of the situation at the end of the war.

> When the war in Europe started in 1939, America was struggling, battered and bruised, from an economic recession that was far deeper and more wounding than anything known in Europe. . . . At the end of World War II, by contrast, America bestrode the narrow world like a colossus. Its military machine, enjoying scientific and technological advances far beyond those available to any other fighting men, had won two wars, each a wide ocean away from home. On the twin rocks of its economic and military might, America then built a society which was the envy of the world— a society in which ordinary working people could enjoy a standard of living, with spacious homes and modern appliances, beyond the dreams of those in other nations. The outside world was kept at bay, like children pressing their noses to the panes of a party to which they have not been invited.

How could those seers at the end of World War II have been so wrong? Put it down to the mindset developed during the Great Depression and sustained throughout the war. How could they have failed to perceive the strengths the nation possessed, such as the activities of the returned veterans, a key element in the prosperity that would mark the scene in post–World War America?

The arithmetic that led the pundits to anticipate a depression was compelling and convincing. Absent massive federal public-works programs larger than anything attempted in the 1930s, the United States would sink back into depression. Samuelson was convinced that "peace-time prosperity could be assured only if the slack left by business investment and expenditures could be taken up by government expenditures."

Before the war, Samuelson had been an ardent New Dealer, and his highly successful textbook reflected his beliefs in the wisdom of government intervention in the economy. Later, in the 1960s, he would argue for a major government role even when all was going well with the private sector. Not so historian Richard Hofstadter, generally categorized as a moderate who, unlike Samuelson, did not offer prescriptions for reform or play a political role. Writing in *The American Political Tradition and the Men Who Made It* (1948), which like Samuelson's economics textbook became a best-seller in the late 1940s and afterwards, Hofstadter started by stating, "Since Americans have recently found it more comfortable to see where they have been than to think of where they are going, their state of mind had become increasingly passive and speculative."

Hofstadter also wrote:

An awareness of history is always a part of any culturally alert national life; but I believe that what underlies this overpowering nostalgia of the past fifteen years is a feeling of insecurity. The two world wars, unstable booms, and the abysmal depression of our time have profoundly shaken national confidence in the future. During the boom of the twenties it was commonly taken for granted that the happy days could run on into an indefinite future; today there are few who do not assume just as surely the coming of another severe economic slump. If the future seems dark, the past by contrast looks rosier than ever.

Academics and government officials were not alone in believing the end of the war would usher in a new depression. Scores of perfectly respectable and intelligent businessmen agreed. Perhaps the most visible of these was Sewell Avery, the CEO of Montgomery Ward, one of the nation's leading retailers.

In his 1945 message to shareholders, Avery predicted hard times ahead, for which Montgomery Ward was well prepared. Avery's beliefs were not derived from the sources referred to by Samuelson and government economists. Rather, they came from the writings of Geoffrey Moore, an eccentric business-cycle theorist, who noted similarities between credit growth in the 1920s and what was happening in the immediate post–World War II period, leading him to conclude that a bust was in the making. In addition, Avery kept charts and statistics on his desk going back to the Napoleonic Wars, prepared to show and explain them to any and all. After doing so, he would invariably ask, "Who am I to argue with history?" As a result, Montgomery Ward did not expand in the late 1940s and early 1950s, while arch rival Sears Roebuck purchased land in suburbs throughout the country and erected department stores that helped destroy Avery and his company.

Avery might have had better fortune in defending his position by observing that Congress seemed to agree with him. By large majorities in both houses, a rather conservative Congress passed the Employment Act of 1946.

Originally it was called the Full Employment Act of 1946 but in its final form the "Full" was dropped, because Congress was fearful of defining "full employment." This was to be a typical compromise bill. The old New Dealers were interested in full employment, but also in eliminating poverty in America. The thought at the time was that if unemployment could be ended it would dispose of the issue, since a person who was employed was, by definition, not poor. The legislation declared:

> It is the continuing policy and responsibility of the Federal Government to use all practicable means . . . to coordinate and utilize all its plans, functions, and resources for the purpose of creating and maintaining, in a manner calculated to foster and promote free competitive enterprise and the general welfare, conditions under which there will be afforded useful employment opportunities . . . and to promote maximum employment, production, and purchasing power.

Leon Keyserling, a member of the Council of Economic Advisers created under the terms of the act, addressed the issue in 1947, in an article titled "Must We Have Another Depression?" His answer, almost two years after the war had ended and when the nation's major macroeconomic problem was inflation and not depression, was not particularly encouraging: "While all economists do not agree as to the causes of the last depression, a listing of the causal factors generally agreed upon indicates that many of these factors are again present now or will be present within a few years." He went on to list some of them:

The tendency of our productive capacity to out-run our mass buying power, the chronic weakness of such bellwether industries as residential construction, the seeming reluctance of capital investment to expand as dynamically as once it did, the uncertain elements in foreign trade, the enormous disparities in the price and wage structure, and huge differentials in the price of the enjoyment of national income by regions and individuals.

So it was that a virtual army of analysts, both governmental and private, from all parts of the political spectrum, believed there would be a conversion effort similar to that which followed World War I, which is to say that, absent military threats, the United States would return to the essentially peacetime, non-military economy it enjoyed during the 1920s, and that the economic results would be disastrous. But there was no such conversion, as the depression-scenario analysis was dashed by events on the foreign landscape.

America: 1945

What kind of a country did those veterans find when they got off the troop ships and returned home? For one thing, it was shabbier than when they left. Maintenance of private property had been neglected for a decade and a half. There was little in the way of new clothing in the stores. Some foodstuffs were still rationed, as was gasoline. Tires were recapped, often several times. If the veterans looked closely at women's legs, which of course they did, the newly discharged servicemen might have realized that the look of what appeared to be stockings had been achieved though the application of cosmetics.

The city centers were still there, where one might shop in department stores, and towns and villages had centers as well, often with a "Main Street." There one might find "first-run movie houses," where a single film was showing. In the neighborhoods were second- and third-run movie houses, with double features, an "A" and a "B" film, which changed weekly. Depending on the neighborhood where one lived, the moviegoer who did not venture far might have seen a steady diet of Warner Brothers, Metro-Goldwyn-Mayer, Twentieth Century–Fox, or Paramount films, since the chains had affiliations with the major studios. In 1945, 85 million Americans went to the movies each week, approximately 2 out of every 3 adults and children.

Radio was even more important to that generation. Practically every home had a receiver, since this was the most inexpensive form of entertainment and information. Few homes had more than one, however. The radio was placed in the living room, and the family gathered in the evenings to listen. Later on, when television made its appearance, the running joke was, "What did we look at [when listening to the radio]?" The answer was, "The radio." There were three major networks, two owned by RCA's National Broadcasting Corporation, and the other by the Columbia Broadcasting System, as well as several regional networks and many independent stations. Some isolated areas could receive few stations, but in the cities more than a dozen were available.

Radio and motion-picture fare was decidedly opti-mistic. The heroes always won in the end, while the villains suffered defeat. If there was extramarital sex, the perpetrators would be punished for their actions. This was the way it had to be, since motion pictures operated under a code of conduct, and radio was licensed by the government. The upbeat messages were what audiences of the time had come to expect.

Most theaters were not air-conditioned (as distinguished from air-cooled) in the summers. Neither were the homes. In tenements, sleeping on fire escapes was widespread, and on hot summer nights urbanites would escape to the parks, or to air-cooled movie houses, equipped with large fans placed on the stage. Nor did the automobiles of this period come equipped with air-conditioning.

The serviceman heading home with his duffel over his shoulder would have seen boys and girls dressed informally, but not the adults. Just about every male who was not a day laborer wore a jacket, tie, and hat, while women wore dresses or suits. Slacks were permitted for women working in factories, but not in offices. To appear in public not wearing the correct clothing would have seemed improper, even disrespectful. If the serviceman was going to a middle-class apartment house, he would find the elevator there operated by a uniformed man or woman.

Mail arrived twice daily. Telephone calls were made with rotary dials, and long-distance calls involved making contacts with three systems, were expensive, and so were rare. One was struck with fear when told by an operator, after the phone rang, to hold on for a long-distance call. It had to be bad news. Likewise, the appearance on a residential street of a Western Union delivery boy on a bicycle could only mean someone had died. The boy's bicycle might have been driven past the milkman making his rounds on his horse-drawn wagon. Sights such as these were seen well into the automobile age, and were there when the Allies defeated the Axis powers in the war.

Children played games in the streets, but grown men rarely indulged in sports. Tennis and golf were for the wealthy. Fathers of children might watch them play, but generally would not do so themselves.

One didn't think too much about calories when it came to food and drink. Middle-class Americans ate a lot of pasta. Macaroni and cheese, canned soups, canned tuna fish, and other inexpensive foods were regular fare, as were hot dogs and peanut-butter-and-jelly sandwiches on white bread. Meat for those making $2,000 or so a year meant hamburger and liver. Americans ate more starchy foods and drank more sugared soft drinks in 1945 than they would toward the end of the century. Americans of that period smoked many more cigarettes—when they could get them—and preferred the standards: Camel, Lucky Strike, and Chesterfield. The men drank beer, most of which had been brewed locally, and every city of any size had at least one brewery, while some, like New York, had more than a dozen. National brands were in the future. With all of this, Americans went less often to doctors. The reason was not that they were healthier, but rather that in an era before near-universal health insurance, doctors were almost a luxury.[3]

3. This was changing. During World War II the War Labor Board held down wage increases. Employers hoping to attract workers offered fringe benefits, which were not restricted, and among these was health insurance. By 1945 the hospital admissions rate was 120 per 1,000 of the population, more than twice what it had been in 1939. These plans expanded rapidly after the war. By 1948 $10 billion was spent on health services and supplies, or $68 per capita, more than twice the expenditures in the pre-Depression year of 1929. By 1960, 80 percent of all workers were covered by employer-supplied health plans. Such coverage, often not taken into account, was a major contributor to the growing wealth of the American people.

If the new civilians attended Major League baseball games—the sport had continued during the war—they would see teams stocked by players who were underage, overage, or rejected for physical reasons by the armed services, along with a few who had night jobs at defense plants. They also would cheer players who lived in the cities for which they played and had off-season jobs there to make ends meet. The uniforms would be made of a heavy flannel-like cloth, and were quite baggy. Male tennis players performed in white flannel slacks and sports shirts. Women players wore dresses. Tennis was not a particularly popular sport, except among the well-to-do. Likewise golf, although middle-class executives were filtering into the sport, and many public links were created during the Depression.

College basketball existed, but it was not as popular as baseball. The players were almost all white, anyone taller than six feet stood out, and there were two styles of play. Midwestern basketball was deliberate, with pattern plays. The New York games featured the fast break, developed at City College of New York. Grantland Rice, the dean of sportswriters, thought the fast break appeared there because so many Jews were on the CCNY team, and they were a sneaky lot. One could say and write such things during this period. Games often ended with scores of 20–18 and the like. A big scorer was one who had "double digits." College football was very popular, and so was the professional game. Those players, too, were white. Black players might appear on all-black college teams. A few made their way to non-black college teams, but not many. This would soon change.

When they attended those games, many of the veterans who had white-collar jobs would do so in suits, ties, and hats—even in hot weather. This was a uniform that distinguished them from blue-collar workers. In the immediate postwar period, after wages and prices were decontrolled, the gap between white- and blue-collar workers diminished even more than it had in the 1920s and 1930s, but the distinction remained. The family breadwinner of 1946 might wear his jacket at the dinner table, but increasingly it was removed, though the tie might remain in place. In this respect, as in many others, the mores and folkways of prewar America continued on into the postwar period. But again, not for long.

Postwar Images

As noted, those who feared a new depression started out by assuming that the economy would return to what it had been prior to the increase in arms procurement that began in 1938. But such was not to be. Although the GNP did dip slightly in 1946 and the nation underwent its worst wave of strikes in history, followed by an inflationary spiral as wartime controls were ended or eased, pent-up consumer demand was satisfied easily, so production increased, and the GNP rose to $231 billion in 1947 and $258 billion in the following year. There followed a minor recession in 1949—the GNP came in at $257 billion—but soon economic growth resumed. This was due to a combination of factors, one of the more important being government spending, the chief ingredient that those who had predicted bad times had said was necessary to avoid a return to the prewar economy. As it happened, government spending, direct and indirect, would remain an important factor in economic performance—and in the continuation of the boom—from then on to the present, and probably for the future as well.

A good part of this spending helped in the recovery of Europe and Asia. In 1946, the State Department turned over more than $8 billion in American property to the newly reconstituted nations of Europe for relief and reconstruction. The following year, Secretary of State George Marshall announced a plan for the rehabilitation of Europe, which between 1948 and 1951 contributed more than $13 billion in American economic aid to the continent. Such grants not only stimulated Europe's growth but also provided that much, and more, in contracts for American firms. Outlining his plan at Harvard in June 1947, Marshall said:

> The truth of the matter is that Europe's requirements for the next three to four years of foreign food and other essential products—principally from America—are so much greater than her present ability to pay that she must have substantially additional help or face economic, social, and political deterioration of a very grave nature. Our policy is not directed against any country or doctrine but against hunger, poverty, desperation, and chaos. Its purpose should be the revival of a working economy in the world so as to permit the emergence of political and social conditions in which free institutions can exist.

The coming of the Cold War, following on the heels of the Marshall Plan and other aid programs, both economic and military, threw all of the pessimistic assumptions of Galbraith, Keyserling, and others into a tailspin. By the mid-1960s, 1 out of every 8 workers was employed by federal, state, or local governments, and their purchases accounted for more than 20 percent of the GNP. Government agencies expended $170 billion in 1963, and the rate was rising. By 1966, governments were spending more than $1,000 per annum for every man, woman, and child in America.

Some government programs, such as interstate highway building, which added to the major new construction of the middle 1950s, were geared not only toward economic betterment, but also were aimed at compensating for the job loss. In 1946, Congress passed the Federal Highway Act, which authorized the expenditure of $1.5 billion over a three-year period on interstate highways, while at the same time the states proceeded on their own to develop toll superhighways. During the 1950s, President Dwight D. Eisenhower was a strong proponent of the interstate system. With his encouragement, Congress authorized construction in 1956 of a 41,000-mile controlled-access superhighway system to link all cities with populations of more than 50,000, to be constructed over a thirteen-to-sixteen-year period, at a cost of $41 billion. In addition, Eisenhower asked for and received appropriations for the St. Lawrence Seaway, which would open the Great Lakes to the Atlantic Ocean much of the year. At the same time, however, Eisenhower insisted on balanced budgets, and even surpluses, to repay the national debt. In 1944, the last full year of the war, the national debt came to $218 billion, and expenditures to $110 billion. In 1948, when it seemed some semblance of prewar normalcy might be restored, the debt was $271 billion, and expenditures $55 billion.

Cold War spending was such that Eisenhower could not slash the debt, which in 1959—his last full year in office—reached $349 billion, while expenditures that year were $135 billion. So while the kinds of New Deal programs that appeared to be bringing America out of the prewar depression were not renewed, the government role in the economy was firmly in place. The Great Depression would not have a second act. Nor would the New Deal. Free enterprise was not dead, or even somnolent. Rather, it was to appear in a somewhat different form that few anticipated or predicted. The old New Deal coalition had enough vitality remaining to permit a virtually unknown Democratic nominee in the 1952 presidential election, Governor Adlai Stevenson of Illinois, to win 27 million votes against Dwight Eisenhower's 34 million. That Stevenson fared as well as he did against the preeminent hero of his generation was a tribute to the Roosevelt-Truman heritage. Eisenhower, however, proved extraordinarily popular. After winning a second term in a landslide (35.5 million popular votes against Stevenson's 26 million), Eisenhower was lauded by labor leader George Meany. "American labor has never had it so good," he said. "Everything is booming but the guns."

From 1947 to 1950, defense spending averaged approximately 5 percent of GNP and more than one-third of federal spending. At the height of the Cold War, in the late 1950s and early 1960s, military expenditures accounted for approximately 10 percent of the nation's gross domestic product, reaching 14 percent in 1953, the last year of the Korean Conflict. This made defense, in its totality, the nation's largest industry. Between 1946 and 1967, the government spent more than $1 trillion on military procurement alone. By the 1950s, sales of ordnance to foreign countries became an important component of the economy. If the pursuit of wealth led many companies into the burgeoning civilian market, it caused others to seek profits from the sale of war-related materials. The

American economy was not based as much on military and related spending as were some of the nation's companies dependent on it for their well-being. In the process, as might have been expected, companies and the individuals who worked for them prospered—as did shareholders, suppliers, and a host of others.

In addition, there were complications resulting from the conversion effort that came with the arrival of peace in 1945. Most of the ordnance suppliers that had prospered during the war halted their conversion efforts and accepted lavish military contracts. The situation in aviation was dramatic. With the end of hostilities, more than $21 billion in contracts were canceled, and factories that produced warplanes soon converted to civilian uses. The sixty-six plants devoted to aviation were down to sixteen by 1947. The giant Willow Run facility, erected by Ford with government aid to produce B-24 bombers, was sold to Kaiser-Fraiser, which used it to manufacture automobiles. In 1947 the total American expenditure for warplanes and supplies came to $1.2 billion.

The importance of military spending was not lost on the nation's political leaders, who were concerned about its impact, both economically and politically. In his farewell address to the nation on January 17, 1960, President Eisenhower warned against the powerful nexus that had grown among the leaders of the armed forces, the war production–oriented corporations, and the nation's universities:

> Until the latest of our world conflicts, the United States had no armament industry. American makers of plowshares could, with time and as required, make swords as well. But we can no longer risk emergency improvisation of national

defense; we have been compelled to create a permanent armaments industry of vast proportions. Added to this, 3½ million men and women are directly engaged in the Defense Establishment. We annually spend on military security more than the net income of all United States corporations.

The conjunction of an immense military establishment and a large arms industry is new in the American experience. The total influence— economic, political, and even spiritual—is felt in every city, every State house, every office of the Federal government. We recognize the imperative need for this development. Yet we must not fail to comprehend its grave implications. Our toil, resources, and livelihood are all involved; so is the very structure of our society.

In the councils of government, we must guard against the acquisition of unwarranted influence, whether sought or unsought, by the military-industrial complex. The potential for the disastrous rise of misplaced power exists and will persist. We must never let the weight of this combination endanger our liberties or democratic processes. We should take nothing for granted. . . . Akin to, and largely responsible for, the sweeping changes in our industrial-military posture has been the technological revolution during recent decades. . . . The prospect of domination of the nation's scholars by Federal employment, project allocations, and the power of money is ever present—and is gravely to be regarded. Yet, in holding scientific research and discovery in respect, as we should, we must also

be alert to the equal and opposite danger that
public policy could itself become the captive of a
scientific-technological elite.

State and local governments were aware of the significance of government spending. When the time came for
the Defense Department to award contracts for the TAX
airplane in the early 1960s, the Kansas and Washington
delegations to Congress supported Boeing, whose major
plants were in Wichita and Seattle, while California and
Texas lobbied for General Dynamics, and New York for
Grumman.

Many veterans of the European and Pacific conflict
wound up working for General Dynamics, Lockheed,
Boeing, and other suppliers of military ordnance. The
enlisted personnel worked on assembly lines and in
offices, while high-ranking officers headed to the executive suites, or to Washington, where they were employed
as lobbyists. As of 1969, more than 2,000 retired military
officers with the rank of colonel or navy captain were
employed by the top 100 military contractors. Lockheed,
which led the pack, had 210 of them, while Boeing
(169), McDonnell Douglas (141), General Dynamics
(113), and North American Rockwell (104) followed.
Some ran for public office, and, indeed, a military record
was practically a requirement for those seeking seats in
Congress.

Other veterans found employment at General Electric, Chrysler, and companies thought of as being devoted
to civilian goods, but which also received military contracts. This was the time when computers were introduced to the business public—and to the military. To all of
this was later added the space programs, which made
additional companies, many of them small and highly

dependent on technology, prosperous. This spending had repercussions in the civilian sector as "throw-offs," ranging from airliners to digital dialing, became more common. The public's attention was fixed on the civilian sector, but the economy was more complex than that, as returning servicemen quickly learned.

Partly as a consequence of military spending, the inflation of the period derived from shortages of supply, not lack of demand. Capital investment was rising, not falling, as a result of the reconversion efforts and the need for new facilities to provide peacetime goods not only for the domestic market, but for European and Asian allies as well. Business expenditures on new plants and equipment for 1947 would come to $19.3 billion, more than 20 percent higher than the previous year, and would rise to $21.3 billion in 1948. Exports, propelled by the Marshall Plan, were booming. That year the United States exported $14.7 billion worth of merchandise and imported $7.9 billion, against the 1946 figures of $10 billion and $5.5 billion, respectively. Freed from wartime constraints, wages were rising, and all sections of the country were improving economically.

All of which underlines why so many eminent and influential economists who had predicted bad times after the war turned out to be so wrong. Even when it was quite apparent that the good times would continue, pessimistic talk did not abate. United Automobile Workers president Walter Reuther spoke of his doubts. When the economy started to slip in 1949 in what proved a minor correction, Reuther said, "Nineteen hundred and twenty-nine can happen again in nineteen forty-nine." Liberal senator James Murray (a Democrat from Montana) joined with conservative representative Wright Pattman (a Democrat from Texas) to introduce a measure providing for government aid to depressed areas. These men and others continued to misread the signs and ignored the more positive aspects of the economy at this time.

The GI of Bill of Rights and Its Unanticipated Impact

On June 22, 1944, President Roosevelt signed into law the Servicemen's Readjustment Act, more commonly called the GI Bill of Rights. Today the measure is best known for its educational provisions. All veterans who were not over the age of twenty-five when inducted were provided with at least one year of education, with additional time based on service. The government paid for tuition, fees, and supplies, as well as a monthly stipend of $50 for a single veteran and $75 for a married one. These arrangements were liberalized under the Truman Administration, especially after General Omar Bradley became head of the Veterans Administration in 1945.

Strange though it may seem today, the large veterans' organizations, such as the American Legion, were not especially interested in the educational provisions of the act. They were ready to bargain these away for job guarantees, additional insurance, and apprenticeship programs. President Truman was not particularly wedded to the schooling arrangements, and wanted to know whether it would be possible to have some form of federal job program, such as the New Deal's Civilian Conservation Corps, should the country fall back into a depression. Of paramount importance was a provision guaranteeing the veteran his old job back within ninety days of his discharge. The American Legion, noting that the government intended to provide veterans who could not find work with $20 a week for 52 weeks—the so-called 52–20 Club—was prepared to barter the educational provisions for another year of unemployment relief.

Few books of the time written as guides for returning veterans and their relatives went into education in much detail. One of the more influential of these suggested that the veteran "will be interested only in education to help him vocationally, preferring mechanical, business, or mathematical subjects; will want to go into a trade, technical occupation or business. . . . Any government program for his benefit must roughly be based upon this norm, with enough flexibility to meet the deserving special cases." Some students of the subject believed many veterans might register at a trade school in order to get a set of tools, but would either attend classes sporadically or never show up. The *New York Times* education editor, Benjamin Fine, thought some veterans who could not find employment might attend college. If the economy did not perform well, said Fine, there might be as many as 1 million veterans in the colleges.

For good reason. The average age of the veterans was twenty-eight. The combat veterans would have gone through hellish times. World War II was not the crusade World War I had been. The jaunty lyrics of "Over There" and "Good-Bye Broadway, Hello France" were written for World War I; there had been few cheery songs during World War II, but rather "I'll Walk Alone," "I'll Be Home for Christmas," and "Don't Sit under the Apple Tree with Anyone Else but Me." Nor was World War II the conflict for democracy it was later painted to have been. One postwar poll indicated that veterans of the European War had a higher opinion of the defeated Germans than of their

French ally. Then, too, were the war itself not enough to color the attitudes of the veterans, many had lived through the harsh years of the Great Depression as well. Those twenty-eight-year-old veterans in 1945 would have been born in 1917, and passed through their early teens when the Depression struck. Hard times and war were their major memories. They would want to make up for lost opportunities. They believed the rest of their lives would be filled with challenges. The veterans expected to work hard for whatever they wanted. The thought that one day they might be prosperous was far from their minds. Their desires were simple. Logic and surveys indicated that many veterans were not that interested in the idea of going to college. Marriage, a family, and jobs were more desirable than four years on a college campus filled with teenagers.

Statistical and anecdotal evidence seems to indicate that not many GIs, contemplating their discharges, gave much thought to earning a college degree. These were young men torn from their factory jobs or working with their parents or engaged in farming. This was a time when college educations were deemed well and good for the wealthy, for intellectuals, for those interested in a career in one of the professions—but not for others. This was the view of numerous men awaiting their discharges, and also of college administrators contemplating the possibilities these people presented and the problems they could pose.

Such thoughts were voiced by eminent college presidents, the kind who were regularly quoted in the newspapers. James Conant of Harvard wondered what kind of veteran would want to attend college, saying, "We may find the least capable among the war generation . . . flooding the facilities for advanced education."

University of Chicago president Robert Hutchins called the GI Bill "a threat to American education" and "unworkable." But presidents of lesser schools, which had had trouble attracting students during the Depression, were enthusiastic, hoping that sufficient veterans might enroll to enable them to survive. It wasn't long before the presidents in the elite group changed their minds and not only welcomed the veterans, but also praised them for the positive elements they brought to the campuses. Professor George MacFarland of the University of Pennsylvania wrote that "the veteran is acknowledged to be serious, time conscious, industrious, and capable." In a well-regarded study of the group, *Fortune* concluded that the class of 1949 was "the best, the most mature, the most responsible, and the most self-disciplined group of students in history." Conant conceded in 1946 that he had been wrong the previous year. The veterans were "the most mature and promising Harvard has ever had."

Those presidents who feared for the futures of their schools now found their classrooms packed, and they were constructing new classrooms and hiring more faculty members. The returning servicemen were ambitious and optimistic, almost all agreed, and these sentiments transferred to the high school grads who attended classes with them. Prior to the war, those young graduates would have sat in awe while their professors spoke of the Punic Wars and the Age of Exploration. Now their professors knew that among those young people were veterans of Europe and the Pacific, who had seen firsthand the areas they discussed, and had experiences they couldn't match. They were easy to identify. Many veterans took to wearing their Eisenhower jackets and other items of military-issued clothing to classes. Soon the newer high school graduates would haunt army-navy stores to purchase such items. Military garb became fashionable on campuses ranging from the Ivy League to out-of-the-way state teachers' colleges.

GIs helped transform the American colleges in ways that would linger long after they had departed. For one thing, colleges had to expand, and new ones, especially state and municipal institutions, were opened while existing ones were revamped. The state systems in California, New York, and elsewhere were transformed into schools that could challenge the best in the country. The gap between a degree from Harvard or Yale and a Midwestern state college that started out in the nineteenth century as an agricultural school was no longer as wide as once had been the case, a situation that was not lost on employers. Graduates of the state universities of Wisconsin, Ohio, Michigan, and especially California had nothing to apologize for when it came to their educations. In the process, the pool of highly qualified trainees was widened and broadened during the late 1940s and early 1950s. But it took time for that new vitality to be acknowledged.

Henry Kissinger, a World War II veteran and the son of immigrants, expected to attend the City College of New York and become an accountant. But a friend of the family, Fritz Kramer, told him, "Henry, a gentleman does not go to City College. He goes to Harvard." So he did— on the GI Bill of Rights. That gap would not disappear in the postwar period, nor has it today, but it no longer was as wide as Kramer thought it to be in the late 1940s. In 1946 more than 1 million veterans enrolled in colleges and universities, and in 1950, more than 496,000 degrees were awarded, almost twice the 1942 figure. In 1944 there had been 106,000 professors; by 1950 there were 186,000.

The Rise of the Military-Industrial-Educational Complex

That there had developed a nexus among government, some large corporations, and major universities, especially the technically oriented ones, became evident by the 1950s. The most obvious signs of this could be seen at the Massachusetts Institute of Technology (MIT), which by the end of World War II was the largest non-industrial defense contractor. The Electrical Engineering Department there, headed by Dugald Jackson, had strong ties with industry and government agencies, and as one measure of such influence, it was thought that half a professor's remuneration should be earned outside of the school.

In this early postwar period, companies that before the war had been oriented toward the consumer and industrial markets and then became military suppliers continued to play that role. Raytheon, for example, had practically no military business in 1940. In the postwar period, more than 80 percent of its sales were to the military. In 1961, a Boston bank suggested replacing the textile spindle with the Hawk missile as the symbol of the local economy. But the symbol might more fittingly have been the Lincoln Laboratory at MIT, which was emblematic of the interrelations among the companies that festooned Route 128, which circled the city and the campus.

In 1944–1945, many commentators had been troubled by questions relating to the ways the veterans might adjust to civilian life. What might those millions of discharged veterans do if they could not find work? General Frank Hines of the Veterans Administration thought "the greatest danger was that of having idle veterans drifting aimlessly about the country." Such men had provided fodder for the Nazi movement in Germany after World War I, and some American demagogues were thinking along those lines. No less a pundit than Stuart Chase, an economist with a knack for translating academic material into popular prose, agreed. He wrote of the "pent-up resentment and hostility in returned soldiers" that had been seen after every war:

> It is due to the regimentation, the frustration of military life, to lowered self-control from combat fatigue, aggressive tendencies encouraged in battle, to a feeling of injustice at having to face mutilation while another makes $100 a week playing safe. The resentment, in short, is due to many causes—above all, to a sense of status lost. One is no longer a hero, but another guy in a new suit, unsupported by social purpose, or by that tight social group, the Army.

A study by the National Research Council supported this view. The council concluded that millions of men were leaving the armed services "with no clear or realistic goal." They were thought to be rootless. "The community of interest which existed before the war is likely to be sharply reduced," the study predicted. The social relationships developed in the services, thought the council, would be lost and there would be difficulties resuming the prewar ties. The potential for anomie was troublesome. Crypto-fascist Gerald L. K. Smith thought he saw the signs. Smith asserted that his Christian Nationalist Party could not hope for victory in the 1944 presidential election, but expected to sweep into office in 1948, when he hoped for support from discontented veterans who thought as he did.

Of course, he and others were proven wrong. Consider what happened among the nation's political leadership. Accounts of the presidents are familiar, but they merit some repetition in order to get a snapshot of what these men were doing when the war ended and how their careers developed. In 1945, sixty-one-year-old Harry Truman, a World War I veteran, was in the White House. Fifty-five-year-old Dwight Eisenhower became chief of staff that year and, after stints as president of Columbia University and NATO commander, succeeded Truman in the White House. Twenty-eight-year-old John F. Kennedy left the navy and would find work as a newspaper correspondent before entering the House of Representatives in 1947, going on to the Senate in 1953, and succeeding Eisenhower as president in 1961. He and the other veterans who followed in the White House were hardly what Gerald L. K. Smith had in mind. Lyndon B. Johnson, another navy veteran, entered the Senate in 1949, and became president upon the death of Kennedy in 1963. Richard Nixon, discharged from the navy in 1946, ran for a House seat later that year, and then for the Senate. He was Eisenhower's running mate on the national ticket in 1952 and 1956, and he was elected to the presidency in 1968. Upon Nixon's resignation in 1974, Gerald Ford became president. Ford was thirty-two years old and a naval officer on V-J Day. Upon discharge he worked as a lawyer until entering the House of Representatives in

1949, where he served until being confirmed as Nixon's vice president. His successor, Jimmy Carter, was twenty-one when the war ended and a student at the Naval Academy, from which he graduated in 1946. After discharge from the navy, he worked as a farmer, a state legislator, governor of Georgia, and then served as president from 1977 to 1981. Thirty-four-year-old Ronald Reagan was in the army and stationed stateside when the war ended, whereupon he resumed his acting career. Elected governor of California, he took office in 1966, served until 1974, failed to obtain his party's presidential nomination in 1976 but succeeded in 1980, and entered the White House the following year. Eight years later he was succeeded by George Bush, who had been only twenty-one years old and a naval officer when the war came to its end. Bush worked as a salesman for a company in the oil supply industry, for Dresser Industries, and then started his own company, Bush-Overby, in 1952 and Zapata Offshore two years later. Bush entered the House in 1967, and then served as ambassador to the United Nations, ambassador to China, and head of the CIA before running for the vice presidency on the Reagan ticket.

Bill Clinton, born in 1946, the first full peacetime year, who had not experienced the Great Depression and World War II, arrived in the White House succeeding Bush in 1993. He was the first of the "baby boomers" to reach the White House.

For close to half a century after World War II's end, veterans of that war served as presidents. Of course, anyone who rises so high cannot be said to have been typical. But in 1945, when Eisenhower was a hero and Kennedy and Johnson harbored presidential ambitions but knew their chances were slim, most other veterans probably didn't think such success possible. What all the polls and surveys indicated, thought Stuart Chase, was that "the outstanding desire is for a good job, carrying security of tenure as part of it. Not fancy wages, but living wages for the family. . . . Unemployment is the major worry, greater in the veterans' minds than the fear of World War III." Many of them "want to continue education, full time or part time, under the GI Bill of Rights." Married veterans "want homes to live in—not pup tents in Central Park, or a cot in the YMCA and the YWCA." They may be rioting for their demands before these words are in print, said Stuart Chase in 1945.

What some of these seers did not fully appreciate, and others did not understand in terms of scale and scope, was the impact of the Cold War on the economy and on the creation of wealth, and, more important, the drive, ambition, and intelligence of the generation that was mustered out of the armed services soon after the war.

Far more common than those veterans who went on to national and even international fame were the tens of thousands, perhaps more, among those millions who served during the war, who had suffered during the Great Depression, and for the first time in their lives found themselves in a secure place, with decent clothes, housing, and food, and a salary and economic security they had never thought possible. Not all of the servicemen had faced the possibility of death on the front lines. Many became managers in all but name, and, were it not for their uniforms, they could have been mistaken for executives at a Fortune 500 corporation, with major responsibilities for personnel and equipment. One of them, Ray Myers, who was among those discussed in William H. Whyte's *The Organization Man* (1956), which became a basic source for those seeking to understand that generation, was a budding school administrator prior to the war.

His military experiences changed his ambitions. "After leaving the military I knew that I wanted to go back to Harvard," he said, "but not to the school of education." Instead, Myers enrolled at the law school, from which he graduated, and then changed his mind about career goals again. "I had learned from my experience in the service that I had some ability to organize and some ability to relate to other people. So I began to think about getting a job. I decided that rather than using law school as such, I was going to try and capitalize on those abilities." Myers wound up at Continental Illinois Bank in Chicago, where he became involved with estate planning for wealthy individuals.

Images

Then, as now, films were made with "messages," and two of these that dealt with returning veterans merit discussion. The first was *The Best Years of Our Lives*, the most honored film of 1946. Directed by William Wyler, it had a distinguished cast. The film tells the stories of three returned servicemen: Air Force captain Fred Derry, who had been a soda jerk in a drugstore before the war; Sergeant Al Stephenson, a prewar banker; and Seaman Homer Parrish, who had lost both arms in the war. In the film, a disappointed and dejected Fred Derry, about to leave town, finds himself at the air base where hundreds of warplanes are awaiting demolition. Climbing into a bomber, he seems to relive the far more interesting time of war. He comes out of his reverie when a foreman involved with dismantling the planes appears. The two talk, and Derry learns that the metal will be used in the construction of homes. He winds up with a job, the inference being that if those planes can be recycled, so could their pilots. Al Stephenson fights for the right to make business loans to returned veterans who, despite their lack of collateral, have demonstrated their trustworthiness. Homer Parrish marries his sweetheart, and clearly will not permit his disability to destroy his life.

The film was drawn from a story by MacKinlay Kantor, *Glory for Me*, written shortly before the end of the war, when the outlook was not so bright. In the story, Derry almost turns to crime before joining with a friend to open a drugstore; Al Stephenson fails to adjust and leaves banking to become a farmer; and Homer Parrish becomes an alcoholic. *Glory for Me* might seem a truer image of America's hopes and fears as the war came to an end, but *The Best Years of Our Lives* reflected the reality of 1945, and what many expected from the future.

The second film, *Apartment for Peggy*, directed by George Seaton in 1948, follows Jason and Peggy Taylor, a veteran who returns to a state college and his pregnant wife. Unable to find housing in the crowded college town, Peggy talks a retired philosophy professor into renting them his attic. The professor is depressed and considers suicide, and in time Jason becomes discouraged and quits school, where he was studying to become a teacher, and takes a job selling cars. In the end Peggy talks the professor into returning to teaching, and he in turn convinces Jason to quit his job and resume his studies. The *New York Times* movie critic Bosley Crowther thought *Peggy* a "tender and genuine comprehension of a real slice of modern life," but then he had second thoughts, and wrote another review: "He [Seaton] makes you understand the determination of this new generation of the dispossessed to emerge from the cheap and the rootless, both in living and in thinking, that events have imposed." Yet there was more than that, for in the film the value of education and the central role of teachers are stressed. More to the point, Seaton wanted the audience to leave the theater believing that returned veterans would lead America into a better world, that the nation never again would suffer as it had through depression and war.

The Best Years of Our Lives and *Apartment for Peggy* were the upside of the hopes held by Americans after the war. There was a downside too, but of course it was not nearly as popular. In 1949, *Death of a Salesman*, an acclaimed play by Arthur Miller, opened in New York to widespread praise, mostly by reviewers who were highly critical of American capitalism. In the half century that followed, the films would be recalled by their appearances on television, but there were no celebrations of the vision in the specialized or popular magazines. However, *Death of a Salesman* was revived by college drama departments and in Broadway and regional productions featuring such stars as George C. Scott, Dustin Hoffman, and Brian Dennehy as the protagonist, salesman Willy Loman, celebrator and at the same time a victim of capitalism.

Unlike the heroes and heroines of the films, Willy is dismayed by the fruits of his efforts. On learning that there is one more payment due on his refrigerator, which has started to malfunction, he angrily remarks, "Once in my life I'd like to own something outright before it's broken! I'm always in a race with the junkyard." Thus, the capitalist dream is destined to turn to ashes. Willy speaks of his brother, Ben, who went to Africa while in his teens and emerged from the desert four years later with pockets filled with diamonds. So Willy has dreams of success. "It's who you know and the smile on your face!" he confides. To be successful you have to be more than just liked; you have to be well liked. You tell your clients what they want to hear. You aim to please, and if that requires lies, so be it. The ultimate goal is success, measured in terms of money and status. His sons, each of whom epitomizes some of these values, are his hope. Willy will not make it, but Biff and Happy might rise to the top—not by the same routes as the protagonists in the films, but to the top nonetheless, paying prices not visualized by the GI generation.

To suggest that there were two competing visions of the future presented in these works of art is tempting, but such is not the case. *The Best Years of Our Lives* and *Apartment for Peggy* reached huge audiences and were honored by the kinds of awards and praise bestowed by middle-brow critics, while *Death of a Salesman* received its applause mostly from those who thought the American Dream a nightmare, a belief certainly not held by the men who stormed Normandy and the Pacific Islands. The former feared the Americanization of the world, and more than a few preferred the Soviet vision of the future. The latter harbored the kinds of aspirations familiar to those who knew their American history. For them, hard work and dedication would win out over pessimism and dark thoughts.

The GIs would make sure that Willy Loman's visions of the postwar world would not come to be. Biff and Happy would inherit a world of refrigerators that worked, homes that could be afforded, and find rewarding and lucrative work. In addition, the thirties Depression did not return. Although reconversion to a peacetime economy was rough at times, the unemployment rate in the period from 1946 through 1950 fluctuated between 3.9 and 5.9 percent, compared to the rate of 9.8 percent when the United States entered World War II.

American Divisions

Women played a larger role in the general economy and society during and after the war than they did in the 1930s. The social and gender implications of this change were momentous. During the war, more than 6.5 million women entered the labor force. Most of them were married, and in this period marriage for middle-class Americans usually meant the wife would remain at home, taking care of the children and all else related to the homestead, while the husband would be the bread-winner.

The government assumed that the pattern of the future would be similar to that of the prewar period. Accordingly, child-care centers sponsored by the federal government were closed down. But as it happened, more women indicated a desire to continue working than had been anticipated. By 1960 it had become evident that women would play an increasingly important role in the workforce. This change had many economic manifestations, from a decline in the birth rate after the baby boom had worked its way out, to increased family income, to the great popularity of take-out meals and fast-food restaurants. At the time, the increase in female employment was explained as a requirement necessitated by the need to pay for homes, appliances, automobiles, vacations, and the many expenses related to childbearing, but by the 1960s many commentators realized that it was more than that—the relationship between the sexes had undergone major changes during the war, and it was not possible to return completely to the old ways.

As it turned out, such was more the case for educated women than for those who had not gone to college. By 1962, three-fifths of college-educated women were in the labor force, in contrast to two-fifths of those who had high school diplomas but had not entered college, and one-fifth of those whose terminal education was in elementary school. Before the war, most married women, no matter what their education, were homemakers. This shift can be attributed to the World War II experience, which opened new opportunities to women.

This change was noted by many commentators, the most important of whom was Betty Friedan, whose *The Feminine Mystique* (1963) became the spark for what came to be known as the women's liberation movement. In sociological terms, the movement was highly complex and many faceted, but in economic terms the effects were more obvious: the workforce was expanded on all levels. The concept of a working woman with limited family responsibilities, considered abnormal before the war, was accepted by the 1960s. It was the economic equivalent of a new wave of immigrants, only this one came from the kitchen to the factory floor, brokerage desk, and executive suite. Just as each immigrant wave had enriched the country, so would this one. The key difference, perhaps, was that for married women in the workforce, the family income was enlarged, making higher standards of living, on the material level at least, more accessible.

In contrast to the expanding economic role of women,

black people remained invisible to many whites. They had to "know their place" in the South, where lynching was still practiced. In the northern cities they lived in ghettos. The black servicemen who returned home had been in segregated outfits. This was the foremost anomaly in American life, and went virtually unquestioned by white America in all parts of the country and in all social classes.

Racial relations had been poor during the war. Pleas for "toleration," the operative term for racial harmony, often were ignored. As anti-Semitism went under-ground—an expected effect of a war against Hitler—anti-black sentiment flared among whites.

The reasons were not hard to find. During the Great Depression, blacks had been the last hired, the first fired. Black unemployment remained high in 1939–1940, as whites found jobs in war-related industries. By late 1940, however, labor shortages in large northern cities, com-bined with the increasing number of men taken into the armed services, led employers to hire blacks. Lured by promises of good jobs at high wages, many blacks left the agrarian South and headed to northern cities. New York, Chicago, Detroit, Pittsburgh, and Los Angeles were among the major destinations, but Detroit, the nation's motor capital and now the wartime hub of heavy ord-nance-bomber production, received the greatest propor-tion of the newly arrived blacks in relation to the prewar population.

All the while, the rhetoric of freedom intensified. This was a war for democracy and liberation, freedom and equality. War movies often featured what Hollywood wanted the public to think was a typical platoon, filled with stereotyped characters. There was the wisecracking comic from Brooklyn, the preacher from the Midwest, the

Jewish lawyer from New York, and perhaps a bellicose Irish American from Boston, an amorous Italian-American, a white southern bigot, and a quiet, strong, but passive black. After a series of conflicts, both against the Germans and among themselves, the platoon emerged victorious— although the preacher might die, often after delivering a sermon on the democratic nature of the war, and the bigot would come to realize the black was as much a man as he, sometimes after the black saved his life. The racial segregation of the armed forces and that of northern cities, together with white hostility, clashed with this vision.

The new closeness of the races in northern cities created situations conducive to violence. Several riots erupted in 1942, and more followed in 1943. Scarcely a northern city escaped rioting. In January 1943, New York, Chicago, and Philadelphia were hit. In February several black tenants at the Sojourner Truth housing project in Detroit were attacked by whites. That summer 10,000 whites roamed the streets of Beaumont, Texas, beating blacks and burning homes. That year in Los Angeles, a group of "zoot-suiters," Mexicans and other Hispanics dressed in colorful garb, loud ties, long key chains, and long hair, speaking an insiders' slang, were attacked by middle-class whites and several dozen servicemen, who looked upon them as undesirables.

All of this was a prelude to the Detroit race riot of late June, in which thirty-four died (twenty-five blacks and nine whites) and thousands were injured. Entire city blocks were destroyed, as Mayor Edward Jeffries, Jr. and Governor Harry Kelly were paralyzed by fear and indecision. Bands of white youths roamed the streets, beating every black they could catch, and blacks reciprocated. War production ground to a halt as Kelly attempted to prevent federal troops from entering the city, hoping to cool things down with his own forces. Finally, after a week of sporadic rioting, looting, and burning, Kelly relented, and FDR sent two military police battalions to Detroit. They saw little service; by then both races were tired of the violence, and the uprising came to an end. The *Detroit Times* called the riot "the worst disaster which has befallen Detroit since Pearl Harbor." The German and Japanese press saw it as a signal for the beginning of a new American revolution, which would force the nation to leave the war. "We'd better be frank about this," said moderate black leader Louis Marin. "The race riot and all that have gone before have made my people more nationalistic and more chauvinistic and anti-white than they ever were before. Even those of us who were half-liberal and were willing to believe in the possibility of improving race relations have begun to doubt, and, worse, they have given up hope." Adam Clayton Powell, New York's sole black councilman, warned that the Detroit experience could "easily be duplicated here in New York."

Determined that New York would not suffer the agony of Detroit, Mayor Fiorello La Guardia took to the radio to notify the city's inhabitants that he would deal harshly with anyone who fomented violence. For a while the situation was tense, but calm prevailed. Then, on August 1, a riot erupted in Harlem when a black soldier scuffled with white policemen and was shot. La Guardia quickly had the area isolated and prevented white mobs from entering. The police did their job effectively, arresting arsonists and looters, and even the black leadership praised their restraint. At the same time, black leaders warned that additional outbreaks could be expected unless actions were taken to change what they termed the racist nature of American society. So long as there was discrimination in the military and civilian sectors, the nation could not claim to be truly democratic in its fight against Hitler, and until then, blacks would remain militant in their demands for social justice.

There was a government investigation of the 1943 race riots, and in the report black hoodlums were blamed for most difficulties, especially in Detroit. Black leaders had hoped FDR would speak to the nation about the problem in one of his fireside chats, but the President thought it unwise to do so. Writing to New York's radical representative Vito Marcantonio, FDR said he shared "your feeling that the recent outbreak of violence in widely scattered parts of the country endangers our national unity and comforts our enemy." He concluded by writing, "I am sure that every true American regrets them." Such a reply was unacceptable to the National Association for the Advancement of Colored People, which, in the August issue of *The Crisis*, published the following:

> What's you get, black boy,
> When they knocked you down in the gutter,
> And they kicked your teeth out,
> And they broke your skull with clubs
> And they bashed your stomach in?
> What's you get when the police shoot you in the
>   back,
> And they chained you to beds
> While they wiped the blood off?
> What's you get when you cried out to the Top
>   Man?
> When you called the man next to God, so you
>   thought,
> And you asked him to speak out to save you?

What's the Top Man say, black boy?
Mr. Roosevelt regrets. . . .

Blacks were, in the words of novelist Ralph Ellison, invisible. Anti-Catholic, anti-Semitic, and anti-foreign sentiments were heard regularly from quite respectable people. Members of minority groups knew that their economic possibilities were limited. Many private colleges maintained quotas, though this was breaking down in the postwar period. Those minority graduates knew they would have difficulty finding positions at large corporations. Employment by governments, especially when it involved a civil service examination, was a distinct possibility. So were the professions. Doctors, dentists, accountants, lawyers, and other professionals drawn from minority ranks might make a living in their ethnic, religious, and racial communities. Bright young women who did not attend college would aim for jobs as secretaries and sales clerks. Female college students were urged by their parents to become teachers. Not only was the pay decent, but it was "always something you can fall back on" after marriage when the children went off to school.

Those returning Americans—including real-life Jason and Peggy Taylors—did not have exalted ambitions. How could they, given the experiences they had undergone for most of their lives? For them, cosmetics were purchased at the local Woolworth, beer at the grocery. There were no supermarkets in 1945. Wealth, and such perquisites as travel to exotic places, vacation homes, dinners at fine restaurants, private schools for the children, and even a comfortable retirement, were not considered possibilities. In 1900 life expectancy for males was forty-six, and for females forty-eight. Workers of that period did not retire. By the late 1930s, when Social Security benefits became available, the life expectancy for males had risen to around sixty-five. Laborers would work until that age, perhaps longer, live a few more years on the payments offered by Social Security, and die. The idea of leaving an estate for the children and grandchildren was not considered a reasonable goal for their kind of people.

Finally, until the post–World War II period, no systematic methods had been developed to measure wealth. In 1962 Professor Robert Lampman of the University of Wisconsin published his landmark work on the subject, *The Share of Top Wealth-Holders in National Wealth, 1922–56*, in which he noted that one may learn about income distribution through a study of tax returns, but not before 1913, since income tax returns were not filed prior to that time, and until World War I only 2 percent of American households paid taxes, the government relying upon such imposts as the tariff and excise taxes (especially on tobacco and alcohol) for its income. In addition, filings for estate taxes were helpful. Which is to suggest that we really do not know how many truly wealthy Americans there were prior to World War II, or, for that matter, not even in the immediate postwar period. That same year, 1962, Raymond Goldsmith published his *The National Wealth of the United States in the Postwar Period*, based on government figures, in which he concluded that corporate ownership of assets had increased in this period, as had individual assets, but he offered no breakdown of the latter. One could conclude from Goldsmith's work that in the aggregate Americans owned more assets in 1962 than they did prior to the war, but he did not go further than that. This work, and other academic studies of the period, are not particularly useful in determining the success or failure of the postwar generation.

The key to a successful life, for that generation, was

the acquisition of an education that provided the credentials needed for a well-paid job, the purchase of a house and a car, a savings account, and the rearing of children who, assuming all went well, would have an "easier life" that included no worries about paying for their educations. The American Dream has always been the hope that the next generation would have it better.

How can anyone know all of this? Certainly this is a matter of opinion as much as or more than fact. But there are ways of coming to at least a satisfactory conclusion, and this would be by examining some of the artifacts of the time. Two of the most important of these are housing and automobiles.

2

A HOME AND CAR OF ONE'S OWN, AND WHAT THEY IMPLIED

For literally nothing down, you too can find a box of your own in one of the fresh-air slums we're building around the edges of American cities, inhabited by people whose age, income, number of children, problems, habits, conversations, dress, possessions, perhaps even blood types are almost precisely like yours.

—John Keats, *The Crack in the Picture Window*, 1956

Housing a Nation

Almost all of the housing units purchased before World War I were paid for with cash, the buyer having saved the price or borrowed whatever was needed from friends and relatives. Mortgages became more obtainable in the 1920s and afterwards, usually running for less than five years. This innovation powered a housing boom during the 1920s. Even so, most of the middle-class housing put up in the 1920s was not single units. Rather, it was in the form of what before the war had been called tenements, but afterwards became known as apartment houses, whose apartments were rented, not purchased.

Immigrants and their children left the slums of New York's Lower East Side in this period for airy apartments in the Bronx, Queens, and Brooklyn, constructed around thoroughfares such as the Grand Concourse, Ocean Parkway, and Queens Boulevard. The same story was told in other large American cities. The change in the designation of these residences from tenement to apartment was more than simply symbolic. The apartment was supposed to have amenities such as electric lights, fire escapes, and refrigerators, which were not present in tenements. In 1995, humorist Bob Orben joked about this differentiation in one of his routines. "It's amazing," he began. "My grandparents lived in what was called a tenement. My parents lived in what was called an apartment house. I live in what is called a luxury condominium. What's so amazing about that, you might ask. It's all the same building."

Of course the slums remained, especially in the central cities, but fewer Americans had to live in substandard housing than ever before. Even so, the supply of housing did not keep up with demand—or, to be more precise, the need.

Not for the likes of apartment residents were the suburbs that ringed those central cities. These were for the upper middle class and the upper class, which is to say, the houses there were expensive by the standards of the time, costing upward of $20,000. These were the homes that were purchased with the help of longer-term mortgages. There was also some low-cost housing, units that could be purchased from Sears Roebuck and others entering the construction business in those years. But not many.

For the lower middle class and above, the 1920s were golden years for housing. The times were golden in other aspects of American life as well. During that decade Americans enjoyed peace, prosperity, and an increasing standard of living, with many of the miraculous inventions and innovations of the period finding their ways into the daily lives of middle-class Americans. The majority of urban and suburban homes, be they houses or apartments, were electrified. Radio and motion pictures altered perceptions and provided entertainment and information. Record numbers of students entered college, many of them relatively poor, at a time when a college education was perceived as the gateway to middle-class status. Wages were rising, hours of labor declining. Fully 97 percent of Americans did not pay income tax, as a result of four slashes in rates.

There followed a bust in housing construction that accompanied the Great Depression. The period from 1932 to 1934 was a bad time for the industry, resulting from the inability of Americans to afford what the builders could produce. The biggest housing boom in American history had been followed by its biggest collapse. Nor was this all the bad news in this sector of the economy. Americans were being evicted from their homes in record numbers, due to their inability to meet mortgage payments. In 1927 there had been fewer than 100,000 mortgage foreclosures nationwide. This statistic rose with the onset of the Depression, peaking at more than a quarter of a million foreclosures in 1933, and not declining below 100,000 until 1940, by which time economic recovery had taken place.

The 1930s was a period of despair for millions of Americans, but not so for many intellectuals, for whom it was a time of power and influence, especially those who found their way to Washington during the New Deal, or had perches at one of the many important reform journals of the time, such as *Nation* and the *New Republic*.

In preparing for his New Deal, President Roosevelt organized a "brain trust" and raided the faculties of major universities for men and women who would help form and lead the crusade. Social planners on all levels and in varying fields were enlisted to map the future for working-class Americans, who seemed to appreciate what was being done for them and understood that in those plans could be discerned the future shape of their lives. A benevolent government would provide them with what later on would be called a "safety net."

From its start, the New Deal considered housing a priority area for reform, with emphasis on slum clearance. To the New Dealers, it seemed manifest that the destruction of the slums would be accompanied by the creation of attractive new dwellings, the models for which were those being erected in Europe, especially England and Italy. The New Dealers created the Federal Housing Administration (FHA), which lent $600 million to communities for slum clearance and guaranteed mortgages. Another new federal agency, the Home Owners Loan Corporation (HOLC), was empowered to sell up to $2 billion in bonds, with the proceeds used to finance mortgages that would run for up to fifteen years, rather than those shorter-term loans offered by commercial banks at that time. The HOLC assisted more than a million troubled homeowners. In all, the New Deal annealed the concept that housing was a matter for government concern—especially the federal government.

By 1934 the federal government had undertaken slum-clearance projects in Atlanta, Cleveland, Brooklyn, and other areas. At the time, President Roosevelt believed that government housing projects should be concentrated in "green belt" areas in the countryside—the suburbs—which had been the English approach to the problem. Three thousand projects were planned, but only three were actually built. In his second inaugural address, FDR had spoken of the one-third of the nation that was ill-housed. In 1937, under terms of legislation sponsored by Senator Robert Wagner, a liberal Democrat from New York who by then had become closely identified with public housing, the United States Housing Authority (USHA) was established, initially capitalized at $500 million, with a mandate to make loans to other agencies so as to provide more than a billion dollars' worth of construction by 1941. Nathan Straus was named USHA administrator, while Leon Keyserling left Wagner's staff to become the new agency's chief counsel.

Despite the efforts of the USHA, the situation did not improve markedly during the next few years, and the housing stock eroded during the war. During the early postwar period, the New Dealers offered a solution to the problem derived from prewar concepts: a mix of public projects and subsidized private houses, with the focus on the former. This suggests that the Washington bureaucrats still believed the private sector could not do the job, that without government input the housing situation would not improve markedly. It was a reasonable assumption at the time. The generation that was raised during the Great Depression and had experienced World War II did not return with high hopes. But this would change, and when it did, the government's programs and plans would be abandoned for a more optimistic scenario.

The challenge was daunting. From 1920 to 1939, the interwar period as a whole, the nation's builders had constructed 9.7 million units of housing and demolished

800,000, so the net addition came to 8.9 million units. During this span, more than 9.5 million new nonfarm families were created. Thus, on the eve of World War II, there were fewer homes for the American people than after World War I. There was not much by way of family growth during World War II, but there was even less construction. On balance, the housing problem of 1946 was greater than that of 1939.

Postwar Housing

By 1945, the housing units constructed in the 1920s were a generation old, and given the economics of the times, in need of repair. The American housing stock was aged, shabby, and scarce. Only half the homes had complete plumbing systems—running water, flush toilets, private baths, and the rest—and close to a quarter of them lacked electric power. Writing at the end of the war, housing expert Charles Abrams said:

> Of the 39,000,000 farm and nonfarm family units existing in 1945, 16,000,000 needed major repairs or lacked adequate plumbing facilities. Some are beyond repair, some repairable. It may be assumed that two-thirds, or about 10,500,000, must be torn down. Another 500,000 must be torn down in the process of replanning substandard neighborhoods. A million more will become obsolete or unuseable because of family migration from depressed industrial areas and desolate farm areas. This leaves 27,900,000 standing and useable. For a population of 140 million, that came to five people per unit. Put another way,

there were an estimated 36.9 million families in the United States in 1945, for which there were those 27.9 million standing and useable units.

Another authority, Robert Lasch, thought that "thanks to fifteen years of underbuilding, first because of the depression and then because of the war, America has fifteen million houses to build in the next ten years." This represented an average annual construction of 1.5 million houses, compared to the Great Depression average of 273,000.

Such was the situation faced by those 10 million returned veterans and their families. Jason and Peggy Taylor's difficulty in finding campus housing was quite familiar during the immediate postwar years. The government moved to act, and provided plywood houses and surplus barracks for veterans. Some of the latter were Quonset huts, which resembled large cigarettes cut lengthwise, each housing two families. There were reports of veterans living in basements, garages, and even automobiles, but not many, since cars were quite scarce. In St. Louis there were plans to transform the river packet *Golden Eagle* into a dormitory for bachelor veterans. California defense plants set up stopgap housing in the fuselages of bombers no longer needed after the war. All over the country, motels transformed themselves into long-term housing units. A man strangled his wife in Norwood, Ohio. Within a day after the news was released, the police received telephone calls from people who wanted to know if the house was up for sale. Authorities from all segments of the political spectrum agreed that during the next ten years the nation would require more than 16 million new housing units.

As difficult as it seemed at the time, the target Lasch set was reached and surpassed. The private market responded to the demand. In 1944 there were 142,000 new housing starts, and there were 326,000 starts in 1945. This was followed by a record 1 million starts in 1946. It was an impressive showing, though not yet enough. Toward the end of the decade, the 2-million-housing-start-per-annum mark seemed within hailing distance, and in 1950 close to that number was posted.

This did not mean the housing problem was resolved. A government study prepared during the late 1940s indicated that overcrowding, defined as more than $1\frac{1}{2}$ persons per room in nonfarm housing, had declined from 6 percent to 4 percent for whites and from 18 percent to 15 percent for blacks, a good start but hardly a solution to the problem. Likewise, the percentage of dwellings requiring major repairs or lacking baths and flush toilets went from 34 to 22 for whites and 75 to 61 for blacks.

Matters would improve, the result of a two-pronged effort by government and the private sector. In 1945, after a decade and a half of the New Deal and government leadership in war, it seemed that Washington would do the job better and accomplish more. Writing in 1965, in an article titled "The Twentieth Century Began in 1945," social critic Irving Kristol had come to this conclusion as a result of the victory of Keynesian economics in the intellectual community, which held that "the overriding function of government is to secure perpetual economic growth."

This thesis is now universally accepted by all political parties and all governments—whether they call themselves capitalist, socialist, communist, or any variant of these categories. It is the distinctive political creed of the twentieth century. Governments that sponsor economic growth are deemed successful; those that do not are deemed failures—no matter how virtuous and agreeable, no matter how nasty and reprehensible they may be in other respects.

This is not to say that Kristol was right or wrong. Rather, the belief that government had to play a major role in the economy was taken as a given by a large number of individuals. This included housing. Especially housing.

In 1946 President Truman named Wilson Wyatt, the former mayor of Louisville, Kentucky, as his "housing expediter" at the NHA. This was at a time of extreme housing shortages, especially for the returned servicemen and their families. "The veteran's wrath is rising," reported a New York housing bureau established to find housing for them, while a joint legislative committee in Albany reported that their resolution of the problem might not be confined to "peaceable acquiescence."

Wyatt began by acting as though he were in charge of a wartime procurement office. "We can meet this need only by bringing to bear the same daring, determination, and hard-hitting teamwork with which we tackled the emergency job of building the world's most powerful war machine four years ago," he said in one of his first speeches on the subject. Having to deal with outdated labor practices and materials shortages, he was soon embroiled in a forest of red tape. Wyatt tried to overcome this with $600 million in premium payments to producers of building supplies.

Congress recognized the extent of the problem. This was not a matter of ideology, but a condition that had to be rectified regardless of philosophy. For the time being, the private sector had lagged, so even such conservatives as senators Robert Taft of Ohio and Allen Ellender of Louisiana were willing to join hands with Wagner, to craft and then help pass the Wagner-Ellender-Taft Bill, which made the NHA a permanent federal agency. Conservative Republicans had to chose between what to them seemed the preservation of the American family and the principles of free enterprise. In this contest, they were able to unite with liberal Democrats in support of the measure.

Under terms of the legislation, the NHA's task was to make grants to local communities and to provide for the construction of public housing for low-income families, those considered incapable of being served by the private sector. In the bill was a proviso for the creation of 500,000 new public housing units within the next four years. Tenants would pay one-fifth of their incomes for rent, which was to be 20 percent less than the prevailing rents in the neighborhood. So this was to be government-subsidized housing for middle-class renters. The provision for rent may seem a trifle strange to Americans today. When the war ended, a majority of Americans rented their dwellings, whether apartments or houses. So the measure passed without much debate. When faced with a situation where 19 percent of American families were obliged to double up, including 2 out of every 5 married veterans, and were looking for places to live, Wyatt had to consider all possibilities, and perhaps delay slum clearance for a while.

Wyatt had a difficult task. His original plan was to

help construct 1.2 million units in 1946 and another 1.5 million in 1947. One-fifth of the total was to be for temporary units. He intended to construct 900,000 conventional units, 600,000 of which would utilize the mass-production techniques pioneered by Henry Kaiser and others during the war. Of these, 1,150,000 would be for units selling for less than $4,000 or renting for $35 a month; 560,000 for houses that sold for $4,000 to $6,000 and apartments that rented for $35 to $50. There were to be 345,000 in the $6,000–$8,000 range and rentals from $50 to $65, and, finally, 645,000 for more than $8,000 and rentals of more than $65.

In order to appreciate what these figures suggest, consider that the median American family income in 1935–1936 was $1,075. By early 1945 it had risen to $2,600, as a result of wartime prosperity and the appearance of two-income families. The rule of thumb in this period was for potential homeowners to seek homes costing twice the annual family income, or rentals at one week's paycheck per month, which in the case of the median family in 1945 worked out to $54. But consider that take-home pay declined after the war. When the reconversion effort ended, overtime pay disappeared. A survey taken in Trenton, New Jersey, in late 1945 indicated that workers who earned $60 a week in war-related jobs were being offered peacetime jobs at $40 and lower.

The program was a disaster. Wyatt was plagued by bottlenecks in supplies and shortages of workers ranging from plumbers to carpenters to lumberjacks. The unions posed problems. So did the banks. Wyatt was looking for builders who could meet his quality standards and produce houses to sell for $3,000 plus $500 for each bedroom on the lower end of the scale (excluding the costs of land

and erection). Wyatt asked interested parties to submit plausible plans, and to produce a specified number of homes in the first year. He told reporters that the government was prepared to take losses of from $25 million to $50 million if the builders cooperated. Few met the standards he established.

Even so, advocates of public housing continued to press forward. For them it was not only a matter of slum clearance, which it had been prior to the war, but rather an extension of the kind of central planning that had informed the New Deal. Abrams, who helped spearhead the concept, wrote optimistically of the future as he saw it:

> Housing has now become, in America, the opening wedge to comprehensive city planning. It has not always been so. Relocation of industry may sometimes serve as a spearhead; transportation and public works may also. But the vastness of the housing program assumed the role today in America that relocation of industry is assuming in England. A comprehensive housing program can influence or determine many aspects of the planning process—densities of living areas, suburban overspread, relation of housing to transportation and industry, integration of our neighborhoods into democratically heterogeneous communities, adaption of schools, roads and other public works to neighborhood locations. Almost every point in the planning process is affected. We are on the verge of rebuilding America. We have an opportunity to fit the parts into a congruous whole, an opportunity such as we have never seen before—but we falter.

Abrams believed the government would have to take an even more direct role in erecting housing than Wyatt proposed. The public seemed to agree. In one poll, conducted by Elmo Roper, 80 percent of the respondents favored low-interest government loans to purchase mid-priced houses, and 48 percent wanted the government to enter the business of building homes, while 42 percent opposed, with the rest undecided.

Such was the vision and the constituency that motivated those involved with the government's housing programs. Certainly living in their own minimal homes or apartment houses was preferable to what many Americans had experienced in the postwar period. A two-bedroom, one-bathroom apartment on the twentieth floor of an elevator-equipped building, erected with government subsidies, with rents fixed at a percentage of income, must have looked highly desirable to a majority of urban Americans. In an era of modest expectations, this was what they wanted and needed—in the view of those who presumed to do the thinking for the masses.

In the end, Wyatt resigned without having realized his ambitions but, even so, a housing boom had begun. Some of it was in public housing—but more was to come from the private sector.

While apartment construction continued, the ease of obtaining mortgages on private houses changed the outlook toward them considerably. As noted, the FHA did guarantee approved mortgages, but the postwar picture seemed so grim that the mortgage program wasn't as effective as its sponsors had anticipated. Now this program was joined by the housing provision contained in the GI Bill of Rights, which provided for "VA Mortgages." Originally, the Veterans Administration guaranteed the first half of the loan up to a limit of $2,000, but this was soon amended until the guarantee was for $25,000, or 60 percent of the loan, whichever was less.

The arithmetic of the situation was compelling. A veteran might rent an apartment, but with a small down payment and monthly charges not much higher than the rent in non-government-supported projects, he might own a house. The mortgage interest and real estate taxes would be tax deductions, and each month part of the mortgage would be repaid. Meanwhile, the house most likely would go up in value. The problem was getting the down payment and finding an affordable house. The VA and FHA mortgages were indispensable parts of the picture, accounting for $15 billion of the $38 billion of loan guarantees on single-family units.

Then, as well as later, the industry was highly fragmented, with most builders constructing no more than a dozen or so private houses or one or two apartment complexes a year. The industry was in need of new ideas, but many of these were much too unconventional for most potential buyers.

Wyatt and others involved in the government program made two basic assumptions: that many of those units would be in government and private ventures, and that most of the houses would be prefabricated. However, even more of the units would eventually be built in apartment houses.

During the Depression, states and even municipalities constructed housing units for individuals in the lower income groups, almost all in the form of apartment houses. There were New Deal programs to assist in the construction of such housing, often known as "projects." In this period social reformers thought these projects were the proper response to what they saw as the most serious issue in housing: slums.[1]

By the end of 1939, which is to say at the beginning of World War II, there were twelve completed United States Housing Authority projects, which provided homes for 30,000 former slum dwellers. At the time—and after the war—this seemed the template for the future. It was believed that hundreds of thousands of refugees from tar paper shacks, homes erected from scrap lumber without indoor plumbing or electricity, would find refuge. There they would learn the ways of middle-class existence and be lifted from their former status. Such were the bureaucrats' hopes at that time.

Privately Constructed Housing

Privately erected projects existed before the war. They first began after World War I, when a shortage similar to that of the post–World War II period appeared. Back then the New York legislature passed a law enabling insurance companies to invest part of their reserves in housing that would rent for no more than $9 a room, with the sweetener of permitting municipalities to exempt such housing from taxation for ten years. The Metropolitan Life Insurance Co. promptly put up a project consisting of fifty-four five-story walk-ups in Long Island City, New York. The

1. In contrast, those concerned with housing at the end of the twentieth century thought homelessness the major problem, which is quite different in both size and scope. Either a person has a home or does not, and by any calculation, there are fewer homeless people now than there were people living in what for the time was considered slums or blighted areas after World War II.

project was a huge success, and others like it followed. Then the law was permitted to expire, and no more housing of this kind was erected in New York until the Great Depression. In 1937 the New Deal housing program revived the concept on a national level, and Metropolitan responded by erecting Parkchester in the Bronx, a conglomeration of apartment houses built on land purchases from the Catholic Church, which was a large landlord in the area. By the time of its completion in 1945, Parkchester housed 35,000 people. This project was aided by the passage of the New York Redevelopment Corporation Law of 1943, which provided financial incentives for construction. Metropolitan then constructed Stuyvesant Town and Peter Cooper Village in Manhattan. These were well constructed, tenants were screened, and the buildings themselves were kept in good repair. Rules were strict—no pets, for example. A half century later, Peter Cooper Village and Stuyvesant Town apartments remain in great demand. Parkchester declined, and in time the company transformed the complex into condominiums and cooperatives. When they had been planned, the apartments were designed to fill the needs of urban workers. The apartments were small, the regulations sometimes grating. There was no place for the children to play, and no area to hang out the laundry. But these privately constructed projects provided far better housing than most of the new residents had known. It was the pinnacle of their expectations. As one Parkchester housewife put it in the spring of 1946, "For the lower middle class—I guess that's our class—it's fine."

That the public projects, geared for those a step below the lower middle class, would become stigmatized did not seem to have occurred to the former New Deal social reformers. In his 1951 book, *Two-Thirds of a Nation: A Housing Program*, Nathan Straus, who had left the USHA in 1941 and was not considered an alarmist, wrote:

> Millions of families live in indescribable squalor. Slums and blighted areas are common to every American community. The sight of slums has become so familiar that the eye is dulled and the mind has long accepted slum housing as unavoidable even if unattractive.

Straus saw no reason for Americans to accept such a condition:

> If better housing were available for the same low rentals, slum families would move out and owners of empty buildings would be forced to tear them down and seek other uses for the sites. Slums exist because they are the best we can offer millions of families. Every American slum mocks the idea that private enterprise meets the real need for human shelter.

What of the construction of single-family homes? The New Dealers continued to oppose the concept. Before the war, single-family houses, especially in the suburbs, were associated with the wealthy, beyond the ambitions of average Americans. When they sprang up in the late 1940s, old-line architectural critics immediately attacked them. They did so even before the war, when some prototypes appeared. Stuart Chase wrote about "the incredible, fantastic jerry-built wilderness out beyond Jamaica" in an article titled "The Case Against Home Ownership" in the

May 1938 issue of *Survey Graphic*. But the public wasn't buying that line. For a 1946 poll on housing, *Fortune* asked its sample what solution they would like to see for the housing shortage. More than 80 percent wanted the government to provide low-interest loans for potential home buyers, and 76 percent wanted the government to oblige suppliers to lower the costs of building materials. Only 18 percent wanted the government to build homes and then sell or rent them.

The government was perfectly willing to have at least part of the housing shortage resolved by the erection of private houses sustained by public funding, and assumed that many of them would be prefabricated. The costs for such factory-built homes were far less than those for houses erected at the site. They required much less skilled labor, and could be turned out in a cookie-cutter fashion.

The designs rolled in. Unconventional inventor-designer Buckminster Fuller obliged with the Dymaxion house (Fuller must have liked that term, since he named an automobile he designed Dymaxion as well), with light walls and floors suspended by steel wires from the top of a central duralumin tower, to sell in kit form for $1,500 to buyers who would provide labor and the site. Foster Gunnison, one of the leading forces in prefabrication, liked to say he built homes for "Minnie and Joe," implying the lower middle class. He scoffed at the Fuller design. "It is no concern of Gunnison Homes, Inc., if Minnie and Joe have not learned to want modern houses or tree houses or igloos. I don't care whether a house is traditional or modern, or even whether the roof is pink or green. I just want to sell houses." Gunnison produced eight houses, the smallest with two bedrooms, a kitchen and bathroom, and a utility room for $4,000 plus the costs for land; the largest had a living-dining room, three bedrooms, two baths, a kitchen and dinette, along with the utility room, and sold for $10,000. All used plywood sections.

A. O. Smith and American Rolling Mill wanted to produce an all-steel, two-bedroom house that looked more traditional and could sell for $3,600. Add the site and construction, and the price rose to more than $7,000. General Houses weighed in with its version, while Frank Lloyd Wright and other distinguished architects presented their blueprints. Prefabrication Engineering offered a twenty-four-by-twenty-four-foot house in three sections for $5,000 plus another $1,000 for kitchen appliances. The Willisway Systems home was four feet shorter, looked like a packing box, and sold for $3,500. It clearly was not meant to last, which Jacques Willis cheerfully conceded. "This is an emergency," he liked to tell reporters, "and we have carried out the logic of giving the boys the most house for the least money."

How did the public feel about prefabricated housing? In that aforementioned *Fortune* poll, 70 percent of the sample knew about pre-fab housing and only 16 percent indicated an interest in it, although 27 percent of veterans were receptive to the idea. One-third said they would purchase or rent prefabricated housing only if they could get nothing else. What didn't they like about prefabricated housing? More than two-thirds cited unsatisfactory construction, and another 18 percent thought the homes lacked individuality or were too small. This clearly indicated that there was a portion of the home-seeking public that wanted more than the bare minimum.

In the end, the answer to their needs came from a man and a company that were far more attuned to the interests and expectations of that generation than any of the private builders or the government: William Levitt & Sons.

Levittown

No figure is more closely associated with the post–World War II building boom than William Levitt. No one has done more than he to revolutionize the industry, or to smash the notion that projects were the best solution to the housing shortage, or that radical new designs were the answer for those desiring their own homes.

In this period, the typical builder was not a company hoping to erect and sell hundreds of houses, but rather an ambitious carpenter, bricklayer, or plumber who had amassed a little capital and started out by building a single house. If successful, he might hope to put up a half dozen homes a year with the aid of subcontractors. There were not many in the single-family detached-house segment of the market.

After the war, Levitt wanted to wed the concept of erecting on-site conventional houses with the thought of turning them out by the hundreds, or even thousands, so as to realize economies of scale. Levitt recognized that the VA mortgages would enable families formerly restricted to apartments in New York's outer boroughs to move into houses of their own. "The market was there and the government was providing the financing," Levitt later recalled. "How could we lose?"

New York City real estate was too expensive, however, for the plans he was making. So Levitt quietly amassed 7.3 square miles of land in the Island Trees area of Nassau County, not far from the Queens border, much of which had been potato fields. Between mid-1947 and late 1951, from a design created by his brother, Alfred, Levitt put up 17,500 homes in two basic models, "ranches" and "Cape Cods." Levitt accomplished this by adapting mass-production techniques developed in the automobile industry, and affected those desired economies by making large-scale purchases from the manufacturers. "What it amounted to was a reversal of the Detroit assembly line," said Levitt. "There, the car moved while the workers stayed at their stations. In the case of our houses, it was the workers who moved, doing the same job at different locations. To the best of my knowledge, no one had ever done that before." The original owners agreed. They would refer to their homes as "1948 Cape Cods," as though they were cars rather than houses.

In those days each new house constructed on order differed from the others, since this was what middle-class owners wanted. Not the Levitts. In time there would be changes in the houses, but initially all the ranches were the same, as were all the Capes.

Workers would be organized in teams, each charged with a different task. To reiterate, these were not "factory-built" houses, but rather on-site construction. The only part of the house that was manufactured in a factory were the windows. The workers would put up the houses in little more than a week, after which they would move on to the next section. Each team or worker had specific tasks to perform; one did nothing but bolt washing machines to the floors of the houses. Commenting on the unusual construction methods, a *Time* magazine reporter wrote:

> Every hundred feet the trucks stopped and dropped off identical bundles of lumber, pipes, bricks, shingles and copper tubing, all as neatly packaged as loaves from a bakery. Near the bundles giant machines with an endless chain of buckets ate into the earth taking just thirteen

minutes to dig a narrow four foot trench around a 25 by 32 foot rectangle. Then came more trucks loaded with cement and laid a four inch foundation for the house in the rectangle. After the machines came the men. On nearby slabs already dry they worked in crews of two and three laying bricks, raising studs, nailing boards, painting, sheathing, shingling. Each crew did its special job and hurried on to the next site. A new one was finished every fifteen minutes.

These "Levitts" were purchased by individuals who often were the first in their families to own their homes. The initial models rented for $65 a month with an option to buy for $6,990. Soon the price was raised to $7,990, and after 1949 they could only be purchased, not rented. For this amount the new Levitt owners got a home on what usually was a sixty-by-one-hundred-foot lot, which consisted of two bedrooms, a living room, kitchen, and bathroom, with eight hundred square feet of living space. The house came with an attic that might be expanded into two additional rooms and another bathroom. There were no basements, but instead each house was erected on a concrete slab. This saved money, but it took waivers by the town of Hempstead to make it possible, since such construction was banned. Because of this, the Levitts employed radiant heating, warm water piped through copper pipes embedded in the concrete floor, the heat coming from an oil burner, which was outside the house for some models, in the kitchen for others. The grounds were sodded, and trees planted. There was a backyard for the children where the washing also might be dried. Levitt even provided playgrounds, shopping centers, and schools. Most of those homes were purchased with FHA and GI mortgages, and the veterans who qualified for the latter could purchase their Levitts with no down payment.

All of which drew the ire of a host of critics. Nathan Straus had attempted to demonstrate that such housing was actually more expensive than his project apartments. Such a house, he said, was "cheap to build, expensive to maintain, its limited life requires a high amortization. At no time will it provide good housing." C. E. A. Winslow, chairman of the Committee on Housing of the American Public Health Association, derided the small houses springing up in suburbia. Although he did not single out Levittown in his remarks, he clearly had it in mind. "In most of our mushrooming suburban housing developments today you cannot tell the house from the garage. If we progress much further in this direction, you won't be able to tell the house from the letter box."

In his best-selling book on the postwar housing scene and suburbia in particular, *The Crack in the Picture Window*, social critic John Keats discussed a "typical postwar development operator who figures out how many houses he could possibly cram onto a piece of land and have the local zoning board hold still for it." He wrote of "mean housing developments, conceived in error, nurtured by greed, corroding everything they touch," which had been "vomited up" by heartless speculators who destroy the landscape with their rows of "identical boxes spreading like gangrene." Keats says of his nameless developer:

> Then he whistled up the bulldozers to knock down all the trees, bat the lumps off the terrain, and level the ensuing desolation. Then up went the houses, one after another, all alike, and none of those built immediately after the war had any

more floor space than a moderately priced two-bedroom apartment. The dining room, the porch, the basement, and in many cases the attic, were dispensed with and disappeared from the American scene. The result was a little box on a cold concrete slab containing two bedrooms, bath, and an eating place the size of a broom closet tucked between the living room and the tiny kitchen. A nine-by-twelve rug spread under the largest room wall to wall, and there was a sheet of plate glass in the living-room wall. That, the builder said, was the picture window. The picture it framed was of the box across the treeless street.

The young Americans who moved into these cubicles, thought Keats, "were not, and are not, to know the gracious dignity of living that their parents knew in the big two- and three-story family houses set well back on grassy lawns off the shady streets, of, say, Watertown, New York. For them and their children, there would be only the box on its slab."

Change a few details and you have the house and development Keats was describing: Levittown. "It was not the house of their dreams, nor was the ready-made neighborhood a thing to make the soul sing. It was, simply, the only thing available."

Keats was wrong about more than a few items as well as being guilty of not knowing the population of which he wrote. The parents of the young couple didn't live in those two- and three-story houses, but rather in tenements and two-family houses in the rundown parts of the central city, where the couple had been doubling up with them since the husband's discharge from the service. The house may have been small by the standards of middle-class homeowners of the 1920s, but it seemed more than adequate to those refugees from the outer boroughs of New York and other cities. As it happened, buyers lined up to purchase Levitts instead of project apartments. Nor was the neighborhood depressing. Rather, it was filled with people just like them, the first in their family to own homes in many cases, and they were grateful to William Levitt for what they received.

Today some of those people are living in retirement complexes in Florida, the Carolinas, and Arizona, purchased with the profits they made on their second and third homes. They were the major beneficiaries of the great boom.

What about the charge of shoddiness? Straus believed small houses would prove to be poor investments. "Office buildings, apartment houses, loft buildings, and stores are continuously bought and sold as investments. But financial institutions and wise investors steer clear of small homes," he said. However, Levittown thrived, and half a century later the houses had been so altered by additions that it was difficult to find one that appeared as it first did after World War II. Moreover, by then the houses were reselling for upward of $170,000. Levitt had created wealth for the tens of thousands of Levittowners who bought and sold his houses.

All of those who purchased Levitts originally or in resales in the first decade were white, and most were Christians. Levitt placed a covenant in the contract forbidding sales to non-whites. Blacks were excluded even after the clause was declared unconstitutional. One of the greatest chances in this generation to make a profitable investment was denied to them. The gradual return of confidence that took place in the 1950s excluded this population. This is not to say that there was no black presence in suburbia. Indeed, in 1927, long before middle-class suburbs became the goal of middle-class urbanites, Louis Fife, a white developer, purchased land in Suffolk County on Long Island, an hour's drive from what eventually would become Levittown, on which he planned to erect houses specifically marketed to working-class blacks in Harlem, Brooklyn, and the Bronx. Fife also sold raw land to those who wanted to construct their own homes. There were no paved streets or roads, no electricity, and no running water. It was hardly middle class, even by the standards of the period. Almost all the residents came from cities, and did not appear particularly pleased with the more rugged way of life in which they found themselves. In time, in order to finance these houses, the community, which Fife called Gordon Heights, established its own credit union. But Gordon Heights was a small development, which foundered during the 1930s. And throughout its life it was isolated from neighboring white communities. Gordon Heights was not imitated after the war, so blacks did not have developments of their own and remained barred from the white ones. Nor did this situation change greatly with the civil rights movement of the 1960s and after. Despite a plethora of government and private programs to encourage black homeownership, the problem remained into the new century. In 1993, 83 percent of white families owned their dwelling (of course, most with mortgages), while the figure for black families was 46 percent.

The success of Levittown bred imitation, and others followed the same idea. In 1947, with 60,000 units going up in Los Angeles alone, the nation's ten largest builders each erected an average of 1,400 single-family houses. In the 1950s, Californian Joseph Eichler, a transplanted New Yorker, recognized the potential of selling houses to the 10 million veterans and their families. Working with architect Robert Anshen, he planned a three-bedroom, one-bath, nine-hundred-square-foot dwelling, and the two men constructed fifty-one variants of the house in Sunnyvale, near San Jose. All of their houses, priced at $9,500, sold within two weeks. Eichler was also one of the first to break through the color bar. Later, when he got into the business of constructing multi-family townhouses and apartments, he insisted on opening them to black and Asian families, this at a time when the FHA still endorsed restrictive covenants. But Eichler did not attempt to do so outside of northern California, where such practices were more acceptable than in the rest of the country.

Regional builders, whose fame never spread outside of their localities, appeared in other parts of the country. One of these, Eugene Glick, an Indianapolis, Indiana, World War II veteran, had vivid memories of the Depression and was intent on providing housing for GIs and others after the war. By the time he was mustered out of the army, Glick had a reasonably clear idea of what he hoped to do with his life: create affordable, decent housing for veterans like himself. With the help of the People's Bank, which was willing to provide mortgages and other assistance, he started out to realize his ambition.

The formula for the construction of those postwar homes was simple enough, said architectural critic Wolf von Eckardt, reflecting on the work of men like Levitt, Eichler, and Glick:

> The builders and promoters themselves invest little more than their judgment on where and what to put up. The "where" is easy—on the cheapest possible land near the most crowded metropoli-

tan concentration. . . . The county governments are happy to welcome them and present them with the essential sewers and local roads. Most country councils are dominated by people whose main cash crop is land. . . . The "what" is answered with clever packaging and public relations. Wrap a shoddily built house in a fashionable facade, stuff it with gadgets, put a gaslight or something in front for that extra bit of nostalgia, give it a romantic name and you'll have the suckers beating a path to the sales office.

Once more the experts derided the new suburbs while the postwar builders were applauded by those who purchased their homes.

By the early 1960s, the housing market was being enlarged by another development of the postwar period: mobile homes, most of which, despite the name, were not mobile. Rather, they were constructed in factories and taken to what usually was a permanent site. These homes, made of metal, would age and eventually had to be scrapped. In this regard, their prices behaved more like those of automobiles than homes, since the former declined in price over time while the latter proved good investments. By 1963 more than 150,000 mobile homes were being sold, this amounting to 10 percent of all new housing starts, and there were 15,000 mobile-home parks in America with 150,000 units, and new parks were opening at the rate of three per day.

Try to imagine the mind-sets of the families in the projects, the Levittowns, and the mobile home parks of America in the late 1940s and early 1950s. They lived close to others in their same income and status groups.

97

Almost all were blue-collar workers, or if white-collar workers, schoolteachers. They had come from slums into something far better. People in the projects may have hoped to repair their new apartments when needed, but there were large common areas that often were maintained poorly. The Levittown residents owned their properties, and many were college educated. While there were manual workers in Levittown, a majority were white-collar, and in time a substantial number of teachers on all levels, including those from the local colleges, moved there, where they vied with one another in matters of lawn maintenance, painting, the planting of trees and shrubs, and the like.

During the period from 1946 to 1955, two-thirds of the new housing constructed in the United States was in metropolitan areas; of that amount, 80 percent was in suburbia. The 1960 census revealed that for the first time in American history, a majority of Americans lived in suburbs. Ever since, the suburbs have grown faster than urban and rural areas.

All of which was translated into wealth—for the builders and suppliers of building materials. In 1950 *Fortune* estimated that building was proceeding at a $20 billion annual rate, of which $7.2 billion went into housing, $3 billion into streets and schools, and the rest into supplies.

Two generations later, many of the projects were graffiti-covered, crime-ridden slums, dumping places for welfare cases, or, quite simply, demolished. Others, to be sure, were successful, but even those did not come close to the classless apartment houses dreamed of after World War II. Go to Levittown today and you will see a community in which the values have risen, and reflect that few of the Levittowners of the late 1940s remained there for the rest of their lives. Those young veterans and their families were delighted and grateful for their homes, but in time—often a short period of time—they would want more. As has been noted, they would sell their homes for a profit, and use the money for the down payment on a larger home in a more affluent part of suburbia.

From all of this one should not conclude that the private builders experienced unalloyed successes while public housing suffered from a series of failures; or, for that matter, that the housing boom of the postwar period managed to solve the slum problems that bedeviled the prewar students of the subject. Many of the old slums remained, and some of the new housing created after the war became the slums of the future.

The figures developed by the Census Bureau indicate that of the 55.3 million houses in the United States in 1956, approximately 12.6 million remained substandard with another 2 million in run-down neighborhoods. One in 7 of the substandard houses lacked a bathtub or shower, and 1 in 10 was not equipped with indoor plumbing. Close to a generation had passed since the end of World War II, but there remained many Americans who had not moved from the bottom of the ladder.

Critics of the low-cost housing continued to voice their opposition to the projects, and they did not stop, even when there was an easing of the shortages. In a letter to the *New York Times* in early 1999, a writer took up the cudgels:

> Sprawl has become instrumental in the destruction of any sense of community within both large and small cities across the country. New developments, built to profit developers, have done more

to fractionalize communities along racial, economic and political lines than any other time in our country's history.

Moreover, one need only spend time in a place like suburban Atlanta to realize that the environmental impact of the long, miserable automobile commute most suburbanites must make is in itself reason enough to curtail growth.

But on the op-ed page of the same issue of the newspaper (February 25, 1999), David Ivins argued that defenders of a pristine environment are fostering what he termed "rural sprawl," which denied development, while also not contributing anything of value to society:

Areas that otherwise would be given over to job creation and highly profitable logging, strip mining and oil drilling are being expropriated by wild animals, which are inherently valueless since they contribute nothing to our economy. Once these beasts establish themselves, shielded by hellbent wildlife-protection groups and misguided politicians from Al Gore to Christie Todd Whitman, they can never be dislodged.

But these animals are only the unwitting servants of the quaint-seeming "country folk" whose diabolical plan is to eradicate or make unlivable our suburbs and cities by covering our streets, sidewalks and highways with grass, shrubbery and trees. They want to inundate shopping malls and sports arenas with lakes, ponds and streams; replace our condo developments with "picturesque" villages and hamlets and our suburban tracts homes with drafty old-fashioned farmhouses.

The Automobile Boom

Transportation was another concern, and it was related to housing. When the New Dealers planned suburban communities, they tended to do so without providing for parking, but rather thought in terms of an infrastructure that would support regular bus and trolley services. Cars were wasteful, polluting, and, as far as most of the planners were concerned, unnecessary. Not that the potential automobile owner wanted much; every poll of the period indicated that the small, affordable, prewar Chevrolets, Plymouths, and Fords would do fine.

The housing and automobiles that were produced for Americans of the post–World War II period reflected these aspirations. Americans did not hope for affluence—yet. But they clearly wanted something beyond adequate. For Washington's planners, housing and transportation were part of the same problem. Americans needed housing, but also wanted automobiles. Indeed, the housing they wanted could not easily exist without the automobile.

In the late 1930s, the top 10 percent of income earners purchased 40 percent of new cars. The war and the postwar boom did not change this situation. In 1953, the top 11 percent purchased 36 percent of new cars.

One of the images of this period was of the suburban mother who drove her husband to the train station, then spent the rest of the day driving the children to school and play, in between shopping and going to coffee klatches with other mothers like herself. A car was clearly required for this kind of life. One did not need a car in the projects, which generally were near public transportation. Life without a car in places like Levittown could be difficult. Socializing in the prewar suburbs revolved around the country club; in the new suburbs the key places were playgrounds, shopping centers, and schools. The old suburbs were for families with servants; the new suburbs housed the servants, electricians, carpenters, and others who worked for the wealthy people.

The same individuals who mocked the provincial nature of suburbia also opposed the automobile culture it fostered. They talked of the waste of resources, conspicuous consumption, the visual pollution caused by automobile graveyards and billboards. The critics calculated how much asphalt and concrete was used to construct roads, and how those roads upset the ecological balance and caused floods. Later on, George Romney, an auto executive himself, would deride the need of a 110-pound woman to drive a two-ton sedan to the store to purchase bobby pins.

What these people needed, argued the critics, was mass transportation. Indeed, some of those planned housing projects had no parking facilities, since they did not expect the residents to own cars. Better trains, more subways and elevated commuter lines, buses, and trolleys were required. If they had their way, the Levittown breadwinner would take a bus or monorail to the railroad, which would whisk him into the city and work. The housewife and the children would be taken shopping and to schools by buses. Taxis and jitneys would be there for needs that could not be filled by mass transit.

Some home builders constructed their projects with

an eye toward the kind of suburbanites who would prefer automobiles. In southern California, John Lusk, a banker at the Security Pacific Bank, advised the officers there to grant mortgages to GIs looking for low-priced housing in areas where land was inexpensive but reachable by automobile. In time Lusk would construct more than 40,000 houses in Orange County, and he was one of the first to capitalize on the growth of that part of the country while understanding the link between housing and the automobile.

No cars were produced for the civilian market during the war; the last new cars rolled off the assembly lines on January 20, 1942. Only 222,862 vehicles were produced that year, and many of these went into military service.

Early that year gasoline came under the rationing program established by the Office of Price Administration. According to the plan, motorists were issued stickers to be affixed to the front windshield, marked by the letters A, B, and C, along with books of coupons authorizing gasoline purchases. "A" drivers received two gallons per week, while Bs and Cs, who were doctors and defense workers, got a little more. Some national magazines published articles on how to place cars in dead storage, along with pieces on how to qualify for higher allotments. Gasoline was not rationed because it was scarce; the United States was the world's largest petroleum producer when the war began. Rather, rationing gas was another way to save scarce, imported rubber, which was no longer available from Asian plantations.

The prices of used cars were also controlled, but it was virtually impossible to monitor sales from individuals to individuals, and a 1938 car that originally went for $500 might realize three times that amount in 1943. Repair problems had become acute by then, and motorists and mechanics would haunt junkyards searching for a usable carburetor for a 1934 Chevrolet or a rear axle for a 1937 Buick. Blacksmiths were called into service to forge parts.

In 1941 there were 29.5 million automobiles registered in the United States; in 1942 there were 27.9 million. By the end of 1944 this figure had dropped to 25.8 million, half of which were more than ten years old and most well beyond their useful life. "Every week," predicted *Fortune*, "literally thousands of cars will drop dead somewhere in the United States."

All of the car companies—General Motors, Ford, and Chrysler, which before the war had 90 percent of sales, and the independents, Studebaker, Nash, Willys, Packard, and Hudson—had plans for the postwar market. Uniformly, they agreed that the public wanted pretty much what they had bought before the war: inexpensive, small cars for the many; large cars for the affluent. There would be no new flash and dash, but rather safe and sensible sedans and coupes. In fact, most models would be produced from dies used in the 1941 and 1942 models and then put into storage.

The manufacturers did not expect to have trouble selling their cars, even though they factored in the possibility of depression. The arithmetic was compelling. In no year before the war had more than 4.5 million cars been produced, and that was in 1929, the last year of the boom decade. In 1941, 3.9 million automobiles had been made, and the factories that churned them out would now have to be converted from military production. According to some calculations, it would be possible to sell as many as 8 million cars a year, a figure never before achieved. The conventional wisdom of the time was that every car produced during the next three to six years would be snapped up by eager buyers.

In 1943 Alfred Sloan and Charles Wilson of General Motors put together a ten-year projection, which was distributed to key personnel. The report attempted to predict the extent of the postwar expansion. Not only was there the American market to service, but the European car companies would not be able to get back into operation as quickly as General Motors could convert to civilian production. Thus, the foreign markets would be there for the taking. What kind of cars would be needed? Everything from small Chevrolets to large Cadillacs, and perhaps there would be some new marques. Charles Kettering, the company's leading engineer, had in mind a "market wagon," somewhat similar to the Volkswagen Hitler had promised the German people. The Society of Automotive Engineers conducted a survey in 1945 and found that people in the test cities of New York, Chicago, New Orleans, and San Francisco wanted small, inexpensive cars. Radio magnate Powel Crosley had introduced such a small car in 1939, and had sold some of them before civilian production ended.

Perhaps Crosley had the right idea. Wilson pondered the matter. He had convinced himself that the American people wanted affordable cars. "The higher the prices of automobiles, the fewer will be sold. If people cannot raise the money or credit for new cars, they will simply get along with their old ones. They showed they could do it during the war." Wilson announced his plan to build "a lighter weight and more economical car" in the postwar period. "Because of the necessity of putting war production first, the car is only in the idea stage, and therefore, it cannot be placed in production until a considerable period of time after the close of the war with Japan." His design team came up with the plan for a car that had a wheelbase of 108 inches (8 inches shorter than that of the 1942 car) and weighed only 2,200 pounds, and he gave it the working title of Cadet. Ford had a similar plan, and after that company rejected the opportunity to obtain the Volkswagen facility, Chrysler took a run at it. Studebaker believed it had a winner in the Champion, a small car introduced on the eve of the war. Others were thinking of entering the field, among them Preston Tucker and Henry Kaiser.

In 1945, the industry produced fewer than 70,000 cars. Even this number was remarkable, given reconversion requirements. The following year, 2.1 million cars were produced, and all were sold without difficulty. Indeed, potential buyers were willing to pay more than the government-mandated price, and sellers often found ways to obtain extra money by offering stripped models at the required prices and then selling items like floor mats for hundreds of dollars each.

As expected, these cars were rehashed 1942 models, with somewhat more chromium, brighter colors, and flashier advertising. Quietly, Detroit dropped plans for smaller cars. The executives thought it prudent, under the circumstances, to stick with what they and the American public already knew. Studebaker placed most of its chips on the Champion, but executives there were troubled. The public was asking for such a car, but would customers really purchase them? They need not have worried. The Champion was a hit, but Studebaker's joy was tempered by the knowledge that the public was so car-hungry that almost any vehicle would have succeeded.

This realization was soon shared by most other industry executives. Perhaps some areas of American business would suffer, but not the automobile industry. Emboldened, the companies started to consider a different kind of car.

The End of the Merely Adequate

After the initial car models made their impact, Detroit made them larger, more powerful, and more colorful. In 1958, John Keats, who earlier had skewered the newer suburban houses, turned his attention to automobiles. In his best-selling book *The Insolent Chariots*, he attacked the industry and its products. These automobiles were, in his view, "overblown, overpriced monstrosities built by oafs to sell to mental defectives." Keats wanted to know "Whence, and what art thou, execrable shape?" What did the middle class want by way of cars? Designer Raymond Loewy, whose new Studebaker set off the change, provided the answer: "What it wants is being translated into the flashy, the gadgety, the spectacular." This, too, was a reflection of the higher cravings that would develop after the early fears of a postwar depression were overcome.

Studebaker was the first to break the mold with the 1947 Champion, advertised as "the first genuine postwar car," which it was. The car was low-slung, sleek, with almost continuous windows, leading some comics to comment that there was no way of knowing which was the front and which was the back. Others called it the car of 1970—but predicted that the customers of 1947 wouldn't buy it. On the other hand, the Society of Industrial Designers chose it as the outstanding offering of the year, and the Museum of Modern Art picked it as one of the ten most significant design concepts in the history of the automobile. At the same time, Powel Crosley's 925-pound car that sold for $325 flopped.

Then, in 1948, Cadillac came up with a redesigned car—or at least it was billed as redesigned—with tailfins pushing up the rear. Like the Studebaker, it too became the butt of jokes, but in time most American cars carried nonfunctional tailfins or their equivalents. The public seemed to like them. The 1949 Chevrolet was the first low-priced General Motors car with a postwar design, and Ford also had a new model. Chrysler started to make the change that year, but did so more slowly and in a more conservative fashion than the others. As a result, sales slumped at Chrysler, but not in the rest of the industry. In 1949 automobile sales came to 5.1 million and registrations to 36.5 million; the 1946 figures had been 2.1 million and 28.2 million. More than half of America's families now had at least one car.

The success of the postwar cars was one of the first indications that Americans had started to throw off their fears of a desolate future. Soon there were other positive signs. The thirties Depression did not return, suburbia was expanding, and those wartime savings were being spent on appliances, vacations, and television receivers. Spot labor shortages were occurring as well. Finally, and most important, there appeared another engine for dramatic growth: The baby boom would energize the American economy for more than a generation.

3

THE FAMILY: ITS WORK, PLAY, AND INVESTMENTS

Life will not be a burden for me at thirty-five because I will be securely anchored in my family. My main emotional ties will center on my wife and family—remember, I hope for five children. Yes, I can describe my wife. She will be the Grace Kelly, camel's-hair-coat type. Feet on the ground, and not an empty shell or a fake. Although an Ivy League type, she will also be centered in the home, a housewife. Perhaps at forty-five, with the children grown up, she will go in for hospital work, and so on. . . .

—A Princeton Senior, Class of 1955

Recall those original Levittowners, who in the 1980s and 1990s were to retire to warmer locales. Most rightly could have considered themselves successful, in that their accomplishments had exceeded the hopes and dreams they had entertained during the immediate post–World War II period. Another reason for their contentment rested in their families. In that generation they usually remained together, although this tendency frequently has been romanticized and overstated. The raw numbers tell the story. The marriage rate in 1944, the last full year of war, was 10.9 per 1,000 population, then rose to 12.2 in 1945, and peaked at 16.4 per 1,000 in 1946 before declining to below 10 by 1950. The divorce rate per 1,000 was below 2 in 1939. It rose to 4.3 in 1946, doubtless due to marriages disrupted by wartime separation and then put on hold until the war was ended, fell back to 3.4 per 1,000 following year, slipped to below 3 and remained there until 1969. Toward the end of the century, 1 out of every 2 marriages was destined to end in the divorce courts.

What did this infer for the nation? It is a given that in general two-parent families are more stable economically and socially than single-parent families. The former was very much the rule in the 1940s and 1950s for the GI generation, but not so for their grandchildren's. And there were other differences. In the earlier period, couples might consider remaining married "for the sake of the children." This was less common later on. The concept of living together without marriage was more acceptable in the late 1990s than the mid-1940s; the pressures upon young people to marry were greater in the earlier period than the later.

In response to allegations that his solutions to some economic problems did not take long-run considerations into account, economist John Maynard Keynes famously replied, "In the long run we are all dead." A perceptive journalist remarked that it was the answer only a person without children could make. At the time and afterwards, commentators reported, some approvingly, others critically, that American life in this period not only was centered around the family, but around children in particular.

If one might be forgiven a generalization that cannot be proven, it may be that individuals who despair of the future are not particularly interested in having children.

Those who have families are obliged to take long-range considerations into account. The middle-class parents who took their infant home from the hospital may have reflected that they had entered into a covenant with eternity, or, at the very least, with the next few decades.

Individuals without such relationships may feel that short-term considerations are of paramount importance. Not so the parents of youngsters. To sociologists this would become one of the basic ways to differentiate the middle class from the lower class. Those newlyweds went on a baby binge after the war, and from then on, at least for those whose families remained together, the welfare of their children was a primary concern when it came to most decisions, especially those that involved their economic well-being.

The Economics and Politics of the Baby Boomers

So loud was the postwar economic boom that it reverberated for generations, affecting both the economic and political life of the nation through the end of the century. When it came to politics—especially the politics of the economy—the indelible imprint left on the GI generation by the Depression and war set it apart from the two generations that followed, the baby boomers and their children. The relative conservatism of the GI generation, combined with their wealth and influence, helped bring to the White House a new Republican regime in one of the great political realignments of the twentieth century.

Just about every poll taken during this period indicated that the GI generation was largely Reaganite and voted for him twice—against Jimmy Carter, who seemed to them to have New Deal leanings, and against Walter

Mondale, who appeared to be a liberal New Deal type. There is no doubt that Reagan was a different kind of president than the nation had experienced since the end of World War II. In the first place, unlike the others, he did not appear to be a pragmatist willing to accept half a loaf in his reform efforts. He possessed a clear ideology and vision in areas of foreign and economic policy. Reagan had strong ideas regarding the role of government and the obligations of citizens. Whether he intended to follow through on these convictions might have been questioned, but that he had a philosophy was quite evident during the 1980 campaign.

On coming to the presidency, Reagan called for massive tax cuts over a three-year period, along with major decreases in spending in the civilian sector and increases in the military budget. He was able to get much of his tax program passed; the 1981 Congress approved a reduction in federal rates by 5 percent the first year and 10 percent the following two years. Military spending rose in the Reagan years, from $134 billion in 1980 to $290 billion in 1988.

Congress rejected most of the Reagan spending cuts, which was the other half of his program. The President asked businessman J. Peter Grace to chair a commission to look into government waste, and in the final report Grace identified potential savings in the hundreds of billions of dollars. But few of his recommendations were ever implemented.

The new marginal tax brackets were set at 15, 28, and 33 percent, which meant that the very rich had the lowest marginal tax rate for their bracket since World War II. At the same time, however, virtually all the existing tax loopholes were plugged, so that in fact most wealthy Americans actually paid more taxes than before. Critics charged that the rich were getting richer and the poor poorer due to the new tax program. But the share of personal income taxes paid by those in the $100,000-and-above bracket actually rose from 29 percent to 35.9 percent. As for the poor, their income taxes were eliminated. By 1988, the 68 million Americans earning less than $25,000 a year paid $47 million in taxes, while the 2.6 million who made more than $100,000 paid $152 million. Federal revenues rose from $517 billion in 1980 to $909 billion in 1988. Along the way, the government increased the national debt, which rose from $994 billion to $2.6 trillion.

Defenders of the Reagan economic record had difficulties coming to terms with charges that the prosperity of the period had been made possible by imposing major debts on future generations. Critics were unable to explain why a national debt that was 31 percent of gross domestic product at the end of the Reagan years was unbearable, while one that was 125 percent of GDP was not considered to be impossible to sustain in 1945. Both could agree, however, that the President had stood steadfast in the face of the very strong anti-inflation medicine Federal Reserve Board chairman Paul Volcker was administering to the economy in the early Reagan years.

When a Fed-induced recession continued, Reagan refused to intercede, even when unemployment reached into the double digits. It was the kind of economic program bound to be unpopular, but it seemed to be working by 1982, when U.S. inflation began to subside. Early in his first term, Reagan was favored by happenstance. He was wounded in a failed assassination attempt, and the oldest president in history came through with grace and humor. The public was reminded of the tragedies of prior assassinations, and reflected on the "Reagan luck."

At the same time, some economists were pointing out that prosperity depended more upon a sustained level of spending than one of savings. This was a throwback to the Keynesian "liberal" arguments of the 1930s, and seemed to have some justification in the direction of the economy during the Reagan years. Businessman Waddell Catchings and academician William Foster had stated the concept in its boldest terms in a 1926 *Atlantic Monthly* article, "The Dilemma of Thrift," that caused sharp debate at a time when the gospel of savings was popular:

> Since, therefore, the final end of all economic activity is consumption, and since it is always possible to produce far more than we consume, consumption regulates production. There is no use building more wooden ships, when hundreds are lying idle at the wharves; no use running all of our spindles, when it is impossible to sell the cloth we have already made. Too commonplace to mention, the fact may seem; yet it is the basic fact in the whole economic problem. . . . Sustained business-depression accompanied by adequate consumer demand is no more possible than drought accompanied by heavy rains.

Daniel Bell, one of the most influential social scientists of the time and author of *The Cultural Contradictions of Capitalism* (1976), claimed that this switch should not have surprised any close observer of the American political scene, since the seeds for it had been planted in the 1950s:

> The culture was no longer concerned with how to work and achieve, but with how to spend and

enjoy, despite some continuing use of the language of the Protestant Ethic. The fact was that by the 1950s American culture had become primarily hedonistic, concerned with play, fun, display, and pleasure—and, typical of things in America, in a compulsive way.

Lost in the debates of the Reagan years was the impact of higher consumption and lower savings on the national psyche. Of course, the Reaganites hoped that lower taxation would spur Americans to save more—but was that a solution to the economic problem? In any case, despite the rhetoric of individualism and self-reliance, it seemed that the public ethic that had guided middle-class America since World War II was being eroded.

Along with tax reform and attempts to shrink government, Reagan continued the movement toward deregulation that had begun under Carter. He did so more by means of naming individuals who opposed regulation and cutting budgets to key positions than by eliminating bureaus and commissions. Regulatory budgets were slashed, enforcement of regulations was ignored, and in the process safeguards in food and drugs, highway safety, the regulation of nursing homes, and banking were lessened. The greatest changes came in the area of the environment, where he attempted to make large-scale sales of public lands and open the continental shelf to offshore drilling. At the same time, Reagan was an ardent supporter of private enterprise's attempts to develop new technologies.

The America into which the grandchildren of the World War II veterans had graduated was one where engineers who could resolve problems, handle data, and make the proper presentations could write their own tickets. But it was also a world where reluctant college students who had been unprepared for difficult work could not find employment they thought utilized their talents and recognized their virtues. One way the educational establishment met this problem was to attempt reforms of curricula and the hiring of professors.

A large part of this change was motivated by reactions against the reforms of the 1960s and 1970s. At that time, students on some campuses demanded an end to the paternalistic attitudes toward them on the part of faculties and administrations, and they won a measure of freedom as a result. By the 1990s, some students started to reject this freedom, and called for higher standards that would please potential employers and graduate schools. By the end of the decade, several technological centers were going still farther, organizing consortia to present candidates in school board elections, supporting charter schools, and making other efforts to raise standards so as to produce the kinds of graduates their companies needed.

The Baby Boom and the Baby Bust

The birth rate in 1929 had been 21.2 per 1,000 population, after which it leveled off and started to decline. The low point in the cycle came in 1933, 18.4 per 1,000, at the bottom of the Depression, when the way ahead seemed uncertain, the outlook bleak. It started to rise afterwards. In 1941, as war neared, young Americans responded by marrying. There were 1,679,000 marriages in 1941, which worked out to 12.6 per 1,000—a new record. The following year there were 3 million births, 400,000 more than the previous year. In 1942 the number of births declined, but still bettered the 1929 mark at 22.2 million, and it stayed at that approximate level throughout the war. For 1945 it was 20.4 per 1,000. In 1946 the rate leaped to 24.1 per 1,000. Dr. Benjamin Spock published his *Baby and Child Care* that year; it would sell more than 5 million copies during the next eight years. The birth rate went to a record 26.6 per 1,000 in 1947, which worked out to 113 offspring per 1,000 for women between the ages of fourteen and forty-four. None of this surprised sociologists, historians, and demographers. The birth rate had risen immediately after the Civil War and World War I, but this time it was different. The high birth rate continued. It would remain above the 1945 level until 1965.

The high rates of marriages and births along with the low divorce rate combined to create an atmosphere of family stability. In 1954 *Cosmopolitan* gave the condition a name: "togetherness." The magazine asserted, "From a little cloud, like a woman's hand, it has risen to blanket the consciousness of an entire nation, popping up everywhere from Macy's to the halls of Congress." Togetherness implied children, life in the suburbs in a house complete with a two-car garage, and steady employment.

The babies born between 1946 and 1964 were a huge statistical anomaly on the demographic charts. During this interval, 76 million babies were born. They would both stimulate and change the nation for the rest of the century. It began with inadequate hospital space, followed by increases in the manufacture of child-related products from toys to baby clothing, and shortages of baby-sitters. Diapers, which were not yet disposable, were a $32 million industry in 1947. Ten years later, diapers reached a level of $50 million, in the process providing not only a

needed service, but also economic opportunities for entrepreneurs. Baby foods, which were sold at a 270-million-
jar-unit pace in 1940, reached 1.5 billion in 1953. The
effects of the baby boom were felt in clothing, toys, bicy-
cles, and all other related consumer products. And in
each, perceptive businesses were able to reap rewards. Or
fail.

Some enterprising and imaginative individuals, realizing that elderly people on limited diets had to eat foods
not that different in texture and nutritional value from
baby foods, attempted to market them as such to the geriatric population. They failed; grandparents were averse to
the suggestion they consider eating the same foods as
their grandchildren. But this was an entry wedge into a
new market—the seniors, who were living longer and
were in need of a wide variety of services. This was due in
part to better nutrition, new drugs, and an increasing
awareness of health. The life expectancy of a person born
in the late 1920s and early 1930s hovered around sixty.

In the suburbs the baby boom helped create and pop-
ularize drive-in movies, where the babies slept in the back
of the car. Then there were the shortages of elementary
school teachers and classrooms. There had been 19.4 million elementary school students in 1920 and 21.3 million
in 1939. In 1940, as a result of declining birth rates during
the Great Depression, there were 18.8 million, approximately the same as in 1916, when there had been 30 million fewer Americans. In 1950, when the vanguard of the
baby boom entered elementary schools, the figure was
19.4 million. By mid-1950, there were some 25 million
children in the elementary schools. The number of
schoolteachers rose from 828,000 in 1944 to 1.2 million in
1956, and shortages led to higher salaries and expanding
colleges. Levittowners needing a second salary to help pay

for the new products and services often decided that the wife of the family should take courses in the schools of continuing education at nearby Hofstra, Adelphi, or C. W. Post in order to qualify for a teaching license and, with this in hand, the wives became substitute teachers at attractive per diem salaries. So it went, at every stage of the bulge's development. Toward the end of the twentieth century, some funeral directors predicted a large increase in their business by the year 2015 or so.

By then the saying "Demography is destiny" had become widespread. So it was. In a time when statistics were becoming more important, these were the key ones when it came to many aspects of American life in the years that followed, including the accumulation of wealth, and how it was spent.

Consider that by 1970 the American population had reached 205 million, having risen from 130 million at the beginning of World War II and doing so without any sizable increase in immigration. Of this number, those born after 1946 came to 95 million. The cohort of people between the ages of twenty and twenty-four in 1970 was 17.2 million; that from fifteen to nineteen, 19.1 million; and the largest category, from ages ten to fourteen, 20.7 million. Only slightly smaller were those between the ages of five and nine, at 20.6 million, while those under the age of five came to 17.6 million. This was what demographers called the "baby bust." They did not think it would last for very long, since the original baby boomers were at the age where they would marry and presumably have babies of their own. So another baby boom was expected.

A 1970 survey by *Scholastic* magazine indicated that the parents of the baby boomers resolved to make certain their children would not suffer the deprivations they had experienced during the Great Depression. And they made up for their own lack of certain amenities and luxuries by showering them, when possible, on their children. To the generation that experienced the Great Depression and World War II, security was important. They were not great risk-takers, and this sentiment was passed down to at least some of their offspring. To a large degree they succeeded, at least when it came to the desire for secure futures. In a survey taken of executives in their fifties in 1989, children of World War II veterans indicated that 3 out of 4 expected to end their careers where they were currently employed.

Discussing the teenagers of the 1970s, *Scholastic* observed:

> Eighty-six percent of teenage boys and girls own or use a camera. Senior high school boys own 2 million razors. Teen-age boys and girls own 10 million phonographs, over a million TV sets, and 20 million radios. They consume 20 percent more food than adults, drink 3½ billion quarts of milk every year, eat 145 million gallons of ice cream a year. It is estimated that it costs almost twice as much for food for a 16-year-old girl as for a 3-year-old, and more than double that to feed a 16-year-old boy. Food for a teen-age boy costs 30 percent more than for his father, 25 percent more for a teen-age girl than for her middle-aged mother.

"Among senior high school boys it is estimated that over 20 percent own cars," wrote *Scholastic*.

All of which was good news for those companies who made such products and foodstuffs—and for those who worked for them, and their stockholders, and suppliers. The care and maintenance of this new generation became a major source of growth for the American economy.

The New Egalitarianism

Disparities of wealth often occur in times of major technological change, as those who successfully introduce the new techniques, products, and services become wealthy while those who are displaced may be impoverished if they cannot adjust. The creation of a national market for many goods at the turn of the twentieth century saw the creation of massive industrial and financial wealth at the top of the economy, while workers and farmers at the bottom suffered. The Morgans and the Fricks had mansions, while Jacob Riis wrote of how the "other half" lived in slums. In time, wealth filtered down to the manual workers in occupations not amenable to unionization, while tax laws and other changes cut into the wealth at the top.

There was more of an appearance of egalitarianism after the war. The college graduate who was doing well selling insurance for a national company drove a Buick. His neighbor, who was a high school dropout and might work on the General Motors assembly line, owned a Chevrolet. But both had cars, and each considered himself successful by prewar standards.

A vague kind of statement like this has to be qualified. While some government agencies offered *estimates* of wealth, none of them actually collected and published such data, including the Bureau of the Census, the Treasury, and the Bureau of Labor Statistics. As noted, in this period no agency sent out questionnaires asking Americans to add up their money and possessions. Even had they done so, the responses might not have been very useful. Scholars can agree that certain assets comprise wealth, but are not sure which do not. Money in the bank or in stocks and bonds clearly is wealth. But what about a legal or medical education, or a mechanical skill? These may create wealth, or might be considered an asset or an investment, but cannot be placed on a balance sheet until and unless they are translated into figures. For example, a General Motors worker might have earned more in 1950 than a freshly minted attorney, and even have more visible assets, but who would argue that he possessed greater wealth?

What can be measured, however, is income, though even here there are problems because different individuals and groups use different data. One organization that accumulated such statistics, the Council of Economic Advisers, reported the following:

Income of the American People in 1951

Quartile	Income Level	Percentage in Cohort
First	less than $1,000	10.6
Second	$1,000–$2,000	14.5
Third	$2,000–$3,000	20.6
Fourth	$3,000–$5,000	33.6
Fifth	$5,000 and more	20.7

SOURCE: *Economic Report of the President*, 1951.

A small number of the fifth cohort, about 2.9 percent, had incomes of more than $10,000.

Clearly no one wanted to be in the first quartile, but

in this group there were not only low income earners, but also farmers who consumed a part of their crops and did not report it as income, small businessmen who had several bad years but then bounced back, older people no longer working full time, and young people just entering the labor force. Single-parent families may also have been in this group. In time, some would work themselves upward. They were in the next quartile, along with more of those out-of-luck businesspeople, old people, and single-parent families. The ability and willingness of a spouse to become a substitute teacher might easily enable the family to move up in income range.

More than half the population was in the next two quartiles, and they were what at the time passed for the middle class. In it were white-collar and blue-collar workers alike. During this period, the average annual income for all manufacturing workers came to more than $3,000 a year, with steel workers receiving, on average, $4,500.

In order to better understand statistics such as these one must have some knowledge of job and work opportunities. An entry-level position at a major corporation remained the goal of many college graduates, while assembly-line openings, often obtained with the help of a relative or family friend, were attractive to those with high school educations. The ambition of many in both cohorts was starting businesses of their own—a corner delicatessen, a hardware store, or something similar for the high school grads, and an accounting, legal, or medical practice for the professionals. For every CPA who hoped for a position at a major corporation or accounting firm, there must have been scores who dreamed of setting up their own practices, either individually or as a partnership. In the post–World War II period, there was a halfway house that would become more attractive as time passed: the franchised business.

The high school seniors of the late 1940s had well-defined ambitions. Within a few years they would be able to get married, support a family, and purchase a modest home. As suggested, down the road were a used and then a new car, rental and then ownership of a vacation place, and a boat. The family would be able to dine once in a while in modest restaurants, and take vacation trips. They would acquire a television set. In 1948, 3 percent of American homes had one, and they were considered luxuries. By 1956, 81 percent had receivers, which then were becoming necessities. The family might live in a community very much like Levittown. Toward the end of that development's construction, William Levitt included televisions in his houses. The family who owned a TV might have watched a popular weekly program of the period, *The Life of Riley*, which started on radio and then was switched to television. It starred William Bendix (and later Jackie Gleason) as a factory worker who moved from Brooklyn to Los Angeles and found work there. Riley, clearly high school educated at best, had found his way to the middle class. He had arrived. Chester Riley rarely wore a suit, but rather slacks and a sports shirt. His speech was ungrammatical, but Riley had the proverbial heart of gold, and he and his family seemed quite content with their lot in life, a life that was better than that of their parents.

This was about as far as they would go. Perhaps their children would get into that fifth quartile, but it was not *their* lot in life. Even so, in the aggregate, incomes were rising steadily through the first decade and a half of the postwar period. Hard work and savings were an assumed part of the picture.

Inheritance and Wealth

Inheritance played a role in those standings, as did increases in the worth of holdings. Personal residences were part of this, and real estate values rose substantially from the late 1940s through the 1990s. According to one estimate, 30 percent of the wealth of the American people in 1983 was represented by their homes, and it should be considered that the owner of a $100,000 home in 1983 that cost $40,000 in 1950 may have refinanced the mortgage, and had a $30,000 or so stake in the home, meaning that a rise in value from $100,000 to $130,000 actually doubled his or her wealth. Holdings in nonincorporated businesses accounted for another 27 percent of wealth, nonresidential real estate 15 percent, stocks and bonds 11 percent, savings and checking accounts 8 percent, and trusts 4 percent. In time, when the government created individual retirement accounts (IRAs), some 6 percent of Americans' money went into such investments, as well as insurance and other savings items. Of the $1.5 trillion in debts owed by Americans, more than three-quarters were for real estate, namely mortgages. Along the way, middle-class Americans realized that Social Security and even home equity would not provide them with the kind of lives they wanted to live upon retirement. IRAs and other forms of savings might perform that task. The pursuit of wealth would continue through these vehicles, among others. But the employees who entered into IRA contracts were not to become the very wealthy—nor did they expect to be.

Sociologist C. Wright Mills, whose *The Power Elite* (1956) is a key document on the subject, believed that the corporate leaders, rather than the inheritors, represented a new class that was to become increasingly important:

> The propertied class, in the age of corporate property, has become a corporate rich, and in becoming corporate has consolidated its power and drawn to its defense new men of more executive and more political stance. Its members have become self-conscious in terms of the corporate world they represent. As men of status they have secured their privileges and prerogatives in the most stable private institutions of American society. They are a corporate rich because they depend directly as well as indirectly, for their money, their privileges, their securities, their advantages, their powers, on the world of the big corporations.

Mills was discussing power, not wealth, and there was a difference. A small businessman of that period might amass substantial wealth without accruing power outside of his local community. Moreover, he might not care for such power. The "good life" as epitomized by a suburban home and a two-car garage was what he really wanted, not influence in the community or beyond. To be sure, as Mills stated, influence was being accumulated by a new class, which did not have the proper social connections, though they often obtained them, as indicated by entries in the *Social Register* and their children's admissions to prep schools and universities. More important for most Americans, however, was income, which was steadily rising in this period. According to the Dunhill International List Co., of New York, in 1956 there were 28,000 Americans whose net worth was more than $500,000, which was double the amount in 1945. So some Americans did prosper financially soon after the war.

Even so, an entry-level position at a major corporation remained the initial goal for the college graduates who were not heading toward the professions, and this was reflected in numerous books and articles on the subject, some of which were made into motion pictures. Among the better known were David Reisman's *The Lonely Crowd* (1950), Sloan Wilson's *The Man in the Gray Flannel Suit* (1955), and David Packard's *The Hidden Persuaders* (1957). From academics came others: John K. Galbraith's *American Capitalism* (1952), Irvin Wyllie's *The Self-Made Man in America* (1954), *The American Business Creed* by Francis Sutton et al., (1956), and Mills's *The Power Elite*. In these books and others the authors challenged claims of entrepreneurship and originality sent forth by defenders of the modern American corporation, charging that conformity, not originality, was the most important trait in executive suites. All of this notwithstanding, executive offices were what many newcomers to the corporate scene strove for in the 1950s.

Most of these analysts discerned a difference between these new "organization men" and their predecessors, or, for that matter, the values they claimed to hold and the reality. William H. Whyte's *The Organization Man* (1956) was perhaps the most celebrated of the genre, and the title of his book passed into the language. Whyte based his book on observations of middle-class executives who lived in the suburbs of Park Forest, Illinois, many of them discharged World War II GIs. He noted that they gave lip service to such matters as self-reliance, independence, and entrepreneurship, although this did not mean they personified such matters in their daily lives. Rather, they seemed to typify the new values of loyalty and dedication to the company, and they sought security and "belonging-ness" rather than independence and freedom. The new organization man, Whyte thought, "must not only accept control, but he must accept it as though he liked it." Such individuals had to be less "goal centered" and more "employee centered." "Be loyal to the company and the company will be loyal to you," was their mantra, accord-ing to Whyte. Such executives were the backbone for what Galbraith called "the technostructure."

Critics then and later chided the organization man for "having sold out," implying that such individuals sacri-ficed their souls for position and wealth, which was nei-ther fair nor accurate. Rather, these management men accepted the ethic of the corporation voluntarily, perhaps knowing there was a price to be paid in terms of inde-pendence, which they paid willingly, often for the sake of family growth and financial stability.

Small Businesses

On V-J Day there were some 6.7 million individual busi-nesses in the United States, most of which were "mom and pop" operations, such as neighborhood delicatessens and dry cleaners, and they had receipts of $382 million. Some 85 percent were sole proprietorships, accounting for 20 percent of receipts, and 10 percent were partnerships, with 12 percent of total receipts. The rest were corpora-tions, whose receipts were more than half the total. One-third were in manufacturing, and less than one-fifth in wholesale and retail trade, while 10 percent derived from finance. In what was supposed to be the age of giant cor-porations, small businesses did quite well. By 1977 there were 14.7 million of them as classified by the Census

Bureau, a majority of which were owned or managed by a single person, and they employed a third of the nation's workers.

Consumer Prices and Average Weekly Earnings of Production Workers in Manufacturing Industries, Selected Years, 1939–1959

Year	Consumer Price Index 1947–1949 = 100	Net Spendable Weekly Earnings, Worker with Three Dependents	
		1960 Dollars	1947–1949 Dollars
1939	54.9	23.62	39.76
1940	59.9	24.95	41.65
1942	69.7	36.26	52.05
1944	75.2	44.06	58.59
1945	76.9	42.74	55.58
1946	83.4	43.20	51.80
1947	95.5	48.24	50.51
1948	102.8	53.17	51.72
1949	101.8	53.83	52.88
1950	102.8	57.21	55.65
1951	111.0	61.28	55.21
1952	113.5	63.62	56.05
1953	114.4	66.58	58.20
1954	114.8	66.78	58.17
1955	114.5	70.45	61.53
1956	116.2	73.22	63.01
1957	120.2	74.97	62.37
1958	123.5	76.05	61.58
1959	124.6	80.36	64.49

SOURCE: United States Department of Labor, *Economic Forces in the U.S.A.* sixth ed., pp. 73, 80; and United States, *Statistical Abstract, 1960*, USGPO, p. 336.

Not only were wages rising, but fringe benefits were becoming more important. This newer form of compensation for the average worker was one of the most significant innovations of the postwar period. Benefits included discounts on company-manufactured goods, paid vacations, assistance in making home purchases, and the important provision of health insurance, all of which derived from careful bargaining between management and labor, often involving labor's willingness to sacrifice wage increases for those non-taxable benefits. Executives received even more valuable benefits. Perhaps the most important of the fringe benefits were the pension plans.

Pension Plan Socialism

One of the earliest pension plans, that of Sears Roebuck, began by employees investing in its stock, so that by the mid-1960s they owned a controlling interest in the company. More companies followed. Without a national debate or an election, employees had created their own form of socialism, in a purely capitalist environment, although none of those involved with the functioning of American business appeared to think of it in such terms. In this manner, the Sears Roebuck employees had achieved greater wealth than they might have imagined before the contract establishing it had been signed.

Another major company that put a pension plan into operation, one that became a model for others, was General Motors, which had considered and rejected a complex profit-sharing program. At the beginning of the negotiations there was talk of having pension funds invested in General Motors stock, an idea that was rejected by the

United Automobile Workers Union, since this would tie workers closely to the progress of the company, and so clash with their roles as workers. Existing pension plans were for the most part invested in corporate and government bonds, a policy considered prudent by a generation wary of anything that smacked of speculation. Moreover, the "prudent man rule" in many states mandated the purchase of high-quality bonds and, in some cases, preferred stock. This was eased, however, as the older trustees retired. By the late 1940s, some pension funds were nibbling at common shares. In the end, the GM plan was to be administered by an outside, independent body and be concentrated in stocks.

At about the same time, several New York life insurance companies petitioned for the right to invest up to 2 percent of their assets in common shares, and the state agreed they might do so. Other states soon followed suit. By 1955, the life insurance companies alone owned more than $3.6 billion in common stock, while the property and casualty companies, which always had the right to own common shares, held another $5.4 billion. Pension plans became another source of demand for common stock. In 1949 such plans owned $500 million of common stock; in 1971 this figure rose to more than $900 billion, while the total for all institutions went from $11 billion to $219 billion in the same period.

In 1952 the assets of private pension plans came to $8.5 billion, of which $1.2 billion was in stocks, and of that amount, $301 million was in the stock of the company for which the plan had been established and $927 million in those of other companies. At that time, 76 percent of all covered employees and 70 percent of those with vested benefits had plans that would return them less than $25,000 a year. By 1958, the plans had $22.1 billion in assets, of which $6 billion was in common shares, with $646 million in the company and another $5.4 billion in shares of other companies. Clearly, the expectation that pension plans would enable workers to control the companies for which they worked was an illusion.

In its 1952 shareholder census, the NYSE found that only 11 percent of all shares were owned by institutions and nominees. By 1976, various pension plans alone owned more than a third of the nation's equity capital. The result was that many Americans who in the 1950s were certain they had no exposure to the stock market found out they were very much in the market—through their pension programs.

Their number included the likes of the fictional Riley family, which through pension plans became major participants in the growing wealth being created in the United States.

The Rileys shared other differences from their prewar counterparts. For one thing, they lived in suburbia—as did the casts of most situation comedies, including *Leave It to Beaver, Father Knows Best*, and *The Adventures of Ozzie and Harriet*. The exceptions were the urbanites, as depicted on *The Honeymooners* and *I Love Lucy*—which concerned couples who in the former case were childless and in the latter had a child during the course of the show. In *The Honeymooners*, bus driver Ralph Kramden wore his uniform even when not on the job, and looked out of place in a suit. All the others, middle-class to the core, were rarely without ties, and most of the time wore suits. In the seventies Archie Bunker appeared, almost always jacketless and tieless, with one child. Return now to the division of families into quartiles, that practice pioneered by the

Council Advisers after the war. The Rileys were definitely second quartile.

In the adjoining apartment might have been another high school graduate who owned a small business, who would dip down into the first or second quartile, especially when competition or bad times appeared. He worked for himself, and took pride in the fact. Unlike Chester Riley, if business required it, he wore a suit and, at home, a tie and jacket or a cardigan sweater. Down the road was the college graduate, whose car was a bit more expensive than Riley's, and whose house was larger than the Riley's apartment. He might be an insurance broker, such as the protagonist in *Father Knows Best*. Those suburban fathers and mothers in the situation comedies were fourth-quartile types. They might have been among those who attended college on the GI Bill (in 1950 close to 500,000 degrees were awarded, twice the 1942 figure). Such individuals wanted more, and had reason to expect it. But not in their most vivid imaginings could they comprehend just how much they might receive by the time they retired.

Finally, there were those who had more than $10,000 a year in salaries and other earnings. These included professionals after a few years of practice and executives at large organizations. The fabled Texas oil millionaires were in the upper reaches of this group, along with successful bankers and the like. But there weren't many of them, and despite tax shelters, the government took much of what they made, since income taxes were more sharply graduated than they would become in the 1980s. In 1939, two-thirds of a million Americans paid 90 percent of all income taxes. By 1960 that percentage was paid by the top 32 million taxpayers. As John Brooks noted in his seminal work, *The Great Leap* (1996), "To put it another way, while the population was rising by 38 percent, the number of persons who had to chip in to supply the bulk of federal receipts had increased by no less than 4,600 percent." From 1952 to 1961, Brooks went on to say, when the population went from 160 million to 180 million, the number of Americans who reported less than $5,000 income on their federal tax returns decreased from 43 million to 33 million.

In 1953 the IRS estimated that there were some 27,000 millionaires. In this period most of them had achieved that status through inheritance, not earnings. According to the IRS, in 1972, 2 out of every 3 households with incomes of more than $100,000 had inherited assets, and of these, 57 percent of the tax returns indicated that these inheritances constituted an important part of their assets. The nation's 100 wealthiest Americans in 1968 included J. Paul Getty, Howard Hughes, Ailsa Bruce, Paul and Richard King Mellon, John Dorrance, Mrs. Alfred Du Pont, and a slew of Rockefellers, all of whom inherited their wealth, though some increased their inherited holdings substantially. But also on the list were many newcomers, who arrived by virtue of the buoyant economy as well as their own intelligence and application. Among the postwar wealthy were Edward Land, Daniel Ludwig, Howard Ahmanson, Sherman Fairchild, William Hewlett, David Packard—and Bob Hope.

The Ways of the New Rich

What were their lives like? Lewis Lapham, in his book *Money and Class in America* (1988), presents the budget provided to him by one George Amory, not his real name, but clearly a member of the old-money upper class in the early 1980s, and a Yale graduate. The budget is like the one Tom Wolfe presented for his hero, Sherman McCoy, in *The Bonfire of the Vanities* (1998), who couldn't pay his bills on an annual income of $980,000. Says Amory, "I'm nothing. You understand that, nothing. I earn $250,000 a year, but it's nothing and I'm nobody."

Maintenance of a cooperative apartment on Park Avenue	$20,400
Maintenance of the house in Southampton	10,000
Private school tuitions	30,000
Groceries	12,000
Interest on a $200,000 loan	30,000
Telephone, repairs, electricity	12,000
Full-time maid and part-time laundress	25,000
Insurance	8,000
Lawyers and accountants	5,000
Club dues and bills	5,000
Pharmacy	5,000
Doctors	4,000
Charitable donations	6,000
Clothes for wife	5,000
Clothes for children	7,000
Cash expenditures (taxis, newspapers, coffee shops, etc.)	8,000
Children's supplies (computers, stereos, allowances, books, dancing school, etc.)	30,000
Own supplies	3,000
Taxes	75,000
Total	$300,400

At the turn of the century, the very rich, like Amory, had lived in mansions and dressed the part. When they shopped for automobiles the choice might be a custom-made Packard, Peerless, or Pierce-Arrow. They dined in fine restaurants, and took tours of Europe, which started by sailing in a first-class cabin on large and luxurious ocean liners. Their daughters had coming-out parties, their sons attended Ivy League colleges, and the latter often entered the family business upon graduation.

The middle class of a century ago did not have cars, and when they finally did, they were Model Ts or Chevrolets. They lived in tenements, ate inexpensive food at home, and their sons and daughters dropped out of elementary or secondary school to find work. They did not go on vacations, and certainly never to Europe. A day at Coney Island or some similar place was dreamed of and remembered long after. Their 1950s and 1960s counterparts had no ambitions (or even desires in many cases) to emulate Amory; rather, they sought bourgeois comforts.

One could not tell the difference between the insurance broker and the banker by clothes alone. The latter's suit may have been purchased at Brooks Brothers and the former's from Sears Roebuck, but at a distance they looked the same. In 1952, 60 percent of the leaders at America's large corporations were college graduates, but a majority of these had degrees from non-Ivy schools. Frank Abrams, the CEO at Standard Oil of New Jersey, had graduated from Syracuse. General Electric's president, Charles Wilson, had a degree from Carnegie Institute of Technology. Leroy Wilson, soon to take over at American Telephone & Telegraph, had his from Rose Polytechnic, and so it went at many other large corporations. In comparison, less than 30 percent of their 1929 counterparts were college graduates, most of whom attended the prestigious institutions. But this was a fairly new phenomenon. Major tycoons of the previous generation did not have college degrees, among them John D. Rockefeller, Andrew Carnegie, E. H. Harriman, George F. Baker, and H. H. Rogers.

In this period, many publications contrasted the earnings of those who had degrees and those without them. In 1971 elementary school graduates had average incomes of approximately $7,400, compared with $10,700 for high school graduates, and $16,700 for persons with college and post-graduate degrees. One might assume from these figures that a college education was a good investment. This was not necessarily so. The cohort of college grads included those from wealthy families who attended as a socializing experience, middle-class students who went on to law and medical schools and whose remuneration was high due to their employment, not necessarily anything else, along with those from poor families who got by on their brains and training. But if an observer went through the reports filed by the nation's largest and most successful corporations, he or she would have learned that virtually all the officers and board members were college graduates.

The observer also would have realized that the remunerations of such individuals were high, but, given the fact that they controlled their boards, could have been still more lavish. The executives of the 1950s and afterwards eschewed salaries in favor of stock options (which when exercised would be taxed at lower capital gains rates), and the wealthiest of the lot often established foundations that received their money, and so were able to control wealth without having to worry about taxes or inheritance problems. For individuals such as these, a generous expense account is far more important, and desired, than a boost in salary. That included access to private hunting lodges, the use of airplanes and yachts, membership in country clubs, tickets to sporting and artistic events, and more. A government estimate of the worth of such perquisites in the fifties came to between $5 billion and $10 billion, all of which was tax-free. In 1952 the wife of such an executive complained about the lot of one married to someone with an expense account:

> Even when he was only earning $7,500 a year he used to be sent to Washington all the time. He'd go down in a Pullman drawing room and as J. R. Robinson of the General Company, take a two-room suite. Then he used to be asked by some of the company officers to a hunting and fishing lodge that the company kept in the north woods. When he went to New York, he'd entertain at Twenty-One, the Barberry Room, and the Chambord. Me, meanwhile I'd be eating a 30-cent hamburger and, when we went away together on vacation, we would have to go in our beat-up old car or borrow my sister's husband's. This taste of high life gives some of these characters delusions of grandeur.

By then those mansions of the old rich were either torn down or transformed into museums. The wealthy executives of 1951 lived better than the middle class, but despite the perceptions of that corporate wife of 1952, by then it was a matter of degree, not kind. They dined in fine restaurants, and soon would fly first-class to Europe on their vacations. The restaurants of the middle class were not as opulent as those frequented by the wealthy, but they were much more so than before the war.

This is to suggest that after the initial postwar period came a time of middle-class growth. The American social and economic pyramid prior to World War II resembled just that, a pyramid, with few at the top and many at the bottom. After the war it looked more like a puffed-up tube, with few at the top and bottom and many in the middle.

Even so, the very rich stood firmly at the top. The top half of 1 percent of the population in terms of wealth (420,000 in number) accounted for 35 percent of gross wealth. If homes were excluded, the rich owned 45 percent of the wealth, 58 percent of unincorporated businesses, 45 percent of stock not held by large funds, 77 percent of personally owned stock, and 62 percent of stock and local bonds. How did this affect wealth? From 1946 to 1975, capital gains on stocks, realized and unrealized, came to $2.7 trillion.

The second half of the top 1 percent—another 420,000—held net assets of more than $1.4 million and less than $2.5 million, which was only one-fifth of what the top half of 1 percent owned.

What about the top 10 percent of all families? They were not exactly living in penury, since the typical family had net assets ranging from $206,000 to $1.4 million, and comprised 7.5 million households. Taken together, the top 10 percent owned more than 71 percent of the total wealth of the American people. Before concluding that the rich and poor will always be with us, reflect that the makeup of both had changed. Americans who would have fallen far below the top 10 percent prior to V-J Day were solidly in that category by the 1980s. The elevator goes down as well as up. Some of the wealthy of the earlier period had fallen a notch or so. In addition, the average wealth for the bottom 90 percent of the population had increased from $27,400 to $39,600 from 1963 to 1983.

It remains to be said that those investments made in

the rearing of the children of the baby boomers paid off. While their ascent into the middle class and above was not as dramatic as that experienced by the World War II veterans, it did happen. But there were statistics that indicated otherwise, in particular when it came to debt. Unlike their parents, the boomers were not averse to accumulating debts to finance their journey to the good life. Between 1977 and 1983, when the boomers were making their mark on the economy, the average net worth of all American households, adjusted for inflation, calculated by the government, rose from $41,000 to $47,000. But for households headed by a person aged twenty-five to thirty-four, the proportion of income needed to repay consumer debt increased from 67 percent to 77 percent. In 1984, more than a third of all households headed by a person under the age of thirty-five had no savings aside from non–interest-bearing checking accounts. Only 13 percent had assets in the form of equities or mutual funds. At a time when 3 out of 4 of the GI generation owned their homes, the average value of which was $55,000, only 34 percent of the boomers were in that category, and the trend was downward.

The Franchise Phenomenon

How can one universalize about the ambitions of more than 10 million returning American veterans and those of high school and college graduates in their cohort during the second half of the 1940s? Some hoped to enter the professions, others the family businesses, and large numbers so wide a variety of occupations as to defy classification. Such is the problem in analyzing a society dedicated to freedom of choice. Even so, several generalizations may be made.

Urban youngsters of this period often had "hangouts." In a large city it might be a corner candy story, a pool hall, a diner, or a school yard. Their rural counterparts had fewer choices, but they too found places to gather and exchange ideas. In the process, they likely formulated strategies on how to mold their futures.

For those who did not plan to seek work at the nearby factory, apply for positions at large corporations, or in some other way work for an organization, the alternative was to ask that candy-store owner whether he needed help or join with a friend to open a similar place in an area where it was needed. Many would like to have their own businesses, or at least find some way by which independence could be achieved. To want to work for oneself, to be independent, is deeply rooted in the American psyche. But of course there are problems along the way. The would-be entrepreneur may lack experience, knowledge, the proper contacts, the personality for such an endeavor, and, most of all, the capital required. Failures galore are a part of the American small-business scene, the existence of which might be expected to discourage others, but somehow this rarely happened.

In the Northeast and Midwest, it seemed that thousands of Italian-American males hoped to open a pizzeria. By the 1970s it was all but impossible to walk more than a street or two in any downtown area without passing one of them. Some were successful, but many failed, the moment of truth arriving when dealers in used restaurant equipment appeared and began to haul away ovens, tables, and chairs that had been purchased with the assistance of loans that were being called in. A few weeks later a new pizzeria owner would appear at the dealer's establishment, take over that equipment, and another pizzeria was born.

The rise of suburbia and the advent of the automobile economy added more ingredients to the mix, one of the more significant of which was the appearance of fast-food restaurants. The phenomenon began in southern California, where before World War II drive-in facilities specializing in chicken, barbecue, and hamburgers attracted a repeat clientele. A few of these were chain operations. White Castle, which specialized in hamburgers, opened its first unit in Wichita, Kansas, in 1921. Food Master began its Jack in the Box hamburger restaurants in 1941, and Friendly Ice Cream appeared in 1935, none at that time with an outreach beyond its original locale, or with a guiding philosophy or large-scale aspirations.

This was the inspiration behind a far more common development of the postwar period, which would revolutionize the world of small business: franchises.

During the immediate postwar period, Americans transacted a great deal of business with franchised companies, but most of them did not realize what they were, and didn't make the distinction between franchises and big— not small—businesses.

There were several forms of franchises, the genre itself having begun more than a century earlier. In its basic form, a franchise is a retail or wholesale business whose operator has obtained the right to provide a product or service from its parent company, for a designated period of time in a specified geographic location under agreed-upon terms. The McCormick Harvesting Company before the Civil War and the Singer Sewing Machine Company afterwards started it all. Lacking the funds and personnel to organize a distribution and servicing network across the country, McCormick and Singer, for a specified sum, would provide its franchisees with product, services, and assistance. Both companies monitored their franchisees, making certain that quality and customer satisfaction were maintained. In time, what was known as the "agency" system declined, but it soon revived as automobile companies took it up, with modifications. Alfred Sloan, the guiding force at General Motors, thought this the best method to distribute automobiles, writing in his autobiography, "I believe that the franchise system, which has long prevailed in the automobile industry, is the best one for manufacturers, dealers, and consumers."

Gasoline stations operated under franchises from the petroleum companies whose products they sold. Soft drink companies such as Coca-Cola and PepsiCo sold franchises to bottlers, and hardware and drugstore chains and automotive aftermarket stores offered franchises in the 1920s. Rexall drugstores were franchised, as were Western Auto Supply and Ben Franklin stores. One of the more familiar franchises was the Howard Johnson restaurants, the first of which, then an ice-cream stand, appeared in 1925. The parent company charged its franchisees a modest fee, which started out at $1,000 and by the late 1930s had reached the $25,000 level. But the parent obtained more income from items it produced and sold to the licensees. Customers who flocked to Howard Johnson during this period usually had no idea that the proprietor was a licensee and not a representative of the parent company.

The franchise concept in restaurants and other areas ranging from motels to rental tools to videocasettes did not take hold in any important way until the mid-1950s, and for good reason. Students of merchandising have long debated whether demand creates supply or the reverse. Thus, the question is whether there was a large unvoiced demand for fast food in this period, which was noted by imaginative and ambitious businessmen, or whether those businessmen helped create the demand by offering willing consumers their product. Certainly, the appearance of so many units in suburbia implies that there is a strong causal relationship between the two phenomena and, since the suburbs developed first, they created the climate that prompted the development of the fast-food franchises. Indeed, franchised motels of this period must have been the result in large part of the needs of those families, now car owners and in search of vacations, to have places along the road to stay.

The purchaser of a franchise did so for the best of reasons. For a fee and the loss of some independence, he or she would be able to open a business selling a product or service already known (and presumably trusted) by many potential customers. The person who enjoyed the product in Rhode Island knew it would be pretty much like the one in South Carolina. The same could not be said for a slice of pizza purchased at Ray's on Twenty-third Street in Manhattan and one purchased at another pizzeria called Ray's on Fifty-sixth Street. This was so because the franchiser, anxious to preserve a reputation, would make certain such was the case. So in return for those considerations the franchisee would obtain a measure of certainty regarding the success of his enterprise. Also the franchiser, be it Mobil or Ben Franklin stores, would not be obliged to tie up large amounts of capital or be responsible for payrolls and the like. In other words, both sides in the arrangement were relinquishing some control and profits in return for a more certain return on capital and what amounted to what later would be known as "sweat equity." As some commentator observed, in transactions between two intelligent consenting adults, both sides win.

The signal year for franchising was 1954. It was then that Ray Kroc, a salesman who specialized in disposable goods and mixers for fountain sales for restaurants, came across the McDonald brothers' drive-in hamburger take-out operation in San Bernardino, California. Kroc approached the McDonalds with a proposal to buy them out. He succeeded, and started transforming McDonald's into a national chain based on franchising. The original contract provided for Kroc to receive $950 for each franchise he sold plus 1.9 percent of the store's gross revenues, with half of that percent going to the McDonald brothers. By 1957 Kroc had franchised thirty-seven sites, and in the next two years, 164 more. The McDonald's restaurants were huge successes, and Kroc added eat-in facilities. He also sold franchise rights for large territories to entrepreneurs who then would sell them to those who became the actual operators. By 1980 McDonald's restaurants were an integral part of the American scene. There were more than 6,500 of them in operation, with revenues over $6.2 billion. By then, too, Kroc was making more money from real estate deals—finding places to establish new restaurants—than franchise fees.

Kroc's formula had a major impact not only on the industry, but on American life as well. McDonald's became a path of entry into the workforce, and an introduction to capitalism, for millions of Americans. In 1998 the company asserted that 1 out of every 8 Americans had worked or did work for McDonald's. The purchaser of a McDonald's franchise in the 1980s—for more than $250,000—received instruction on how to operate at the company's "Hamburger University," and continual supervision by company representatives, and, once more, the other chains followed suit.

In 1954 James McLamore and David Edgerton also

opened their first Burger King in Miami, Florida, and it soon became a national chain. McLamore and Edgerton pioneered in the "wholesale" approach by making large-scale grants of territories, in the hope that by so doing they would expand more rapidly. A Burger King franchise initially cost $25,000, including equipment, plus 1 percent of gross sales. The approach worked. In 1967, when there were 274 Burger Kings, all but thirty-five of which were franchised, the owners sold the company to Pillsbury for $28 million. By the mid-1980s a Burger King franchise cost $400,000 plus 4 percent of sales, and a large majority of the stores were franchised.

In 1952 Harland Sanders, who had sold his chicken at his restaurant, rejected what he considered a boring life in retirement and started offering franchises on his Kentucky Fried Chicken, initially for nothing at all. In time he would market the concept to would-be restaurateurs willing to pay him five cents a bird for access to his secret recipe for fried chicken and for the right to use his products and trademark. Two years later, now living on Social Security, he worked at it full time, and although the company was sold to Heublein and later to PepsiCo, he remained the company symbol until his death in 1980. By 1971 there were 3,317 KFC outlets, up from approximately 400 in 1964.

While fast foods were the most visible and best known of the franchise operations, others were even more lucrative. One was in the area of motels and hotels. Especially motels, of which there were some 13,500 before the war and 41,000, of quite a different type, by 1958. In the same period, revenues rose from $36.7 million to $850 million. The prewar motels were shacks hardly larger than walk-in closets and lacked indoor plumbing, while those of the late 1950s not only had all the amenities but also air-conditioning, and often swimming pools.

American travelers had their choice of motels before World War II. Most of these were owned and operated by the same person (or family) who lived on the site. The exceptions were the motels that were co-owned. Howard Johnson had 130 co-owned restaurants by 1940, which while not quite the same as franchises, were somewhat similar. After World War II, the company opened some motels at their restaurant sites, offering co-ownership to outsiders. Travelodge was another pioneer in the field. Scott King, its owner, opened King's Court in San Diego in 1935 and a Travelodge in the same city in 1940, again on a co-ownership basis. In this case the co-owners shared equally in mortgage payments and costs, while the co-owner received a management fee of 10 percent of gross revenues. Profits, when they existed, were shared equally. As can be seen, this was quite different from being a franchisee, and more akin to working as a manager. Other motel operations with similar arrangements were quite common in the postwar period.

There clearly was a demand for inexpensive motels a family and businesspeople could drive to and be assured of certain quality standards. These were lacking in 1946, at a time when families started taking vacations in their newly purchased automobiles. Some businessmen recognized the need and acted to fill it. Kemmons Wilson was the most important of these. He was well prepared for the task, having constructed military housing in the Memphis area during World War II. Being quite wealthy, he might easily have opened motels on his own, with 100 percent ownership. But he did not do so, opting for franchising instead.

The inspiration for Wilson's entry into motels came in

1951, when on a family vacation to Washington he found it difficult to locate a decent place to stay at a reasonable price. He saw a gap in the market, a need, that he would fill. In speaking to his wife about his plans, Wilson said that he intended to build hundreds of motels across the country. Wilson spoke of his project to Wallace Johnson, the vice-president of the National Homebuilders' Association. Together they developed a prospectus.

The first site was the highway that ran between Memphis and Nashville. The motel was to have 120 rooms, with a restaurant, a gift shop, and a swimming pool. The rooms would be air-conditioned and have television sets. The charge was to be $4 a night for a single and $6 for a double. There would be no extra charge for children. This was what he had tried to find on that vacation, and this was what he built, for a cost of $280,000.

Within the next two years Wilson constructed three more motels in the Memphis area. All was going well, but Wilson now had to face two problems: obtaining funds to build other motels, and finding managers for them. He might oversee motels in his home area, but what about those far from Memphis? Wilson found prospects in the World War II veterans. They had access to some capital, but not enough to finance their own businesses. They also lacked experience and realized the high failure rates of new businesses. The answer to their problems was at hand in the form of franchising. Thus, Wilson was an entrepreneur who was impelled to start a franchising business in motels, and those veterans and others who wanted to be their own bosses were potential franchisees.

Searching for a name for the motel, he decided to call it the Holiday Inn, after a motion picture of the time. For a $500 fee a franchise buyer would be granted the right to own a Holiday Inn in his city. In addition he would pay a user's fee and five cents a night per room. The innkeepers would have to maintain certain standards, and agree to permit Wilson's company to have the construction contract. Initially Wilson constructed at costs of $3,000 per room, which were sold to the franchisee at $3,500.

The franchisers learned from one another. Ray Kroc insisted that franchisees follow his guidelines: failure to do so would mean the loss of the golden arches that had become the McDonald's symbol. Likewise, those franchisees that did not live up to the Holiday Inn standards risked loss of that valuable trademark.

Johnson recalled the situation in his memoir:

> We built several Holiday Inns in Memphis, Tenn., and they were quite successful. But Kemmons realized that to build this nationwide system, we would have to start a franchise program.
>
> Kemmons and I were both homebuilders. So we invited seventy-five of the nation's leading homebuilders to Memphis to hear about our plan. About sixty showed up. They were enthusiastic. Said they would begin as soon as they got home, and would send their franchise checks for $500 and five cents a room for advertising.

Holiday Inns were a huge success. Eleven were opened in 1954, including the first franchised operation. Three years later, Wilson had an underwriting of his stock, selling 120,000 shares at $9.75. The stock did well, as did the company. The motels were sought out by travelers, and often were sold out weeks in advance, prompting others to enter the field. Those families now went along the highway without reservations, knowing that down the road was a motel. Marion Isbell, who headed Ramada, one of Holiday Inn's competitors, was once asked how he went about selecting locations. "It's really simple," he replied. "All I do is go into a city and find out where Kemmons Wilson has a good Holiday Inn and I put a Ramada Inn right next door."

Motels and franchising changed the face of America. Motel receipts in 1939 had been $37 million. By 1958 they came in at $850 million. This was only part of the story. Successful motels made their franchisers and franchisees wealthy, but in addition their availability greased the wheels of commerce, in that they provided handy and affordable places for businessmen to room. In addition, the wealth was spread to a small army of suppliers. One of these was Benjamin Ellman, who sold hotel and motel fixtures. While on a business trip, Ellman stopped at the Holiday Inn in Des Moines. Impressed by what he saw and experienced, Ellman asked the manager about the company, and learned it was based in Memphis. "And I got so excited that the next morning instead of continuing on out West to Omaha, I turned around and drove to Memphis, Tennessee," where he went to headquarters and introduced himself to Wilson:

> Kemmons Wilson was the type of person who liked to talk to young people like me. And we spent about three hours where he talked to me about the future. Cuz in those days, according to the statistics, probably 98 percent of the people in this country had never traveled more than 25 miles from where they had been born. And he said this was all going to change. And all of the things we take for granted today he told me about in 1961. He then turned me over to their

director of purchasing and they specified for use at Holiday Inn restaurants and coffee shops my fixture, an Eagle light fixture. That happened in the early 1960s. I never forgot that conversation. And of course I used that to go ahead and build my business as to what was going to happen in this industry. But in addition that light fixture of mine was specified in—Holiday Inn put out a very thick book of specs about how you're supposed to build these things. And in one corner of one page, the specifications for the light fixtures happen to be my company's light fixtures.

In this way, Ellman was on his way to national success, by selling not only to Holiday Inn, but to other motel chains as well.

Ten years later, franchised companies accounted for 10 percent of the nation's GNP, and by 1980 there were close to half a million franchised outlets of all kinds, which provided more than a third of a trillion dollars in sales. By then thousands of Americans who in earlier periods might have tried to make it on their own had become wealthy through the operation of franchised companies. The classified advertisements of large newspapers informed them of the opportunities that existed, usually under the heading of "Franchising & Business Loans," and the costs and methods of financing them. One qualification that was not included for those who wanted to purchase a franchise was a college education, the value of which continued to exist, but just what those letters at the end of one's name implied was being challenged.

All of these forces inferred that the population, in the

aggregate, was growing more affluent. They had money to spend, and by spending, created a new demand for supply, and so supported others who were involved at that end of the continuum. Writing in June 1946, a *Fortune* columnist observed:

> So the Boom is on, the biggest in American economic history. Almost all the curves are up, the market is bull—or was when this went to press. There is a powerful, a consuming demand for everything that one can eat, wear, enjoy, burn, read, patch, dye, repair, paint, drink, see, ride, taste, smell, and rest in. The nylon line is the symbol of 1946—at any given time of day, all over the U.S., thousands of women are patiently shuffling through the hosiery stores.
>
> Throughout the nation there is at large a vast force of spending money, surging violently about the economy, like an Olympian bull in an old curiosity shop, battering its way in and out of stores and through the banks and into the stock market and off to the black market and on into the amusement industry. Everything that is made is bought up as fast as it appears. There seems to be no bottom to the demand, no bottom to the American purse. Toulouse-Lautrecs at $30,000, mink coats at $15,000, men's wrist watches at $1,000—all sell just about as fast as egg beaters, table radios, and pork chops.

So it appeared, although the writer obviously exaggerated. What was clearly so, however, was that many thousands of Americans—perhaps hundreds of thousands—were achieving economic and social successes in this period. If it was not the promised land, it would do (in the words of a popular song) until "the real thing" came along.

4

THE CREATION OF WEALTH ON WALL STREET

Take a nice little company that's been making shoelaces for 40 years and sells at a respectable six times earnings ratio. Change the name from Shoelaces Inc. to Electronics and Silicon Furth-Burners. In today's market, the words "electronics" and "silicon" are worth fifteen times earnings. However, the real play comes from the word "Furth-Burners," which no one understands. A word that no one understands entitles you to double your entire score. Therefore, we have six times earnings for the shoelace business and 15 times earnings for electronics and silicon, or a total of 21 times earnings. Multiply this by two for Furth-Burners and we now have a score of 42 times earnings for the new company.

—Jack Dreyfus, 1960

The techniques employed in accumulating wealth have concerned America's leaders at least as long as there was a nation. Writing of this in 1988, social critic and essayist Lewis Lapham reflected on the wide variety of thoughts on the subject advanced by the founding fathers. "Money, not morality, is the principle of commercial nations," said Thomas Jefferson, at a time when he was doing what he could to encourage the export of American grain. James Madison worried about the agitation for "an abolition of debts, for an equal division of property and other wicked projects." John Jay thought "the people who own the country ought to govern it." John Adams opined that the "great functions of state" should be reserved for "the rich, the wellborn, and the able." Charles Pinckney believed no one would be worthy of being considered for the presidency unless and until he could prove he had a net worth of at least $100,000, which would be more than $10 million in today's prices.

This is not to say that all or even some of these men believed in rule and control by a permanent class of the wealthy, but rather that wealth, whether achieved through inheritance or through one's own accomplishments, should be a prerequisite for the bestowal of power in the new nation. It was thought at the time that wealthy people would not seek high office to achieve a status they already enjoyed by virtue of their financial assets or their family name. Nor would they become involved in new businesses made possible by their political status in order to become wealthy—since they already had achieved that estate. Analyzing the situation in 1968, journalist George Kirstein wrote, "Rich men may engage in exactly the same commercial pursuit as the non-rich—after all, Henry Luce continually worked as hard creating Time-Life as any of his employees—but he did not have to. The rich may compromise their own standards of morality or taste, but they are not forced to in order to provide for their families."

The Quest for Wealth

Writing in 1956, at a time when it had become evident that Americans were in the midst of a major wealth-creating period, historian Robert Heilbroner reflected on the phenomenon in one of his books, titled *The Quest for Wealth: A Study of Acquisitive Man*:

> As far back as there is history, men have dreamed of wealth: to what heights have they not reached—and to what depths have they not sunk—in quest of those golden dreams! High treason and low trickery, great affairs of state and petty squabbles over an inheritance, marriage and murder: what aspect of the tragicomedy of man has not been touched by the love of gain? Truly the drive for riches must be adjudged as powerful and protean a stimulus as any to which the human mechanism responds.

Perhaps so for those who aspire to enormous wealth—the notables who make the front pages of newspapers and the history books, and who earn large incomes that require the services of a cadre of tax and estate lawyers. While few of the postwar generation would spurn such fortunes, these dreams were not omnipresent. Rather, most individuals yearned for a "comfortable" life that included the purchase of a new Buick rather than a used Chevrolet, a four-bedroom air-conditioned house with a swimming pool in the backyard rather than a two-bedroom Levitt with a pass for the neighborhood pool, enough money to pay the tuition exacted by a nearby university rather than the sure knowledge that the limits of the family budget mandated a state school. Such individuals did not count on inheritances from wealthy relatives. If they experienced a windfall, it would come from a winning lottery ticket, not success in selecting one's forebears.

Most studies of the increase in wealth after World War II indicate that while inheritance played an important role for old wealth, savings from wages and other income were more significant in the creation of the newly affluent—but not savings by themselves. Had Americans merely placed their savings in banks and permitted them to grow through the slow accumulation of interest, no real wealth would have been created. But this turned out not to be the case. Rather, after the war many Americans went on a binge of investments, beginning with their own homes, even though they did not consider them to be investments per se.

One of the unanticipated results of this situation was the enrichment of white purchasers of suburban homes but not blacks, who, in the late 1940s and 1950s, were effectively excluded from ownership. As noted, Levittown's initial contracts contained covenants forbidding owners from selling to blacks. Of the somewhat more than 65,000 Levittown residents in 1960, almost 100 percent were white. By then the covenant against sales to blacks had become publicized, and William Levitt was called upon to comment. "We can solve a housing problem, or we can solve a racial problem, but we cannot combine the two," he responded. The civil rights movement and changes in the law did not alter this very much. In 1960 the only black residents of Levittown were a few domestic servants, who were permitted to live there under terms of the covenant. By 1990, there were still only 118 blacks in Levittown, or 0.03 percent of the population.

On the other hand, civic groups in Shaker Heights, on the outskirts of Cleveland, older than Levittown and more upscale, mounted a campaign to attract black buyers, which enjoyed some success. Moreover, contrary to predictions, land values rose rather than fell. While Shaker Heights hardly was integrated, by the 1970s the sight of blacks no longer was considered unusual.

At a time when their white counterparts were making one of the most important investments of their lives, blacks were excluded. This is one of the more significant financial truisms for that generation. Another was the virtual exclusion of blacks from the early stages of the franchise boom, and the failure of brokerages to admit blacks at the start of the bull market, thus excluding many of them from another great wealth creator of the second half of the twentieth century.

In time the most important investment vehicles came to be common stocks. One of the forms of savings not ordinarily categorized as such were pension plans. The increase in the common stock holdings of such plans and their growth in net worth were important components of the wealth of the American people by the closing years of the twentieth century. The securities markets would enrich more Americans than the franchise boom, as did the increase in the value of real estate, which boosted the wealth of a wide variety of middle-class Americans in every part of the country.

Those associated with the franchise boom included franchisers like Kemmons Wilson and Ray Kroc, but also the businesspeople who provided the Holiday Inns and McDonald's that dotted the landscape with their supplies, ranging from towels to potatoes; the franchisees who joined with them in building their empires; and those who became their customers. Such individuals and others, who may not even have frequented the McDonald's and the Holiday Inns, also invested in the securities of the companies they served and serviced, or merely heard about, and in the process shared in their growth.

Likewise, among the Americans who profited from the stock market were investors and speculators as well as many Wall Street personnel who catered to the needs of these individuals. During the early postwar period many of the brokers at the nation's established and respected investment banks were newcomers, recruited to the brokerages by a new breed of manager that appeared after the war. Those holdovers from the earlier period would have had difficulties acclimating to the new atmosphere on Wall Street. In the postwar years, after an initial adjustment, more Americans than ever—including the halcyon days of the 1920s—became interested in securities. The conventional brokers prospered; but there were others, akin to the fly-by-night brokers of the 1920s, who catered to the desires of those with a strong gambling instinct. As it happened, these brokers and their customers did far better than their more conservative counterparts during the late 1950s, and set the tone for bull markets of the future.

The brokers were only one component of the new stock-oriented investment community that prospered. The investment banks that served the needs of new companies wanting to sell securities, researchers in back rooms who churned out reports on the state of the market and its component parts, traders in banks who attempted to make money for their employers by purchasing and selling securities, and armies of clerks and other support personnel also did well financially. One survey of the early 1950s indicated that 2 percent of the population owned 58 percent of the common stock. More than 55 percent of families earning more than $10,000 a year owned securities, while less than 20 percent of those earning between $5,000 and $10,000 owned them. As for those with earnings below $5,000, the figure was 7.4 percent. Ownership was still confined largely to the upper and the middle classes. Even so, the expansion of wealth was impressive. And between 1940 and 1958 interest in the securities markets was growing apace. The circulation of *The Wall Street Journal* grew from 32,000 to 540,000.

The Birth of the Bull Market

Wall Street was a wasteland in the 1930s and 1940s, when solid, blue chip firms with good records were selling at depressed prices. After more than a two-year decline following the 1929 Crash, stock prices bottomed at Dow 42 on July 8, 1932, bounced around, and then struck 50 on February 27, 1933, and continued to rise. Why? Because Franklin D. Roosevelt's promised activist program instilled confidence, which is to say investors and professionals alike started to consider the possibilities of a brighter future. This marked the advent of a now-forgotten bull market that lasted two years; on March 10, 1936, the Dow topped out at 194.

Yet this quadrupling of prices did not result in euphoria or attract hordes of investors to the brokerages. Volume for all of 1932 came to 425 million shares, which is what is traded on an ordinary day in today's markets. The stock ticker would remain silent for a quarter of an hour at a time, and in this period it took only 80,000 shares to make the daily most-active-stocks list. The reason was the lingering memory of the 1929 Crash, which would not be crowded out by the good economic news on the front pages of newspapers. After the traumas inflicted in October 1929 it would take more than a market rise to bring investors and speculators back to Wall Street. In addition, even though the economy was recovering, there was disturbing news from overseas. Adolf Hitler spoke constantly of his territorial ambitions, and soon acted on those pledges, with little or no reaction from neighboring countries. How far might he go? Would anyone have the will and fortitude to stand up to him? Questions such as these sent prices downward; on March 31, 1938, the Dow dipped below 100. There followed a rally to 152 on January 3, 1941, on low volume—the daily trades for 1941 averaged 619,000 shares, and would decline to 455,000 in 1942.

Following an old Wall Street tradition, both bulls and bears looked to the past trying to understand the present so as to divine the future. The bulls noted that prices rose during World War I, due in part to wartime orders for equipment, while the bears recounted tales of the Great Depression.

The market performed dismally during World War II. On December 6, the day prior to the Japanese attack on Pearl Harbor, the Dow closed at 117, and on Monday it fell to 115 and continued downward. At war's end the index was only at 147, even though the American economy had doubled in size during this period and corporate profits were more than 250 percent above their 1929 levels.

This situation continued after the war when, as noted earlier, many economists predicted a depression once military orders were canceled. One survey indicated that more than 40 percent of the public thought another depression was on the way. This attitude showed up in the kinds of securities that investors brave enough to venture into the market seemed to prefer. In 1949 the five best-performing stock groups were leathers, utility holding companies, papers, soaps, and ethical drugs, which were largely the kinds of stocks that had steady earnings in both good and bad times, and paid good dividends. The market advanced for the year, led by more glamorous stocks, but the public clearly wanted safety and yield, and was unwilling to take chances in order to have growth. Investors of this period were influenced more by memories of the 1929 Crash than by the potential of new products, such as electronics, computers, and, especially, television.

In spite of investor apathy, TV receiver sales boomed as the new medium showed the rapid growth characteristics later associated with the Internet. In 1946 a grand total of 10,000 television sets were manufactured. Three million receivers were sold in 1949, and for 1950, more than 7.5 million, as television soon became a household utility. Motorola's sales rose from $23 million in 1946 to $82 million in 1949, while net income went from $620,000 to $5.3 million. A host of other companies, from Admiral to Zenith to GE to RCA, posted similar results. But the stocks of these companies languished as investors, who perhaps recalled the radio boom and bust of the 1920s, remained cautious. As late as 1950—a time of strong economic growth with sharply higher corporate earnings and rising dividends—the Dow's P/E ratio stood at 7.0, lower than it had been at any time in the 1920s or 1930s.

The economic throw-offs from companies involved with new technologies and products were also impressive. Television provided well-paid jobs for tens of thousands of technicians, assembly-line workers, artists, advertising agencies, salespeople, and others. Through the 1950s and afterward, television provided an avenue of growth and a passage into the middle class and beyond for many Americans then entering the workforce—even more so than radio. Television became an engine of social change in the United States. But for the growing army of investors, its major impact seemed to be on the securities markets, whose revival coincided with, and in some ways was caused by, the advent of television.

In time the shriveled hopes of the 1930s would be replaced by the high expectations that accompanied this new consumer culture sparked by television. During the immediate postwar period it was possible to argue that prosperity would be short-lived. Such no longer was the case in the early 1950s, by which time investors had started to return in force.

Making Fortunes on Wall Street

Not that the brokers were prepared for a large increase in their customer base. During the 1920s, Wall Street had been the goal, and careers there the ambition, of a generation of America's blue-blooded young men. All of this ended with the Crash. Wall Street professionals had started to depart during the early 1930s, casting their ballots with their feet for a long-term bear market with little public participation. Before the Crash, Wall Street had been the prime destination for bright Ivy Leaguers. In 1928, 17 percent of Harvard's business school graduates found employment there. In 1942 the figure was 2 percent. During those years, most of the talented bankers, brokers, traders, and salesmen left for other occupations, and when the United States entered World War II, those who remained during the 1930s departed for government jobs or service in the armed forces. "When the crash came in the thirties, no banker would admit where he worked," recalled Citibank's CEO Walter Wriston. "Nobody wanted to work for a bank from 1933 to 1939. Then the war started. So there was nobody coming into the business from 1933 to 1946."

The generalized lack of interest in banking and finance during the late 1940s and early 1950s was made evident in many ways besides the departure of customers, although that aspect was the most visible sign of a loss. Perhaps even more significant was the unwillingness of young people to commit themselves to Wall Street careers. This was quite understandable, given the experience of the Depression and World War II. In 1929 the volume of trading had been 1.1 billion shares. The 1933 volume came to 655 million, and the following year it would decline to 324 million. The bottom, 126 million, would be reached in 1942.

The lack of business led to a decline in the price of NYSE seats. One changed hands at $17,000 in 1942, at which time there were 33,000 employees in the district, against the 125,000 in 1929. Experienced commission brokers were drawing $35 a week. Investment bankers with blue-blood credentials were holding down night jobs as salesmen in nearby department stores and eating sandwiches at their desks.

That such a situation could not continue for long after the war now seems quite obvious. The growing prosperity, the high corporate earnings and rising dividends, along with promises of more to come, would in time inspire new interest in the markets. As it happened, however, a super-salesman appeared who became the herald of a new era, not only to investors, but, more importantly, to legions of talented young men (women would arrive later) seeking careers in the area of stock brokerage.

The Wall Street figure associated with the new market was Charles Merrill. During the boom of the 1920s, he had been head of the firm of Merrill Lynch & Co. But by early 1928, Merrill had become convinced that the high stock prices bore no relation to reality, and in March he suggested to his clients that they lighten their portfolios. "Now is the time to get out of debt. We do not urge that you sell securities indiscriminately, but we do advise in no uncertain terms that you take advantage of present high prices and put your own financial house in order." Shortly after the October 1929 Crash, Merrill transferred all his brokerage clients and employees to E. A. Pierce, and went into semi-retirement.

Lynch died in 1938, forcing Merrill to spend more time in the office. The following year, E. A. Pierce experienced difficulties, and, at the urging of an old associate, Winthrop Smith, Merrill absorbed it and another, much smaller house. Merrill Lynch was transformed into Merrill Lynch, Pierce & Cassatt. In 1941 Merrill purchased a New Orleans–based brokerage, Fenner & Beane, and out of this came Merrill Lynch, Pierce, Fenner & Beane. It was a substantial operation—in fact the nation's largest brokerage, with nearly 100 branch offices.

Merrill came to the office with some degree of regularity, but not on a full-time basis. He was not a healthy man, and he enjoyed the good life far too much to devote himself to business for very long. Merrill suffered a heart attack three years later. He returned soon after, but for the rest of his life he worked part-time. With this, Winthrop Smith assumed day-to-day leadership, which presaged the firm's next designation: Merrill Lynch, Pierce, Fenner & Smith. Merrill concentrated on the development of the firm's sales operations and public relations. It was in this area that he made his signal contribution, transforming the nature of brokerage by helping fashion the first market based upon widespread participation. In effect, Merrill democratized share ownership.

Merrill hoped to convince a public with memories of the market crash of 1929 that investment in stocks was now prudent and that brokers—then perceived as hustlers—could be honorable and forthright. If potential small investors were persuaded that the broker was a professional in every sense of the term, they might be induced to use his services. This was a segment of the population brokers traditionally had ignored; they had discouraged individuals with only a few hundred dollars from investing.

Merrill argued that while newcomers usually started with little, in time, if the experience was salutary, they might become more substantial investors. In effect, he hoped to do for brokerage what the chain stores had done for retailing: make smaller profits per client but larger overall revenues through volume, in this case by luring many more of them to Wall Street.

There was a large constituency for Merrill's services. An NYSE survey disclosed that the average annual family income of a person who purchased his first share of stock in 1959 was $8,600, while 10 percent were earning more than $15,000 a year. The new shareholder was thirty-nine years old, married, and fairly well educated. Four out of 5 had graduated from high school, and 1 out of 4 had a college degree. But they were not educated in the ways of business and finance. Less than half had any idea of the earnings of the companies whose stocks they owned, and only 10 percent knew the name of the company's CEO. Just 40 percent knew the products or services offered by the company. An earlier survey showed that only 20 percent of the population could correctly define common stock, while 60 percent did not know that the NYSE itself did not buy and sell securities. Such individuals needed help, and Charles Merrill's account executives were prepared to offer that and more.

The NYSE mandated minimum commissions; there was no maximum, and most brokerage firms extracted what the traffic would bear. Not Merrill Lynch, however, which not only charged the minimum but campaigned for yet lower rates. Research operations were expanded, and at a time when other brokerages charged for such information, reports were offered free to interested individuals. Although Merrill Lynch was a private company, it issued annual reports starting in 1940. Other brokerage firms had fee schedules for monthly statements, for holding, for clipping coupons on bonds, and for practically any other service rendered. Merrill Lynch waived such charges.

During this period, Merrill Lynch brokers were paid salaries, not commissions, and the brokerage house made certain the public learned about this. Brokers at other firms might use the hard sell to increase their income. Not the Merrill Lynch account executive—a designation Merrill insisted be applied to all new brokers.

Merrill substituted a true trainee program for the casual ones then prevalent. Constantly he stressed his first precept: "The interests of our customers MUST come first," said an early Merrill Lynch training brochure.

Merrill Lynch was not the first brokerage to advertise, but it carried the art to new heights. Earlier advertisements were either simple statements of services available or blatantly sensationalist. Merrill Lynch was interested in educating potential customers. One of their ads, "What Everybody Ought to Know about the Stock and Bond Business," was a long essay that read more like a textbook than an advertisement. Merrill Lynch was besieged with requests for reprints, eventually distributing more than a million copies. The firm also published a series of booklets on investing, offered free for the asking. One of the more popular of these was "How to Read a Financial Statement," and a version of this publication, first available in 1946, is still being distributed today. The firm also warned novice investors away from exotic trading, which was more suitable for sophisticated accounts. Accordingly, another brochure was titled: "Hedging: Insurance Policy or Lottery Ticket?"

During the era prior to the 1929 Crash, investment bankers ruled Wall Street, and for the most part they arrived from the nation's premier colleges and established families. Investment bankers, the aforementioned blue bloods, were key figures in the district. In the 1930s and 1940s, specialists (who make markets for stocks on the NYSE floor) were important, and many came from families of specialists, in some cases going back for generations. Now it was the turn of Merrill's registered representatives. Such positions were open to virtually any young man who was well educated, personable, willing to work hard and learn the methods of the firm, and serve the customers who appeared at his desk. Better still if they were good at making "cold calls" (to those who in any fashion indicated an interest in knowing more about securities). Family and friends who would open accounts were desirable. But in the end, intelligent, affable young men could hope for financial careers at a time when customers were being lured back to the Street.

There were two other caveats. The young man had to be white. Blacks were not welcomed at the brokerages in the early 1950s—not even as customers. And women were not welcome. There were some female brokers, but not many.

This approach worked. Merrill Lynch became a powerhouse of finance. By 1955, the firm handled 10 percent of the transactions at the NYSE and 18 percent of the odd-lot business (purchases and sales of less than 100 shares), which was often the way small investors started out. Its gross income came to $45.6 million in 1950; four years later it was $73.3 million. By then, too, most of the other brokerages followed his example. Merrill had changed the face of Wall Street.

While not as important as Merrill, Keith Funston proved to be one of the best salesmen securities-based capitalism ever had. A tall, silver-haired, loquacious man with a patrician bearing but a plainspoken way of dealing with people, Funston became president of the NYSE in 1951. He arrived there from the presidency of Trinity College, the candidate of Sidney Weinberg of Goldman, Sachs & Co., the man known as "Mr. Wall Street." Funston's only drawback was that he knew next to nothing about the securities business. No matter. At the time, the real power on Wall Street rested with the investment bankers, men like Weinberg. Merrill was the representative of commission houses, the brokers who would benefit financially from an influx of new customers. Funston represented the community as a whole, rather than any one particular segment of it.

Funston glorified what he called "People's Capitalism," and was its most enthusiastic booster. The term signified free-enterprise capitalism in which a large portion of the population owned securities. Funston contrasted this with the situation in the earlier years of the twentieth century, when ownership was far more concentrated. He believed that through the acquisition of stocks Americans could become capitalists and share in the growth of the nation.

Wall Street's goal, said Funston, was public ownership of the means of production, not through government, but rather through an army of shareholders; he hoped to build "a nation in whose material wealth every citizen has a vested interest through equity ownership." This was the period when the Cold War was starting to occupy the interest and concerns of many Americans, and anti-communism was in vogue. Speaking in New York in mid-1952, Funston asserted that "the way to fight communism is through American prosperity." He stated that "we're trying to broaden the base of stock ownership and thus strengthen the basis of democracy." Or as an NYSE vice president put it, "A regular dividend check is the best answer to communism."

In the first years of what was a protracted bull market, activity concentrated on the two extremes: those apparently risky, low-priced stocks that appealed to speculators, and the bluest of the blue chips for the new investors. Then, as activity increased and profits were made, investors sought out more speculative issues, and this trend continued throughout the late 1950s and into the 1960s.

Earnings improved for the well-known companies, to be sure, as did their dividends, but not nearly as rapidly as the expansion of price-earnings ratios, which propelled stocks to new highs, beyond the 1929 level by late 1954. Stockholders were receiving excellent returns on their investments, not from dividends, but from capital gains.

Prior to this great upward sweep, stocks yielded more

than bonds, a reflection of their greater risk, justifying the old maxim, "The greater the risk, the greater the return." In 1950, for example, the dividend yield on the Dow Jones Industrials averaged 6.9 percent, at a time when AAA tax-free municipals yielded an average of just 1.7 percent, long-term U.S. governments averaged 2.3 percent, and AAA-rated corporates offered 2.7 percent. Increasingly, these traditional investments were either forgotten, ignored, or consider the relic of a bygone era.

Consider the case of RCA, the star of the 1920s bull market, which started 1950 at $12\frac{1}{2}$, with a dividend of 50 cents, and soon after reported 1949 earnings of $1.58. U.S. Steel was at $26\frac{1}{8}$, earned $5.39, and had a payout of $2.25. General Motors sold for $71\frac{5}{8}$, earned $14.64, and paid $8.00. RCA was prospering as a result of television receiver sales. U.S. Steel was operating at full capacity in an industrial boom, and General Motors could not keep up with the demand for its cars. Yet in all three cases, the dividend yield on the common stock was much higher than that on the companies' bonds. Their P/E ratios were 8, 5, and 5 respectively, while the yield came to 4, 9, and 11 percent.

The situation changed dramatically in the next decade. In 1959, the Dow Jones Industrial's P/E ratio reached 18.4 and the P/D ratio, 30.5. By then RCA's P/E ratio had advanced from 9 to a high of 23, and its yield had fallen from 4 percent to 3 percent; U.S. Steel's P/E rose from 5 to 19, its yield declining from 9 percent to 3 percent; and General Motors' P/E rose from 5 to 23, its yield collapsing from 11 percent to 4 percent. Meanwhile, bond prices declined (the Dow bond index was 101.43 at the start of 1950, and 86.36 on January 2, 1959), and yields advanced. Equities were favored, bonds shunned.

This was quite a change from what had been the conventional wisdom of earlier periods. It seemed to run counter to the old logic that had once governed investments. In 1940, Benjamin Graham and David L. Dodd, in their classic work, *Security Analysis*, had set down the accepted dictum regarding dividends, which they called the "overshadowing factor" in common stock investment:

> This point of view was based upon simple logic. The prime purpose of a business corporation is to pay dividends to its owners. A successful company is one that can pay dividends regularly and presumably increase the rate of return as time goes on. Since the idea of investment is closely bound up with that old dependable income, it follows that investment in common stocks would ordinarily be confined to those with a well-established dividend. It would follow also that the price paid for an investment in common stock would be determined chiefly by the amount of the dividend.

Yet in the postwar era, the conventional wisdom did not hold, as investors shifted their focus to capital gains. The purchase of common stock in the hope of capital gain represented quite a change in investor (as distinct from speculator) psychology. In the past, higher stock prices usually had resulted from the realization of increased dividends that would boost yields. But during the 1960s, stocks without dividends rose to spectacular heights. Indeed, part of the new conventional wisdom was that dividends didn't matter, and that corporations would do well not to pay large dividends. The reasoning was that growth companies were continually in need of additional capital for expansion, and that, generally speaking, increased payouts were the mark of companies failing to grow as rapidly as they might.

The Cult of Growth

Thus investors and speculators of the 1950s had to come to terms with two ideas that were new to that generation: that the purchase of securities need not be confined to the very wealthy or the very rash, and that capital gains could be preferable to dividends and interest. For a generation raised during the Great Depression, when prudent individuals placed whatever funds they had in insured savings accounts and then in defense and war bonds, this required a remarkable change in attitude. By mid-decade, the trend was clear enough that *Business Week* could editorialize that "1954 will go down as the year when we conquered the depression phobia." The developing mania for stocks could be perceived in a variety of statistics. There had been fewer than 500,000 shareholder accounts in 1945; by 1959 there were 4.3 million of them. But the most impressive statistics were for new issues of common stock, many of which were for young companies and others for established public companies taking advantage of higher P/Es to raise capital through equity offerings rather than debt. Many of the new glamour stocks sold at P/Es that an earlier generation—including that of the 1920s— would have considered astonishing. In addition, very few of the high-flying glamour stocks paid dividends.

There had been a widespread pursuit of growth during the 1920s, but it was different then, based as it was on speculative hopes associated with the belief that the markets were rigged. The growth philosophy of the 1950s and 1960s was founded on the conviction that the economy was growing, that certain segments were doing so faster than others, that specific companies in those segments would perform superbly, and that the market, now better regulated, would reflect this fairly over time. The more sophisticated readers of the *Wall Street Journal* had the new theory of investing explained to them in mid-1954:

> The good growth company, experience showed, may pay out only a small part of its earnings in cash dividends, using the rest for research, development of new products, and expansion . . . In the growth company, the plowed-back earnings should bring larger earning power—and in the long run bigger dividends—always assuming the company's products or services are well accepted, and that its management is alert and forward looking. And, when the dividends increase, the yield on the original stock investment goes up with them.

This development apparently puzzled the rating services and others who contrasted the current market with what had gone before. In late May 1954, *Moody's* issued a report on the advances posted by several growth stocks. Since January 1, 1953, the Dow had risen 12 percent, the service observed, and in the same period IBM's increase had been 25 percent, Scott Paper rose by 56 percent, Minnesota Mining by 44 percent, and Minneapolis-Honeywell-Regulator's advance was 40 percent. Accustomed as it was to a different kind of valuation, *Moody's* recommended switches to less adventuresome low P/E stocks that paid larger dividends. *Business Week* agreed, and noted another phenomenon: the sharp rise of some secondary issues. "The month is only half gone," it wrote in August, "yet there are more erratic daily fluctuations than the Street has seen in years. Such issues as Avco, International Telephone & Telegraph, General Dynamics, and Martin have shown advances in the double digits, while the Dow Industrials have declined in this period." Moreover, an increasing share of preferred and bond issues were in the form of convertibles, thus adding the "equity kicker" that enabled issuers to sell paper with lower yields.

The inclusion of Avco and International Telephone & Telegraph in the writer's list of fast-moving stocks is significant. These companies were conglomerates, a term one heard often in this period. The conglomerates, as a group, not only were glamorous but set a style that was much admired and imitated. This period was the third in a series of merger movements—the first occurring at the turn of the century, the second in the 1920s. Conglomerate mergers were combinations of non-related companies, the theory being that such companies could mitigate the vagaries of the business cycle by balancing consumer-goods and capital-goods companies, capital intensive firms and "cash cows," firms in industries that did well in economic slowdowns with those that might do poorly, and so on. In addition to Avco and International Telephone & Telegraph, other leading conglomerates included Litton Industries, Gulf + Western, Textron, and Ling-Temco-Vought. Moreover, many well-established firms made non-related acquisitions. During this period rumors of a takeover would boost the stock of the sought-after company. Investors followed "hot tips" regarding the actions and desires of leaders of conglomerates and other companies on the prowl for acquisitions, especially of those companies that attracted several suitors, in which case a contest for control might develop and catapult the stock of the sought-after company to great heights.

The movement rolled on during the rest of the decade, as the prices of conglomerates and other glamour stocks rose sharply, and it rewarded those who owned them and had a good feel for when to get in and out.

By then, too, the electronics boom had taken hold, attracting investors to that sector of the economy. Scientists at many of the old-line companies, as well as recent graduates from some of the nation's best graduate schools, wanted to start their own companies, not only to realize their ambitions, but also to cash in on their knowledge and interests. To serve both, there appeared a new group of financiers known as venture capitalists, eager to finance dreams—for a price. Georges Doriot, who had a long relationship with Harvard and the Massachusetts Institute of Technology, organized a company whose business was to locate and raise funds for such individuals and their companies. Doriot's firm, American Research & Development (AR&D), had more than a dozen investments in "start-ups," the most important of which was Digital Equipment, the brainchild of Kenneth Olsen and Harlan Anderson, both of whom were researchers affiliated with MIT, where in the late 1950s they attempted to develop small computers. Convinced that their products were meeting a market need, they attempted to raise funds to start production, but without much success. They arrived at AR&D, and Doriot provided the partners with $70,000 in return for approximately 60 percent of the stock in the company that was to be called Digital Equipment. In time the value of that 60 percent grew to more than $1 billion.

This was another way Americans who understood the developing electronics economy, and were prepared to take chances, were able to become wealthy. In addition to Digital, Doriot bankrolled such successful firms as High Voltage Engineering and Tracerlab, and had close relations with Raytheon, itself an incubator of new firms. Indeed, among them, Lincoln Laboratories, Raytheon, Sylvania, and MIT produced close to 200 start-ups, most computer-related with military applications. So long as computers were the central focus of high technology, Route 128 would thrive.

Doriot was perhaps the best known of the venture capitalists, but he had many competitors. Frank Chambers was the angel behind such firms as Dataproducts, American Microsystems, and Rolm, but he was most famous for having rejected the chance to help finance Apple Computer. Arthur Rock saw promise in Apple and helped in its creation; in 1968 he provided $5 million for Intel when that company was in financial need. Pitch Johnson, whose organization, Asset Management, became a center for small companies, was quite famous for a while. Jack Melchoir was the first to see promise in Rolm, and was one of those who helped finance it as well as Osborne Computer. Numerous other companies, among them many of the Internet companies, found some of their initial sponsorship in the ranks of venture capitalists.

The new issue market for stocks such as Digital Equipment soared, with the public eager for the common stocks of firms like Automatic Data Processing, Coleco, Control Data, Datapoint, Jack Eckerd, Federal Express, Intel, Levitz Furniture, Mary Kay Cosmetics, Mattel, McDonald's, Polaroid, Smucker's, Teledyne, Texas Instruments, Wang, and Xerox, in addition to that of the conglomerates. The mania for new issues continued into the 1960s, and gathered steam as many of the stocks doubled and tripled within hours of being offered. The quality of the offerings had declined by then, a recognition by under-writers and clients alike that prices were being paid that reflected new standards of valuation.

Much to the surprise of the old-timers, stocks of the young electronics firms took Wall Street by storm. The district seemed to be speaking of nothing but space travel, microcircuits, transistors, klystron tubes, and other esoterica. Analysts found themselves staying up late at night to bone up on college mathematics and physics as well as corporation reports. By March 1959, the American Stock Exchange, where many of the new issues were traded, was recording 3-million-share days with a fair degree of regularity. Meanwhile, at the NYSE, stock splits of such glamour firms as Thiokol, Pfizer, and Eastman Kodak helped propel the market to new highs. By March the Dow crossed the 600 mark, and three months later it was just below 650. Other markets joined the New York advance. By mid-year the London Exchange was up by 58 percent from its February lows, and there were similar patterns at other European exchanges. "We thought it wouldn't happen here, but the whole world seems to be caught by a frenzy of speculation," remarked a Swiss banker. There was a minor dip in the autumn, but stocks came roaring back. By then a rash of new companies had had their initial public offerings, with names such as Astron, Dutron, Transitron, and a host of other "trons" and "electros," and they were taken up by a public fascinated by the new technologies and eager to get in on the "world of tomorrow."

The new investors were a cross section of the population. Some were substantial businessmen and professionals, pillars of their communities, who were interested in purchasing blue chip stocks and securities in the more promising of the new companies in the glamour industries. Others, often in the same category but more adventuresome, wanted to gamble on the young companies and did so through marginal brokerage. The arrival of this new cohort, which seemed quite different from the gamblers of the 1920s, was celebrated by academic students of capitalism. Indeed, People's Capitalism inferred that this time around the people would have a genuine stake in the companies whose products they purchased. "Through stock ownership the people own the means of production," wrote Marcus Nadler, a professor who also worked as an adviser for Hanover Bank.

This was not really so. Indeed, a survey indicated that a smaller proportion of the general population owned stock in 1960 than in 1929. Another study, released in 1952, estimated that there were fewer than 6.5 million direct owners of stock. In 1956 the NYSE claimed there were 8.6 million, and by 1965, the figure rose to 20.1 million. Even so, in 1955 only 7.9 percent of the American population were shareholders, against the 6.6 percent of 1937, hardly a great increase considering the different atmospheres of the two years. And a 1951 survey—admittedly prior to the great increase in shareholder participation—showed that 2.1 percent of the shareholders owned 58 percent of all common stock. Another study in 1960 revealed that only one-sixth of all American families owned any stock at all. On the other hand, institutional ownership of common stock was increasing in this period. In the late 1950s the hod carrier might not own much in the way of stock, but his union owned $10 million in stock, while the Teamsters had close to $25 million.

While investors attracted by the words of men like Merrill and Funston were initially drawn to the old blue chips—General Motors, General Electric, American Telephone & Telegraph, the Pennsylvania Railroad and the like—in time they would turn to younger companies, and to new issues in particular.

Gambling on Stocks

Some of these offerings were made by old-line brokerages. For example, White Weld underwrote an initial public offering for Pocket Books, Shearson Hammill did one for Restaurant Associates, and Lehman Brothers handled an IPO for Vacuum Electronics. Others utilized the services of second and third-tier houses: Peerless Tube was underwritten by Winslow, Cohn & Stetson, and Pneumodynamics by Hemphill, Noyes. The more conventional of the new brokers found places at these houses. The others applied for positions at the newer, more venturesome brokerages, whose clienteles, for the most part, were comprised of individuals seeking a fast return on their "bets." Often these clients opened discretionary accounts, meaning the broker had the right to buy and sell as he saw fit. Indeed, in some cases the brokers would refuse a new account unless it was discretionary. What this meant, then, was that the broker could decide, prior to the actual underwriting, which of his customers would receive shares, and when they should sell them. In such circumstances, the possibilities for manipulation were present, and often this abuse existed. At first, most offerings were made by old-line banks, which wouldn't touch a company with less than a five-year record of successful operations. These banks had reputations to safeguard, and weren't about to trade them for quick one-time profits.

Then, as the mania gathered steam, marginal underwriters sprouted to peddle low-grade merchandise. Their ranks included the likes of Mike Lomasney, Charlie Plohn, and Mike Kletz. They were more salesmen than bankers, small-timers who functioned on shoestrings and weren't in business for the long haul. Their operations were legitimate, but at the same time they were edged with dubious practices.

They were a picturesque crew. "Two a Week" Charlie Plohn crowed, "I give people the kind of merchandise they want. I sell stock cheap. I bring out risky deals most firms wouldn't touch." Don Marron, the twenty-seven-year-old leader at the firm of Marron, Sloss & Co., spoke of his ambition to create a major power in underwriting, and liked to boast of how far he had come so quickly.

Kletz, a wily veteran who had gone through a number of stock manias in his time, was one of the larger underwriters of small new issues, capable of outmanuevering firms many times his size. He called in some markers and underbid several prominent houses to obtain the $1.6 million underwriting for Yale Express, one of the more substantial offerings of the period. Kletz was refreshingly realistic about his prospects. "All we have is me and eleven girls," he told a reporter proudly, adding that it was likely to stay that way, since he wasn't sure how long the boom would last. Kletz liked to talk about "the other-idiot principal": "My clients buy stocks because they know some other idiot will buy it from them at a higher price." And they did, the game continuing so long as the market did not run out of idiots.

One key to their success was Regulation A, which exempted new issues for less than $300,000 from full SEC disclosure. For example, their financial statements need not have been certified by independent accountants, and they weren't required to file "red herring" prospectuses. An SEC representative merely shrugged when asked about the kind of stock issued by dubious houses under these conditions. "We're not here to keep investors from losing money," he said. "The day we start doing that, it'll be the end of the free capital market."

At the height of their popularity, the new-issue bankers had buyers scrambling for shares and pleading to be placed on their customer lists, while scores of small-business men lined up to cash out through IPOs. The underwriters seemed to have a magic touch; as *Barron's* noted, virtually all of their issues rose, sometimes doubling or tripling in a single day. Few of the companies survived, however, and the same was true for the underwriters. That is usually the situation at the tail end of manias.

Getting started in the business was the biggest problem. IPO underwriters needed a supply of contented, eager customers who were willing to follow instructions without asking questions. A couple of successful underwritings, combined with word-of-mouth promotion, usually did the trick.

The customer would telephone, be told of a forthcoming offering of "Xotronics," and be assured it would put IBM out of business. The caller would be informed that he could have no more than 1,000 shares at $5 a share. The underwriter would say when and at what price the offering would be sold. Could the customer sell earlier? Of course, but to do so would be to violate an unwritten rule, and there would be no more opportunities to buy.

The underwriter's methods were quite simple. He would take 2.1 million shares and try to sell 2.0 million at the aforementioned $5. That price was for the customer; the underwriter would pay the client $4 for 2 million shares and keep $1 a share for himself, along with the extra 100,000 shares, for which he would pay a penny a share. One morning on the phones and the underwriter's salesmen would have placed all 2 million shares—and have a waiting list.

On the day of the placement, the salesman would receive calls from that 1,000-share client (and some of his acquaintances), along with the others who were not in on the original deal, trying to buy in the aftermarket. In a twinkling, the price would rise to 10, and the underwriter would start disposing of his 100,000 shares. Along the way he might sell some of the customers' shares as well. Once out of the situation, he would let the price rise or fall on its own. Sometimes it went higher, and often it went lower, but the underwriter didn't care, since by then he was involved in other deals.

Consider a typical distribution of the early 1960s: a Lomasney underwriting of BBM Photocopy, a firm he touted as "the next Xerox." As part of his remuneration, Lomasney received 20,000 warrants, to purchase shares for a penny each. He then sold 100,000 shares of the stock at $3, receiving a hefty commission for his effort. Within a short time the stock was selling for $40, which gave the warrants a value of around $800,000. Thus, Lomasney received just under $1 million for this small deal, while BBM obtained less than one-third that amount from the underwriting. The BBM management wasn't complaining, however, since they owned bundles of a stock that reached $40.

Since then the process has been repeated many times, and most of the companies whose stocks were underwritten are no longer with us. BBM and Chemtronic, for example, are out of business. But their corporate grandchildren were offered weekly in the 1980s and 1990s by the descendants of Mike Kletz and Don Marron. The older, established, and more familiar firms came in only after the market had become more knowledgeable about the category.

By the early 1960s the craze occasioned by the flotation of shares in new high-technology companies had gotten to the point where most new issues, no matter what the business of the companies, went to premiums soon after being offered. Almost any new stock could be counted on to rise by 20 to 50 percent on the first day of trading. This was true for technology stocks, such as Bristol Dynamics and Polychrome, but also for the likes of Mother's Cookie, which came out at 15 on March 8, 1961, and was selling for $24\frac{1}{2}$ on April 14. Alberto Culver, a niche player in the decidedly unglamourous business of hair-care preparations, was offered at 10 to those who were able to get in on the initial sale on April 5, and changed hands at 22 on April 22.

The lesson was clear. Brokers working at underwriting firms could count on long lines of customers seeking to be in on the initial offering, while the customers realized this was one of the easier ways to make money. This situation meant that both brokers and customers would profit in an almost riskless fashion, and so Americans rushed to obtain posts at the brokerages and to get on preferred lists. Such activity could not help but stimulate business formation. The availability of capital from so generous a market and so promising an economy stirred entrepreneurship.

There were, finally, some investment banks that came to concentrate on bringing to market viable companies whose balance sheets, leadership, and economic promise were of a higher quality than those underwritten by the Kletzes and Marrons of the Wall Street world. Among these were Kohlberg, Kravis, Roberts, and Drexel Burnham—especially Drexel Burnham, where Michael Milken would later become celebrated (or reviled) for his use of junk bonds in leveraged buyouts.

In his work as a trader, Milken had become fascinated by the bonds of low-rated companies that he felt were underpriced given their prospects. He was one of the few in the industry who felt this way. Among the others were the managers of several mutual funds, who concentrated on what were then known as "fallen angels," high-rated bonds, that, due to problems at the issuing company, had been downrated. Among these funds were Keystone B4 and Lord Abbott Bond-Debenture, both of which did well in the mid-1970s. First Investors Fund for Income, one of Milken's best customers, was among the top performers in this period. From fallen angels Milken progressed to the underwriting of new companies and the refinancing of some troubled companies, whose financial situations meant they would receive low ratings from Standard & Poor's and Moody's. Among the first of these were Comdisco, Fruit of the Loom, Continental Airlines, Beverly Enterprises, Minstar, Cablevision, Duracell, MagneTek, Mattel, and many companies involved with gaming activities in Las Vegas. Some of these companies failed to perform as expected, while others were quite successful.

The Mutual Fund Explosion

The development of interest in securities and the new-issues craze created great wealth for many who participated. But much more was generated by those who originated, managed, and marketed mutual funds, and by customers fortunate enough to purchase the right one at the right time. The oldest of the modern funds, the Massachusetts Investment Trust, appeared in 1924, but the idea of small investors pooling their money and having a professional manage it through the purchase and sale of securities existed as far back as the Hellenistic Age. During the 1920s there were two versions of the trusts: the closed ends and the open ends. The former had a specific number of shares outstanding, while the latter were prepared to purchase and sell shares at net asset value, plus or minus "load," for those sold with commissions, or net asset value for the "no loads," which soon became the more popular type. In 1940, there were some 300,000 owners of shares of mutual funds, and the assets of the funds in which they invested were $400,000, indicating that some of those accounts were quite minuscule. By 1950 there were almost 100 funds, and the number of accounts had expanded to 900,000, with total assets of $2.5 billion. Then, during the postwar period, armies of salesmen for load funds, comprised mostly of part-timers, sold their funds to individuals interested in participating in the market but eager for professional guidance. Their success was attested to by the numbers—in 1960, according to the Investment Company Institute, an industry organization, there were 4.9 million owners and assets of $17 billion.

In addition, several fund managers became the glamour figures of the new bull market. Fred Alger, who guided Security Equity Fund, had the proper credentials: a Yale education and a father who had been ambassador to Belgium. Howard Stein of Dreyfus Fund succeeded the legendary and highly respected Jack Dreyfus. But Fred

Carr of Enterprise Fund had a checkered career that smacked of scandal, which did not bother those who were able to get in on some of his signature public offerings, including Winchell's Donuts, Kentucky Fried Chicken, McDonald's, Tonka, Jostens, and Kelly Services. The most prominent was Gerald Tsai, a non-patrician who had fashioned his reputation at Fidelity Fund, one of the largest and most successful no-loads. Management, then, was another vehicle through which the parvenue could achieve wealth and status.

At a time when the no-loads were developing families of funds, thereby offering investors the right to switch from one to another without penalties, Fidelity, T. Rowe Price, Scudder, Vanguard, and several others became the stars of that constellation, and managers there were the closest Wall Street would have to superstars in what clearly was the vehicle of choice for those who hoped to combine a measure of safety with the possibilities of growth. By 1965 the 165 mutual funds reported 6.7 million accounts with $35.2 billion in investments. In 1970 the number of funds had risen to 361, the accounts to 10.7 million, and assets came in at $47.6 billion. A means had been found by which middle-class Americans might hope, with regular deposits into mutual funds accounts, for a comfortable if not lavish old age. Such certainly was not the case a quarter of a century earlier. This alteration in public perception was one of the two most important changes of that period, both of which indicated that the bleak atmosphere created by the falloff from the Great Depression was, if not over or nearly so, at least a much less dominant force in American life. The other force was the altered attitude toward debt, as embodied in the creation and popularity of credit cards.

Middle-Class Credit: The Credit Card

The credit card, a ubiquitous part of American life by the 1970s, was introduced by the Bank of America in 1957, but there had been limited forms of such cards earlier. Sears Roebuck and other retailers, gasoline companies, finance companies, and some other consumer-oriented firms had cards that could be used to charge items at their outlets. The Diners Club, a more universal charge card (as distinct from a credit card), could be used at many restaurants that had signed up for the service. Soon after it was followed by the American Express card, also a charge card, which was accepted at many more establishments. These were the first that might be used at the discretion of the holder and not limited to single companies, such as those issued by Shell Oil, Macy's, and the like. Customers were billed monthly, and were expected to pay promptly. There were some attempts to develop a card that would be honored by a group of merchants, but these failed.

The true father of the credit card was A. P. Giannini, who had organized the Bank of Italy before World War I as an institution that catered to the needs of Italian-Americans in the San Francisco area. In 1930 he acquired the Los Angeles–based Bank of America of California, which included twenty-one branches, and this became the base of his activities in southern California. They were all under the umbrella of Bank of Italy, which by 1927 had 300 banks in 185 California towns and cities, with capital of $750 million. By then it was the largest bank west of the Hudson and the third largest in the country. In 1928, Giannini changed the name of the umbrella company to Transamerica, which indicated the geographic scope of his ambition. His commercial scope was even greater. Giannini hoped to create a way whereby small merchants and consumers might have lines of credit at his bank, not too different from that which merchants had at their banks, meaning they would have an available line of credit of, say, $1,000; they could charge up to that amount, be billed monthly, and pay a fee for the privilege.

At the time wealthy Americans, and those on expense accounts, often had charge cards, which were quite different from credit cards in that they enabled their holders to charge expenses but did not extend to them the right not to pay outstanding balances; rather, charge cards obliged them to pay charges at the end of the billing period. Offering credit was a different matter entirely, one that American Express eventually would attempt to do, but not at that time.

In mid-1957 Bank of America executive Joseph Williams presented his idea to the bank's management. The plan envisaged credit limits of between $300 and $500, with floor limits of individual charges from $25 to $100 and above. Cardholders would be required to repay the loan at a specific rate, with the understanding that interest would be charged on balances. On the other hand, cardholders might pay the entire amount of the loan at regular intervals, and in this way avoid the interest charges. Participating merchants would be authorized to accept charges up to that limit, and for amounts above it, they would telephone the central office for approval. They would pay a fee, plus 6 percent of the purchase price. The "Bankamericard" was to be a combination of the Diners Club card and those issued by the retailers. It was a revolutionary idea, but the most radical aspect was to provide middle-class Americans of the postwar period with lines of credit formerly reserved for the very wealthy, who

charged their purchases in the swank stores they frequented, usually without a time limit for payment, as the
English aristocracy had done for centuries.

At this time, Williams thought the Bankamericard
could provide the holder with a convenient way to pay for
small purchases, and could serve as an instant personal
loan for larger ones. He understood the temptation such
cards would present for overspending. This created
another problem for Williams and others who followed.
Initially he mailed the cards out wholesale to Bank of
America depositors and other valued customers, which
resulted in many of them being discarded or used in an
irresponsible fashion. In response, the bank advertised:

> As for its encouraging extravagance, it seems to
> us that this is a problem which every individual
> must resolve for himself. Only you can determine
> to what extent your income and circumstances
> permit you to buy on credit. It is not our inten-
> tion to encourage "easy money" or a "free spend-
> ing program." In fact, we believe our job is to
> assist you in any way possible to maintain sound
> and sensible control of your finances.

Bank of America lost money on the Bankamericard
until 1960, when it showed a modest profit. Then, as
cardholders became more familiar with the ways and
methods of personal credit, additional consumers wanted
such cards, and Bank of America was able to franchise the
cards to other banks. In 1960 there were close to a quarter
of a million cardholders who purchased $59 million worth
of goods and services by using them. In 1968 there were
430,000 cardholders who charged $252 million. As the
cards became more popular, other companies entered the

field, most of which either failed or were merged out of existence. By the 1980s Visa and MasterCard were the most successful and ubiquitous, having signed on a clear majority of the nation's banks to their programs. At the same time, merchants learned that unless they accepted the cards their businesses would suffer greatly. Restaurants that catered to the expense-account trade, for example, could hardly survive without those ubiquitous decals in front windows announcing to their customers that they would accept their cards, thus providing patrons with proof of purchase for their expense accounts. By then, too, companies took to issuing the cards to their executives to ease payments and have receipts for their accountants to use when toting up entertainment expenses for the Internal Revenue Service. Soon companies offered bonuses to win cardholders, the most popular being credits toward free airline trips. Thus, the cardholders would be encouraged to charge purchases, knowing they were accumulating mileage points. By then, too, automobile rental companies such as Hertz and Avis had decided not to rent their cars to anyone who did not tender a credit card, to protect themselves against losses due to damages.

Those who earned large and small amounts from the cards included the Visa and MasterCard companies, the banks that issued them, and the merchants who accepted them. For their part, cardholders found their lives simplified by the convenience of the cards. By the mid-1980s, close to 3 out of every 4 Americans between the ages of seventeen and sixty-five had at least one credit card, and the average outstanding balance was almost $1,500. Many American consumers came to think differently about their spending reserves. In the pre-card period, they would take into account just how much savings they had prior to making a purchase. Thus, a family thinking about a vacation that would cost approximately $3,000 would consider bank accounts and other sources of savings prior to making a commitment. The key question to be answered was, "Can we afford this vacation?" Armed with credit cards, the same family might ask, "Can we afford the payments for this vacation?" which is to say, the $3,000 would be translated into a $500 or so payment on the next invoice. This was not a wholly new experience. When purchasing a home, they would have calculated the costs associated with the mortgage and taxes. Even so, there was a difference. The home was an indication of wealth, a storehouse that increased in worth month by month. Not so payments on the credit card balance, which was determined by enjoyment in the past. Of course, not all of this fell into the consumption category. The family might have purchased a computer for that $3,000 that increased productivity and so contributed to earnings. But most evidence was that consumption, not investment, was the cause of credit card purchases. Mimi Lieber, a consultant to the industry, conducted a study in the mid-1980s that indicated that more than half the sample did not believe it was right to borrow, but that more than 60 percent of them had credit cards on which there were unpaid balances.

The banks had reason to applaud the latter statistic. In the early 1990s, when they were being castigated for having invested in junk bonds, in this way endangering deposits, a government study indicated that only a few banks and S&Ls had substantial holdings in junk bonds, whose financial performance was quite satisfactory. In fact, the financial institutions had better earnings performance from these bonds than from any other investment—

except credit cards, which were far and away the best-performing financial holdings in the banks' portfolios.

Before these postwar financial innovations—the democratization of stock market investing by Charles Merrill and his imitators, the creation of small-investor-friendly mutual funds, and the credit card explosion—the middle class, for the most part, was excluded from the world of investments. For the vast majority of these Americans, their investments (though few used that word) were in thirty-year mortgages and passbook savings accounts, which were predictable and safe. Now, ordinary householders were abandoning the limited ways of the past to participate in an economic boom that would ultimately outstrip even the most bullish predictions of the day.

5

Technique requires predictability and, no less, exactness of prediction. It is necessary, then, that technique prevail over the human being. Get technique, this is a matter of life and death. Technique must reduce man to a technical animal, the king of the slaves of technique. Human caprice crumbles before this necessity; there can be no human autonomy in the face of technical autonomy. The individual must be fashioned by techniques, either negatively (by the techniques of understanding man) or positively (by the adaption of man to the technical framework), in order to wipe out the blots his personal determination introduces into the perfect design of the organization.

—Jacques Ellul, 1964

The development of technologies as such is not the province of a book that purports to deal with the ways Americans became successful and wealthy after World War II, though the creation of industries and companies is an important part of the story. Even so, some mention has to be made of several developments. In the field of consumer electronics, primary importance must be assigned to the appearance of the transistor, developed by AT&T's Western Electric in 1947. Fearful of being charged with anti-trust violations if it capitalized on the invention, AT&T licensed the transistor to Raytheon, Zenith, and RCA in the early 1950s, and then to Texas Instruments, Philco, and other companies. The integrated circuits that followed, along with hundreds of other items, were at first seen as having only military applications. But they soon revolutionized such products as radios, phonographs, recording devices, and television, starting with radios in 1954, initially for a small company called Regency, which sold them for $50, less than the costs of the transistors.

The Electronics Age

The potential of transistors was obvious, at least to some in the electronics arena. In 1955, IBM CEO Tom Waston, Sr., purchased more than 100 of the small radios to give to his top executives. "If that little outfit down in Texas can make these radios work for that kind of money, they can make transistors that will make our computers work, too," he told them. And they did. Two years later, IBM obtained transistors from Texas Instruments to help make its next generation of computers. Even so, as recently as 1963, the transistor and allied devices were used primarily in military-related products. That year, measured in terms of value, $120 million worth of them were in military products, $92 million in industrial products and functions, many related to the military, and only $41 million in consumer products. More than half were in portable and automobile radios, with less than $300,000 worth in television receivers.

Some of the World War II generation who entered the

job market in the 1950s after receiving their undergraduate degrees were familiar with new technologies developed during the war. This was not unanticipated, since war always has been the breeding ground for the kinds of technological and managerial changes later employed in the civilian sector. So it was that aviation, automobiles, radio, a host of drugs, and other fields and products expanded from their World War I flowerings into important industries during the 1920s and beyond, and this was even more the case for the technologies advanced in World War II.

Of these, none was more important than what eventually would be categorized under the rubric of "high technologies" or "electronics." Chief among these were computers in all of their many manifestations. Computers as later understood were not created to meet the demands of war. But the electronics involved in aircraft, the aiming of bombs and of guns, and the navigation of ships all employed technologies virtually unknown prior to the war, and the most significant among them were those relating to computers. This was an industry and product that did not exist except in laboratories and the imaginations of researchers in 1939. A decade later, electronics were the mainstay of several major industries, ranging from consumer electronics to the aforementioned computers.

Startling and significant new inventions and technologies often have multiple births, largely because the innovators are not certain just how they may be employed. Such was the case with early radio, for example, when it was thought of as an instructional medium, with entertainment and information-spreading taking secondary roles. Thomas A. Edison did not harbor great hopes for the phonograph. He believed it might be used to record the last words of people before they died. Even the automobile's promise eluded the imaginations of the early pioneers, who thought of it as a wealthy man's toy, and so it was in the time of the Packard, Peerless, and Pierce-Arrow. Henry Ford did not invent the automobile, but he was responsible for the form it was to take, that of a vehicle for the use of the middle class—and even the lower class.

Similarly, that was the way the computer developed. Its original manifestation was the mainframe, a large machine capable of crunching numbers for companies and governments. Even while mainframes continued to be the dominant configuration of computers for decades, some experimenters were working on smaller versions, which held no interest for the larger companies. In time they would re-invent the computer, and demonstrate uses for the technology that had not been imagined by the founders of the industry.

The mainframe business would involve thousands of workers directly and many more indirectly. The credit card business, for example, would not have been possible to the extent that it developed were it not for mainframes, and many other forms of record keeping, calculation, and planning also depended on them. But personal computers, accessible to all, sparked a period of technological and societal change comparable to the Industrial Revolution of more than a century earlier, with an impact that perhaps in time would become even greater.

During the 1950s, most literate Americans realized that mainframe computers were among the most important technological innovations to appear since the end of the war, although few truly appreciated why this was so and just what computers could do. The popular belief held that computers represented the introduction of artificial intelligence into the factory and office, and in time they might exercise a measure of control over day-to-day life.

In this period UNIVAC was a synonym for computers in the minds of many people, who assumed it was produced by International Business Machines, the most famous company in the industry, the paradigm for the corporation of the future. Actually, UNIVAC was the product of Remington Rand, which, given better leadership, might have become the most prominent in the field. Its Univac Division was one of what often was referred to as the BUNCH, an acronym for Burroughs, Univac, National Cash Register, Control Data, and Honeywell, all of which entered the computer business at roughly the same time. This was an attractive industry, one that held out the promise of major growth and large profits, and it drew other firms involved in the new technologies that had come out of the war. Later RCA, General Electric, and others would make their bid for leadership, but in the end they dropped out, as did the BUNCH. Some American firms opted to mount their challenges in specialized parts of the market. Cray made its bid in the field of supercomputers, while Digital Equipment and Data General tried to best IBM in the area of smaller machines. Japanese firms attempted to compete directly with IBM, with mixed results. Ultimately, however, IBM had the dominant position in mainframes. While this was happening, a host of small start-ups were moving into the market for desktop computers, which, while lacking the power of the mainframes, were more affordable and flexible.

The New Computer Culture

Computer hobbyists, who bore a close resemblance to the radio experimenters of the early 1920s and who tried to develop receivers and transmitters based on the primitive technologies of the time and then improve on them, soon appeared in all parts of the country. The Stanford campus in California was one of the more active areas. One meeting place for such hobbyists was the Home Brew Computer Club, which was comprised of several hundred individuals who met to swap information and exchange ideas. They would purchase parts from electronics supply companies, one of which was the Byte Shop, a business that became so large it encouraged some hobbyists to open retail outlets to serve the population. There were dozens of would-be entrepreneurs in the club. Steve Wozniak and Steve Jobs, founders of Apple Computer, both college dropouts, were only two of the many budding entrepreneurs. Among the others were Adam Osborne, who later founded Osborne Computer, which produced the first transportable computer; Harry Garland and Roger Mellon, who founded Cromemco, which created an advanced desktop; Nolan Bushnell, who gained fame and fortune by virtue of Atari and Pong, the latter the first video game; and Bill Gates, whose Microsoft became a giant of the software field. One of the most important of the pioneers was Air Force lieutenant Ed Roberts of Altair, the model for those who wanted to produce machines, who organized Micro Instrumentation and Telemetry Systems (MITS), which became an incubator for scientists and entrepreneurs, and produced and sold calculators based on the new technologies.

Paul Terrell, who organized the Byte Shop, failed in

his attempt to create a nationwide chain. William Millard, who earlier had founded a computer company known as IMSAI, did better with his ComputerLands in large part because he saw the virtues in franchising. By 1983 there were nearly 500 ComputerLands doing business at a $1 billion clip. ComputerLands were filled with customers, but also with would-be rivals, there to see how it was being done, after which they would open stores of their own. Writing of ComputerLands (and ignoring the E. J. Korvette experience) that year, *Forbes* said:

> ComputerLand's growth has been like nothing seen before in U.S. retailing. Fiscal 1984 store sales will be up 50% at least (to $1.5 billion or so) from 1983's, which in turn were 150% above the previous year's. Today only Tandy's Radio Shack chain, with 1,065 stores handling computers, is larger than ComputerLand. Entre Computer Centers, the second largest franchised chain, has only 75 stores vs. ComputerLand's 474 in the U.S. and 24 in other countries.

Millard and his backers were becoming wealthy, but so were the franchisees. The typical store grossed at least $2 million, with pre-tax margins of 10 percent and more. Some franchisees entered into contracts for several stores, and in the process made more money from computers than did Millard—or for that matter, Jobs and Wozniak, whose Apple II computers were featured at Computer-Lands. Jobs was on his way to becoming the symbol of the microcomputer, or, to those who criticized him, its Pied Piper.

In 1981, during an interview with *Computers & People* magazine, Jobs attempted to rationalize the changes brought about by what he called "the Apple Revolution," but in reality the switch in interest from mainframes to desktops was much more than that.

> The whole concept is this: for the same capital equipment cost as a passenger train, you can now buy 1,000 Volkswagens. Think of the large computer [the mainframes and the minis] as the passenger train and the Apple personal computer as the Volkswagen. The Volkswagen isn't as fast or as comfortable as the passenger train. But the VW owners can go where they want, when they want, and with whom they want. The VW owners have personal control over the machine.
>
> In the '60s and early '70s, it wasn't economically feasible to have the interaction of one person with one computer. Computers were very costly and complicated; 50 people had to share one computer. Back then, you could have the passenger train but not the Volkswagen. But with the advent of microelectronics technology, parts got smaller and denser. Machines got faster. Power requirements went down. Electronic intelligence became affordable. We finally had the chance to invent the personal computer.
>
> Basically, Steve Wozniak and I invented the Apple because we wanted a personal computer. Not only couldn't we afford the computers that were on the market, those computers were impractical for us to use. We needed a Volkswagen.

Wozniak had a different, less romantic, interpretation of the advent of the personal computer:

Our success was due to a number of factors. First of all, we had never manufactured computers before. We couldn't look back and say, "Here's how computers earned a lot of money in the '60s and '70s, that's the style to do." All we thought about was what was going to work out in our own homes. Our motivation was what would be good in the end. If there were a known formula for what would make a successful product and what would make a billion dollars, all the big companies were a lot smarter than we were. What we had was luck. We did the right things with the right coincidences of timing and the right people in the right place together.

Some technicians and scientists at IBM and the BUNCH companies were also captivated by the vision of computers for everyone, and several left their companies and migrated from their headquarters in the East to northern California and other centers to find financial and intellectual support. Alan Shugart, who was a top IBM scientist, went to a start-up firm in the hope of receiving the kind of encouragement he needed; when this failed to materialize, he left in 1973 to form Seagate Associates, which metamorphosed into Seagate Technology. When the new company did not attract funds, Shugart became a commercial fisherman, invested in a saloon, and did some consulting. Finally, in 1981, Seagate Technology had a successful initial public offering, and Shugart was wealthier by $1.2 million. Shugart was not bashful in confessing that he was in the business for the money. "We all work hard," he told an interviewer, "because we all want to make a fortune in a hurry." With him, as with many others, it was a case of easy come, easy go. Shugart was not to remain wealthy for long, and he left only a small mark on the industry.

Desktop computers were quite successful, especially among businessmen and academics. Although the early models had limited capabilities, some 200,000 of them were sold in 1977 by such firms as Apple, Radio Shack, and Commodore, and the market was growing at the rate of 50 percent per annum.

IBM's introduction of its Personal Computer in 1981 marked the "legitimization" of the small machines, and attracted more manufacturers, especially those who produced "clones" of the IBMs. By 1984 there were some 200 clone manufacturers, among them Compaq, which produced a machine that many purchasers considered superior to the IBM while capable of running all of its programs. Industry magazines, such as *PC World*, carried advertisements from scores of suppliers, such as AST and Dell, who offered more power at lower costs than IBM. By the late 1980s it had become evident that personal computers, which were becoming more powerful and less expensive quite rapidly, could replace some of the smaller mainframes. Workstations, a business in which Sun and other firms emerged as leaders, were even replacing IBM mainframes.

IBM seemed a certain winner and pace setter at the beginning of the computer age. It was the leader when interest turned to desktops, but there were other companies that offered strong competition. Moreover, it was becoming increasingly evident that the computers themselves, which is to say the hardware, were not the key to the industry. Rather, the software they ran was essential, and software companies such as Microsoft and Computer Associates became increasingly important in the early 1990s. By then, too, what seemed to be a predictable industry had become quite vital, with changes appearing regularly.

In the 1950s computers were seen as replacements for other machines and humans to execute existing tasks. In the age of the desktop, computers were performing tasks that once had been unimaginable. There were those who claimed they were creating a new civilization, not merely acting as participants. In the process, computers displaced companies as well as workers involved with the old technologies. They were part of the mechanism whereby that new age—with new industrial leaders—would come to the fore.

The New Industrial Paradigm

A goodly number of the computers and other electronic devices produced in the 1970s and later were the fruits of combination research facilities–factories. Such enterprises created a new kind of factory, equipped with clean rooms and all kinds of electronics apparatus, which dotted the landscape near the homes of the scientists and technicians employed there. These individuals did not work on an hourly basis, and many did not have specific tasks. Rather, they came and went as their assignments demanded, and it was not unusual for teams to labor around the clock, depending on the needs of the project. While involved with an undertaking at three A.M. on a Sunday, a young high-tech worker might look down the line and see a Nobel Prize winner with two or three of his graduate students busily exploring one of the master's or student's undertakings. A few weeks later, one of the researchers with whom the student had some contact might offer him a job, complete with a munificent sign-on bonus. Or another researcher might tell him of how he planned to leave the NYSE-listed company at which he was a senior scientist to form his own company. The seed capital was already in place, and there would be a list of individuals who were coming into the new company, along with some of the projects and their industrial sponsors. Why was this young person being singled out to receive such information? Because that senior researcher wanted him there, at a fine salary plus stock options.

Nolan Bushnell, who was to found such firms as Atari and Pizza Time Theatres, explained how it was done:

> A guy wakes up in the morning and says, "I'm going to be an entrepreneur." So he goes in to work and walks up to the best technologist in the company where he's working, and he whispers: "Would you like to join my company? Ten o'clock, Saturday, my place. And bring some doughnuts." Then he goes to the best finance guy he knows, and says, "Bring some coffee." Then you get a marketing guy. And if you are the right entrepreneur, you have three or four of the best minds in the business. Ten o'clock Saturday rolls around. They say, "Hey, what is our company going to do?" You say, "Build left-handed widgets." Another hour and you've got a business plan roughed out. The finance guy says he knows where he can get some money. So what have you done? You've not provided the coffee. You've not provided the dough-nuts. You've not provide the ideas. You've been the entrepreneur. You made it all happen.

Of course, this is an exaggeration. But it was close enough to experience to ring true to dozens who started companies in this period, and who built a research and manufacturing facility in the area.

It was quite different at the Route 128 companies, which tended to be more formal in their approaches. Engineer Alan Michaels, who had worked for companies in both places and had a hand in starting up several of them, including Convergent Technologies, put it this way:

> There is no way that I could have started Convergent [Technologies] in the Boston area. I am convinced that there are definite cultural differences in Silicon Valley compared with Route 128 . . . When I started Convergent, I got commitments for $2.5 million in 20 minutes from three people over lunch who saw me write the business plan on the back of a napkin. They believed in me. In Boston, you can't do that. It's much more formal. People in New England would rather invest in a tennis court than high technology.

Moreover, there was no single dominant firm in Silicon Valley, while Digital Equipment came to be seen as the leader along Route 128. "When you work in Route 128, you see DEC as the center of the universe," was the way one executive put it. "Silicon Valley isn't like that; it isn't dominated by any big company or companies."

In the process, a new form of community was being created, one that, sometime in the 2000s, may come to be seen as the successor to or at least an adjunct to the industrial and commercial city. While they appeared in the 1950s, it was not until the 1990s that attempts were made to provide rationales for them and even a name: technopolises. The technopolis—where many of the children and grandchildren of the GI generation were employed—did not so much remake the world they inherited as adjust existing institutions to their needs and to the demands created by the new technologies with which they labored. They managed this with so much success that one might conclude that they either enlarged the boom they inherited from their parents and grandparents or created a new chapter in the saga of American growth.

Consider that this came after a period, during the 1960s and 1970s, when some pedants voiced fears that the American Century had come to an end, that Japanese and other Asian cultures contained elements that were more appropriate to the new world of technology than anything devised in America. The problem with such an analysis is, among other things, that it did not take into account the American proclivity to adjust to changing circumstances and to absorb ideas and peoples and fit them in with what already existed. In the first place, there was no single American culture, and there never had been one. The counterculture of the 1960s and beyond, despite the name, was as native to America as was the dominant culture. The ability of more than one way of life to coexist has never been fully appreciated by either.

So it was with the coming of the technopolis. While Americans were debating the merits of the Vietnam War, attempting to find ways to satisfy the needs and "demands" of racial and gender activists and come to terms with new ideas from overseas, the "technological imperative," which is to say the demands posed by the new technologies, was also being addressed.

In the midst of this came the most important wave of immigration since the turn of the century. In that earlier period millions of newcomers from eastern and southern

Europe reinvigorated old American industries and helped create new ones. During the 1960s and afterwards, immigrants from Latin America and Asia performed similarly. At one time, some San Diego civic leaders suggested it might be well to construct a new Statue of Liberty in the harbor, on a pivot, which would enable it to face south and west on alternate days of the week. In 1900, critics of what then was being called the "new immigration" complained that the newcomers were altering American life in ways that would make the old traditions and values appear redundant, implying that they would create in America an alien civilization to supplant the existing one. Such was not the case. Rather, the newcomers absorbed the old ways, accepted the values they suggested, and applied them to the new challenges posed by the industrial era. This matter was addressed obliquely in the presidential elections of 1992 and 1996, when candidates Ross Perot and Pat Buchanan suggested that curbs on immigration were needed to prevent the denaturing of the American spirit.

It didn't happen. Instead, those waves of immigrants continued to hit the shores, affecting many industries, but most visibly those requiring high levels of knowledge and training. If one entered the commissaries of many high-technology companies in the 1980s at lunchtime, one might hear conversations held in dozens of languages. The speakers were immigrants, new Americans whose credentials had earned them a place at the American technology high table. Without them, the technopolises would not have worked as well as they did.

It still remains to define the word *technopolis* before examining the more important of them. In much the same way as the industrial cities of a century ago were built around the workplace, so were the technopolises.

Pittsburgh and Detroit, key industrial cities, were erected around the steel and automobile industries. In a like fashion, the workplaces for the electronics age would be the laboratories and graduate schools.

But there were some major differences. Recruiters for high-technology companies would report that likely candidates usually had several concerns on their minds when considering relocation. The first often was the workplace environment. Companies that could not guarantee twenty-four-hour-a-day, seven-day-a-week access to laboratories were at a disadvantage. The interests and abilities of colleagues also counted. Access to top-notch graduate schools and their faculties was almost taken for granted; no area could hope to attract the desired scientists without them. These people also wanted superior educational facilities for their children. It was important to them that excellent cultural amenities be nearby, along with certain kinds of sports facilities. An often unconsidered factor in this is the presence in the area of a motivated alumni community. They maintained their contacts with the university not only as a result of genuine affection for their alma mater, but also because of a recognition that such contacts are good for business. Potential faculty and businessmen seeking a place to build research facilities would be wined and dined by alumni prepared to discuss the benefits that might accrue to all involved.

In the nature of things, government contracts, especially those that were related to military needs, were an important component of the mix. In the late 1960s, six states depended on such contracts for 10 percent or more of their income. These were Virginia, Utah, Washington, California, Alaska, and Hawaii, so defense-related contracts tended to be concentrated in these states. Some metropolitan areas had an even greater reliance on such contracts—with Washington, Boston, Seattle, Huntsville, Cape Kennedy, Los Angeles, San Diego, and Wichita in the lead. The requirements of the government helped redraw the nation's economic and financial map. This is not to suggest that other states and metropolitan areas lagged economically as a result. New York, Chicago, and other large cities depended upon other industries, and because of this were in some respects healthier and more promising economically.

One of the earliest of the new communities developed along Route 128 in Massachusetts, although it did not prove to be the template from which the others were fashioned. Nonetheless, in the early years of the computer era, Route 128 seemed an image of what to expect in the future. It became a mecca for scientists, and the nearby universities, especially Massachusetts Institute of Technology, became the educational centers that were the goals of bright, ambitious young faculty, some of them the GIs who completed their educations by virtue of the GI Bill or were supported by generous fellowships and scholarships. During World War II, the government established the Lincoln Laboratories there, which had pioneered in radar and other wartime inventions. Boston's investment community, second only to that of New York, was able to provide funding for several of the companies that wanted to capitalize on the proximity of university talent, government funding, and other amenities offered in the area.

Scores of high-technology companies located their facilities along Route 128, among them Digital Equipment, Data General, Wang Laboratories, Prime Computer, Analog Devices, Polaroid, Ionics, High Voltage Engineering, EG&G, and others, along with virtually all the high-technology companies that entranced investors in the 1960s and 1970s. By then one might drive along Route

128 and see a parade of the nation's major high-technology companies, which worked closely with MIT, Harvard, Boston University, and the dozen other universities in the area, as well as with the government. Their presence attracted other companies and scientists. From 1955 to 1971, the number of firms in the region leaped from 39 to 1,200. For a while, Route 128 served as the center for the industry that produced small minicomputers, which some thought were capable of supplanting the "big iron" put out by IBM.

This government-academia nexus was challenged in the 1960s by anti-war demonstrators protesting the involvement of the universities with the Vietnam War. By then the government and industry dominated large segments of the universities' research departments. "We were churning out defense-oriented graduate students," recalled one MIT professor.

By the late 1970s Digital Equipment and Data General, two of the firms with facilities along Route 128, between them accounted for more than half the sales of minicomputers. Many smaller companies united to form the Massachusetts High Technology Council, a 124-member group that worked with the state government to provide benefits for its members and had close relations with the area's colleges and universities.

"Almost all of our graduate students who didn't go into university teaching wound up in the missile and aircraft industries," said one professor-entrepreneur. As a result of protests, some of the institutes devoted to defense and industrial purposes were spun off by their parents, and others oriented toward different ends.

Even so, locales with fine universities and pleasant climates held a decided edge. The Santa Clara area was the kind of place in the 1950s and 1960s where experimentation was part of the atmosphere. By 1955 the Stanford campus, in what had become the Stanford Industrial Park, had seven companies in place on land previously used for growing peaches. There were thirty-two companies by 1960, and seventy in 1970. Within fifteen years, the number of companies with offices and/or research facilities there had reached ninety, and there were some 25,000 professionals at work in the park. Out of Stanford's classrooms came the likes of Sun Microsystems, Silicon Graphics, Cisco Systems, and Yahoo!

The park had been the incubator for Beckman Instruments, one of whose founders had been a Stanford chemistry professor, Fred Terman. Terman was the key player at Stanford. Before the war, after receiving his education at MIT (where he studied under Vannevar Bush), Terman had gone to Stanford to become an electrical engineering professor and dean of engineering. Most Americans who had heard of Bush, Karl Compton, and other scientific academics pressed into government service during and after the war probably had never heard of Terman, who was an academic Dr. Strangelove, a calculating politician whose sole ambition was to make Stanford the world's premier scientific university, in the process obtaining employment and status for his colleagues and graduate students. He thought the postwar years would be crucial for the school. "I believe that we will either consolidate our potential strength, and create a foundation for a position in the West somewhat analogous to Harvard in the East, or we will drop to a level somewhat similar to that of Dartmouth, a well-thought-of institution having about 2 percent as much influence on national life as Harvard."

Terman's proposition was simple enough. Ignore the undergraduates because they don't pay dividends in grants and prestige. Concentrate instead on graduate programs, but only in the hot departments. It would be wiser to build a few superb departments than to seek excellence across the board. Or, as Terman put it, it is better for a basketball team to have one seven-footer than a lot of six-footers. On another occasion, Terman spoke of "steeples of excellence," which reflected his belief that academic prestige does not depend on the overall quality of the faculty, but on that of its stars. A steeple, according to Terman, was "a small faculty group of experts in a narrow area of knowledge, and what counts is that the steeples be high for all to see and that they relate to something important." The important something at Stanford, as far as Terman was concerned, was to be the kind of electronics that could be translated into products demanded by government or the private sector. The earnings from the leases of these items were to be used to create a "fighting fund" to recruit and retain star faculty members.

Terman pulled it off. In 1946 Stanford's government contracts came to $127,000; ten years later they were $4.5 million. After the war he lured Lockheed Aerospace, Westinghouse, Raytheon, Philco-Ford, and other established firms to the area, and those companies' technicians interacted with the Stanford faculty in ways that Terman had hoped they would. Within another decade, Stanford was among the top three universities in terms of government contracts.

Terman attracted venture capitalists to the area, which is the reason Silicon Valley is located where it is. Terman also was responsible for the establishment of the Palo Alto Research Center (PARC), which became the incubator for dozens of high-tech companies, many of which had been lured there by Terman and his co-workers and successors. One of these, Xerox Technologies Ventures, became a model of its kind, established in the late

213

1980s with $30 million in seed money, with the understanding that if a group of entrepreneurs came up with an idea for a company, Xerox would have the right of first refusal, after which the founders could do what they wanted with it, the only restriction being that it was located in the Stanford PARC. More firms of this type were organized, including the Center for Integrated Systems in the Silicon Valley.

As has been seen, just as the electronics complex around Route 128 in Massachusetts had been made possible and energized by companies coming out of MIT and Harvard, so Silicon Valley (which was bounded by Palo Alto to the northwest and Los Gatos to the southeast, almost all of which was in Santa Clara County) was made possible by companies formed by Stanford faculty members and graduates. William Hewlett and David Packard, two of the graduates, had formed Hewlett-Packard and received a $538 loan from Terman, who also helped arrange for an additional $1,000 loan from a Palo Alto bank.

Terman provided some of the financial backing for William Shockley, who had participated in the invention of the transistor (short for transfer resistance) while at the Bell Laboratories in New Jersey. Shockley was a native of Palo Alto and wanted to return home, which he did. With the assistance of Beckman Instruments, he formed Shockley Laboratories, which was based there in 1954. He received the Nobel Prize in 1956, by which time Shockley Transistor and then Semiconductor was located at Stanford. Among his early hires were Robert Noyce, Gordon Moore, Sheldon Roberts, Eugene Kleiner, Jay Last, and Jean Hoerni, all of whom were pioneers in the electronics revolution. Shockley proved to be a poor manager, and in 1957 several of his key personnel left to form a research operation closely tied to Fairchild Camera & Instrument, which was based in Connecticut.

Shockley's relationship with Stanford was one of its most important assets. Fairchild was not a particularly productive enterprise, but out of it came several consequential companies. Robert Noyce, one of the early hires at Fairchild, left to help organize Intel. Together with some of the others, Noyce convinced venture capitalist Arthur Rock to invest $2.5 million in Intel, one of the thirty-one high-technology firms organized in Silicon Valley during the 1960s, which included Rheem Semiconductor, Signetics, Teledyne, General Microelectronics, and Advanced Micro Devices.

As mentioned earlier, Silicon Valley began with companies and researchers involved with computers and semiconductors. Some of these were newly formed, while others were outposts of existing companies that hoped to cash in on the brainpower centered there. These were followed by semiconductor operations. By the late 1980s, the Valley entered a new phase, with the appearance of companies and laboratories involved with medical electronics, communications systems, automotive electronics, and biotechnology. One of the key elements of this later development was the sharing of information and researchers and several companies whose work paralleled each other's.

For those who have never been there, it should be noted that Stanford is immense. On other campuses students bicycle to classes; one sees many motorcycles at Stanford. Alongside the classroom buildings, libraries, and administrative centers are outposts of some of the nation's most aggressive corporations. The synergy is complete. Professors are employed at those centers, which also utilize the graduate students in a form of apprenticeship.

Scores of those small, entrepreneurial companies were started and staffed by Stanford people. "When we set out to create a community of technological scholars in Silicon Valley there wasn't much here and the rest of the world looked awfully big. Now a lot of the rest of the world is here," said Terman.

Terman's priorities were clear. Education was fine in its place, but there were more important considerations for those involved. Commenting on Office of Naval Research contracts, he wrote, "Even though much of the basic research work that these agencies support is carried on in universities, the *primary motive is not to aid education* but rather to accomplish their mission." This philosophy is fair enough insofar as the government is concerned, but what is the primary motive of the universities? Having those companies within driving distance made the universities more desirable places for the faculty and students. The universities would obtain the prestige that came from having well-known, celebrated faculty members on the campus along with the companies for which they worked when not with students. Indeed, it is difficult to say what most attracted the faculty members—the ability to teach students who were also employed by top technology companies and so were well motivated and intelligent, or the opportunities the faculty members had to engage in state-of-the-art research at some of the best sites in the country.

The University as Factory

By the 1960s it had become evident that Department of Defense relationships with leading research-oriented universities had reached the kind of level that had troubled President Eisenhower. In 1964 MIT had $47 million in

Department of Defense contracts alone, followed by the University of Michigan ($14.7 million), Stanford ($12.8 million), Columbia ($9.2 million), and the University of Illinois ($7.6 million). Toward the bottom of the list of universities receiving much smaller contracts were tiny Emmanuel College in Massachusetts ($312,000), the University of California at Riverside ($319,000), the University of Louisville ($325,000), the University of Georgia ($327,000), and the University of California at San Francisco ($343,000).

Those smaller grants usually were made to an individual rather than to the institution and could be taken with him if he relocated. Clearly, such grants were not the kind the schools preferred. And in time, there were financial reasons for this, as well as those relating to status. The Technology Transfer Acts of 1980, 1984, and 1986 authorized university and government laboratories to own technologies developed with government funding and to benefit financially from them. Thus, the universities might obtain patents on discoveries and the researchers might organize companies they would own to do the same. In effect, the federal government was providing the research funds for would-be entrepreneurs who, if successful, could cash in on their discoveries.

About 600,000 new firms appeared annually in the United States during the 1980s, and such high-technology start-ups represented only a small fraction of that number. But among them were some of the more successful efforts. Aware of how such firms invigorate the economy and attract jobs and investment capital, several states entered the competition. Not since the late-nineteenth-century competition for railroad rights of way had the competition in financing been as great as it became in this period. And central to all of this, as noted, was the research university. By the late 1980s research and development expenditures were on the order of $132 billion per annum, and the universities and colleges accounted for some 12 percent of this amount. In this regard, the military-industrial-educational complex was alive and well at the close of the twentieth century, even with the end of the Cold War.

With only the development of this complex, Silicon Valley would have emerged as one of the major technopolises, but another element went into the mix. During World War II, California—and the West Coast in general—had emerged as the home of major defense companies, and this continued after war. Clearly, the economic balance of America was shifting westward. By the 1960s, California, by itself, would have been the world's eighth largest economy in terms of GNP. Before the war, ambitious young people headed eastward in search of opportunity. After the war, it was the West that filled this role. Terman was convinced that the nation's future rested in the West and with high technology, to be nurtured at Stanford. Reflecting upon this later, he said:

> The West has long dreamed of an indigenous industry of sufficient magnitude to balance its agricultural resources. The war advanced these hopes and brought to the West the beginnings of a great new era of industrialization. A strong and independent industry must, however, develop its own intellectual resources of science and technology. For industrial activity that depends on imported brains and second-hand ideas cannot hope to be more than a vassal that pays tribute to its overlords, and is permanently condemned to an inferior competitive position.

That national defense was and is necessary is obvious. However, the bond between the universities and its sponsors had a price. "Were they training a generation of scientists and engineers so addicted to the wasteful culture of military procurement that they could never flourish in the cost-conscious world of civilian technology?" Terman got the message. In 1970 he told the Stanford faculty of his hope that the professors would "cease turning out people in their own image but would rather educate engineers attuned to the needs of non-aerospace, non-defense industries by working on research related to the problems of the world."

His advice was heeded. Silicon Valley never would be as closely tied to the defense industries as was Route 128. Later on, when interest shifted from hardware to specialized software and then to the Internet, Route 128 companies would be left in the dust, while Silicon Valley thrived.

Although Route 128 and Silicon Valley were the best known of the research, development, and manufacturing centers for the new technology, there were many more. In addition, individuals interested in opportunities presented by the new technologies, working on their own, could be found all over the country. Of the new centers, one of the more prestigious and productive was the Research Triangle at North Carolina, planned by state officials and the office of Governor Luther Hodges, which drew upon the faculties and facilities of nearby Duke, the University of North Carolina, and North Carolina State. The University of Utah served that role for the Utah Research Park in Salt Lake City (Bionic Valley), which concentrated on medical research, especially in the field of artificial organs, and soon had close to 50 tenants and 2,000 employees. There was an important center in Troy, New York, not far from

Rensselaer Polytechnic Institute (Silicon Valley East). In each case there were three elements: one or more research-oriented universities, government, and industry.

Such centers developed around Dallas–Fort Worth (known as Silicon Prairie), and Austin. It was there that the kind of sharing that was becoming widespread in the Silicon Valley reached its next stage, with the formation of the Microelectronics and Computer Technology Corporation (MCC), which was comprised of companies at work in similar and related areas. As a result of the benevolent attitude of the Texas government toward such projects, in 1988 the American semiconductor industry selected Austin as the location of its research consortium, SEMATECH, comprised of thirteen member companies that worked in harmony with each other. The close collaboration among scientists in all parts of the country was signaled by the naming of Robert Noyce as the first head of SEMATECH. The business community made its contribution as well. There were thirty-two new endowed professorships in the area of science at the University of Texas, half of which were provided by businessmen involved with MCC and SEMATECH.

In order to assure a steady stream of well-prepared and motivated students into their classes, these scientists were encouraged to reach out to the high schools. Businessman and sometimes presidential candidate Ross Perot, in one of his less-publicized efforts, made an attempt to refashion high school curricula and recruit promising teachers. By the end of the century it seemed possible that Texas might replace California as the center for high technology in the early twenty-first century. What a union of the private sector, government, and academia had accomplished for the GI generation in the late 1940s and early

1950s, a similar combination seemed capable of performing for the grandchildren of those veterans.

Phoenix (Silicon Desert), where Texas Instruments and Mostek were key firms, became an important center for work in electronics. With state assistance, dozens of old and new companies located there. By the late 1980s Arizona had a larger share of its workforce engaged in high-technology work than any other state in the nation.

By then, too, Phoenix was the nation's sixth largest city and, in addition, was the destination of more than 2 million tourists a year. While there were several world-class museums in the area and a Frank Lloyd Wright structure (Taliesin West) some twenty miles from downtown, it was better known, perhaps, for its sports teams, the new sign of status: Phoenix Suns (basketball), Arizona Diamondbacks (baseball), Arizona Cardinals (football), and Phoenix Cardinals (ice hockey). In addition, as will be seen, Phoenix became the focus of an interesting experiment in education that by the end of the century appeared capable of revolutionizing the way vocationally oriented students thought of schooling. Phoenix regularly wins awards for being "one of the best places in America to work and live," which certainly helped in recruitment efforts.

Minneapolis–St. Paul (which became a center for supercomputer research); Colorado Springs (Silicon Mountain); Portland, Oregon; Seattle (Silicon Valley North); and Orange County went from being backwaters to the front lines of research. There was Silicon Bayou at Lafayette, Louisiana, which housed companies involved with the petroleum industry. A complex concentrating on software was located in lower New York City, which became known as Silicon Alley, and drew upon the talents of nearby New York University and Cooper Union, along with Columbia University and other schools in the area. By the turn of the century there were more than 600 firms in lower Manhattan, ranging from large ones in corporate suites to one-person software operations, being run out of one-bedroom apartments on a part-time basis.

The movement was exported overseas. There was Silicon Bog (Ireland), Silicon Island (Taiwan), Silicon Tundra (Canada), and Silicon Plain (Finland). Silicon Fen (England), located near Cambridge University, had by the end of the century become home for more than 1,000 companies that employed 27,000 workers, which made it the largest concentration of high-technology businesses and personnel in Europe—but not in the world. Silicon Wadi (Israel) absorbed many of the scientists and technologists who fled the former Soviet Union after the end of the Cold War, and helped make that country a high-technology center. With 135 engineers for every 10,000 people, Israel is far ahead of the United States (18 per 10,000) in this regard. By the end of the Cold War, Israeli companies and freelance workers were accounting for a large share of new high-technology incorporations. At the same time, India and Ireland emerged as major centers for software development. Many of the companies and workers in places such as these were backed by funds generated in the United States. Thus, the great boom in growth that started in the United States after World War II, and continued in Europe and Japan in the 1950s and 1960s, became a global development afterwards.

In fact, there were few sections of the country and then the rest of the developed world lacking such facilities and centers, all raiding the others for talent. Robert Noyce noted that venture capitalists were eager to locate entrepreneurs wanting to start their own companies, and the movement had become a craze peopled by scientists eager for the main chance:

> Venture capitalists from here [Stanford] are willing to go to Boulder to look at a new opportunity. Or Minneapolis. Or Cedar Rapids, Iowa. But there isn't the local sophistication of what it takes to succeed with a new business. There is suspicion of the venture capitalist who comes out from a big city to Boulder. The entrepreneur doesn't have someone at his side to help him talk to venture capitalists. Today I get more and more calls from someone in Podunk asking me who can help them write a business plan.

Such calls were quite common. By the end of the century there were more than 500 business-breeding sites, up from the twelve in 1980, and the services of professionals like Noyce had grown exponentially. Out of them came the Fort Collins (Colorado) Virtual Business Incubator, originated in 1999 to lure companies to the Rocky Mountain city. Maury Willman, who was seeking a place to locate her new company, Ergonomic Health Systems, received not only the help of professionals at reduced fees but also office space at low costs. Other companies, led by Infusion Technologies, followed. In addition to financial help from the city and state, the relationship with Colorado State University helped transform what had been a backwoods school into a new center of high technology.

In like fashion, the city of Orlando, Florida, the University of Central Florida, and the state collaborated to create a technology complex there. Lockheed, Thermo Electron, and Nationsbank, also in the area, contributed money, time, and expertise. Nationsbank was particularly helpful in raising $57 million in venture capital, some of which was used to lure Triton Network, a major Lockheed supplier, to Orlando. By the end of the century, Orlando, which previously had been known primarily as the home of Disney entertainments, was also considered an up-and-coming technology center. According to the *Economist*, on the eve of the millennium, there were seventy-two locales throughout the world that called themselves "Cyber" this or "Silicon" that, by virtue of their clusters of software or hardware companies, electronics research laboratories, and the universities that support them. Even so, none of these could approach Silicon Valley in terms of production or prestige.

Just as new technopolises appeared regularly, so some of the older ones entered periods of decline as the areas in which they specialized lost importance. As long as emphasis was placed on the computers themselves, Route 128 remained a vital and significant place. By the late 1980s, however, more emphasis was being placed on programming, networking, and telecommunications in its widest sense. Route 128 did not make an adequate transition from minicomputers to this new manifestation of the technological age. By then Silicon Valley and other venues had become more prominent and essential.

To return to the comparison of today's technopolis with the industrial city of 1900, it might be said that a century ago America had two economies that existed side by side: the new industrial metropolis and the older agrarian one. Of course, there had been large cities in America throughout the nineteenth century, and farmers always relied on urban facilities for banking, insurance, transportation, and other services. But the new order of things was different, and contemporary accounts indicate that farmers, throughout America, recognized the nature and importance of the challenge. So it was toward the close of the twentieth century. American manufacturers of pots and pans and the like realized their times had come and gone, that in the future the nation would become more involved with the production of electronically based goods and services. In the 1920s, the farmer's son would get a job at General Motors. Today the GM assembly-line worker's son might find employment in Silicon Valley. The father would have been dazzled by the prospect of the interstate highways that were discussed during World War II and came into being after the war. They would create the need for more and better automobiles. His job was safe, or at least so he believed at the time. In like fashion the electronics worker at the close of the twentieth century would consider the prospects of the Internet, which would require electronics gear just as the superhighways would demand automobiles. But neither could visualize just how the game would be played out.

One interesting change in the technological landscape came in the late 1980s, when some of the pioneers and more of those who followed left the technopolises for other locales, some of them rather surprising. These departures indicated that in the new kind of economy that was developing, geography played far less a role than had been the case as recently as the 1960s, as evidenced by the decline of the Route 128 complex. Geoffrey Goodfellow, one of the most respected researchers in the "hot" field of wireless electronic mail (E-mail) left the Valley to take up residence in Prague, the capital of the Czech Republic. "In the Valley, it's all about power and money and work, work, work, work, and the expectation among your peers that you're going to do the next big thing," said Goodfellow. "Eventually I saw that this was a false god." Even so, such departures, while surprising within the industry, were somewhat rare. Rather, Apple's Steve Jobs, Jim Clark of Silicon Graphics, Mark Andreesson, co-founder of Netscape, and others like them remained the role models for young entrepreneurs.

John Walker, founder of Autodesk, a hot technology company, left when he decided the work there and elsewhere in the Valley was "no longer fun." In addition, it was hard on his health. Walker wrote a book titled *The Hacker's Diet: How to Lose Weight and Hair Through Stress and Poor Nutrition* and became a freelancer, also working on projects to test the relationship between technology and parapsychology. Steven Edelman, who had worked for and founded several companies in the Valley, thought, "Silicon Valley had become the kind of place where if you wanted to be somebody you had to be wildly successful." This was not his ambition, so he left for a forest location near Portland, Oregon, where he spent more time analyzing other companies to judge their investment potentials than on technology. Echoing that thought, Paul Saffo, one of the Valley's most successful consultants, said, "There is this pressure to prove yourself over and over again in Silicon Valley. People wonder, 'Was it me or was it luck?' "

Nerdistans?

By the late 1980s, the technopolises were being supplemented by the next step on the evolutionary scale, which insiders called the "nerdistan." The term derived from "nerds," the sometimes contemptuous, sometimes complimentary name applied to the scientists and technicians who worked there. Nerdistans were, generally speaking, suburban enclaves of the type quite familiar to the baby-boomer parents of the new generation, with their shopping centers, malls, decent but not necessarily outstanding universities, proximity to an airport, and perhaps lacking major cultural amenities but with motion picture theaters specializing in art films. There were no inner-city problems in the nerdistans, and little if any crime. At the technopolis, the workplace was usually in an industrial park within driving distance of the homes of the workers. At the nerdistans, the living spaces often were within walking or at least bicycling distance of the laboratories and offices. According to students of the change, the nerdistans were a product of labor shortages. Desirable scientists were attracted to the technopolises because they viewed them as preferable alternatives to urban locales; the nerdistans were the next step upward, with workplaces actually designed by the workers.

Irvine may be the prototype for the next stage in the development. It is a city that does not fit well into any of the rubrics thus far presented. Part of a complex of cities (Costa Mesa–Irvine–Newport Beach), by the end of the twentieth century it possessed more than 22 million square feet of office and business-park space, as well as twelve residential neighborhoods, each with its own shopping centers and recreational facilities, all sharing the facilities of the University of California–Irvine. Irvine is near the John Wayne Airport, which is close to a major hotel, shopping area, and recreational centers. Irvine grew from practically nothing to the home of more high-technology companies than either Route 128 or Silicon Valley. It is also one of the wealthiest areas in the United States. In 1982 the median price of a home in Orange County, of which Irvine is the center, was close to $250,000, the nation's highest. By way of comparison, the New York metropolitan area's figure was $192,000.

Irvine has become one of the several models for the next century, which include such centers as Tyson's Corner, Virginia; City Post Oak–Galleria, near Houston; and the King-of-Prussia–Route 202 complex northwest of Philadelphia. This is not to suggest that sometime in the near future America's technological elites will migrate to these areas. Rather, the aging children and young grandchildren of the World War II generation have come to look upon such places as their progenitors viewed Levittown, which is to say, as a vision of the future—and a pleasing one at that. In describing Corte Madera Town Center, one of these complexes outside San Francisco, one of the developers wrote:

> Corte Madera Town Center's tenant mix has been carefully developed to support and enhance the architectural design of a small town village square. The feeling and synergy of a downtown has been created with financial institutions, restaurants, a variety of services, department stores, speciality stores, a drugstore, and a supermarket. Prominently tagged in the advertising as "The Main Street of Marin," Town Center is Marin's one-stop family-oriented shopping center. As Corte Madera's only "downtown," Town Center has a unique role as a community focal point.

As will be seen, such a vision was at odds with that conceived by other "futurologists," who considered the downtown to be a group of Web sites. Moreover, both downtowns lacked an amenity Americans had come to expect from their shopping and living center: fast-food restaurants.

How could the World War II GIs have imagined such a world? All of this would have sounded like science fiction in 1945. Those involved with the new forms—the dwellers in a technopolis or a nerdistan, or a denizen of the World Wide Web—would have seemed alien life-forms to their progenitors of that earlier period.

The Weakening of Unions: The PATCO Story

That there were no roles for unions in the technopolis was manifest. Among their other functions, unions existed to protect workers against their bosses. In the technopolis, the workers and the bosses were united in their goals, aspirations, and work. Perhaps the workers who were engaged in efforts associated with the industrial age—janitors, assembly-line workers, and some in the offices—would be attracted by unions. But not the technologists whose work was central to the technopolis. Such had become evident in the 1970s, but the most striking demonstration of the new order of things and the difficulties faced by those workers eager to better their remuneration and status—and even retain their jobs—came in 1981.

Americans awoke on the morning of August 1, 1981, to the news that a Major League baseball strike had ended, and that the season would finally begin. The walkout, which had begun on June 12, had cost the 650 players involved an estimated $28 million, while the clubs' losses came to about $116 million.

The previous day the *New York Times* had editorially urged the players to accept the owners' most recent offer, unless they "suddenly mistake themselves for air controllers." The writer was referring to another strike then looming, one that, while not as closely watched as the stoppage of the national pastime, would prove an important turning point in the young Reagan Administration and, more important, for the nature of worker-management relations in the future.

That same morning, both sides in the air controllers' contract negotiations indicated that a strike would take place the following Monday. Transportation Secretary Drew Lewis asked the leader of the Professional Air Traffic Controllers Organization (PATCO), Robert Poli, for an extension, but was rebuffed.

The PATCO story received less attention than that accorded the end of the baseball strike, but economically it could prove far more consequential. Every day some 800,000 passengers took off and landed aboard the 14,000 scheduled domestic and foreign flights, and to this should be added the 10,000 tons daily of air cargo. The industry employed 340,000 workers, and indirectly many more. Any stoppage, even for a few days, could ripple through an economy already beset by recession.

Poli sensed that if all the 17,500 controllers walked out together, air travel would be impossible, even if as expected the government called in military controllers and supervisors. Such a strike would paralyze the country and force the administration to seek an accommodation. While these considerations were important, Poli's ace in the hole was the fear of accidents that might occur if and when the strike was called. When Poli last met with Lewis, he remarked, "You're responsible for safety. If passengers are killed, it's your responsibility."

Lewis left the negotiations confident that he couldn't lose in this confrontation. Since 1947 it had been illegal for government employees to strike; each of the controllers had had to sign an oath to that effect: "I am not participating in any strike against the Government of the United States or any agency thereof, and I will not so participate while an employee of the Government of the United States or any agency thereof." The penalties could be severe: fines, imprisonment, and dismissal.

Lewis had another reason to believe he was in a strong position. For months he had been studying the air traffic situation, and he had concluded that there were about 3,000 more controllers than were actually needed for the tasks involved. Also, the controllers spent only half their work time at the radar scopes, the rest of the day being used for clerical and administrative tasks. The government had 3,000 controllers and supervisors in the military capable of manning the scopes, and they could be deployed where needed. If all the controllers walked out they might cripple the system, but if even fewer than half remained at their posts, the system could function.

Finally, there was the political dimension. Lewis understood that President Reagan's economic program, which just then was being signed into law, required large-scale economies in order to pay for the proposed tax cut and to balance the budget. The President simply could not afford to grant such a whopping increase, which was bound to be looked upon as a template by other unions, both in the public and private sectors. He already had replaced a temporary freeze on hiring with a new, permanent ceiling. His massive budget was working its way through Congress, and to falter in the face of the PATCO confrontation would invite failure on Capitol Hill. Other federal unions were carefully monitoring the situation. Moe Biller, the fiery president of the 600,000-member American Postal Workers Union, had started negotiations for his union's new contract. If Reagan caved in to the PATCO demands, Biller would have a cue to become militant in his negotiations.

While Reagan enjoyed great popularity after he was shot on March 30, the nation still hadn't seen him perform in a political crisis. Some foreign leaders saw him as an untested neophyte. Was he tough enough for the job? It remained to be seen.

The picture the public received on television that evening was unmistakable: the government was being reasonable, hoping for some kind of compromise, while the union was unbending and adamant. PATCO's public image wasn't enhanced when Poli boasted, "This country cannot operate without those thirteen thousand people to monitor the traffic." Thus, PATCO pictured itself as holding a gun to the nation's head. All indications were that the public didn't like it.

Until then, Reagan had remained pretty much in the background, leaving it to Lewis to speak for the administration. That he had decided to confront the union should have been obvious, however. Reagan had gone through something like this while governor of California. When 500 state employees went on strike, he gave them five days to return or be fired. On that occasion, they backed down.

Poli knew the law and the Reagan record, and he probably knew about those other controllers who could be used to fill in for those who left their posts. He should have realized that some of the members wouldn't go on strike. It is difficult to fathom how he could have misread the situation so badly.

Reagan had spent the weekend at Camp David, planning strategy for his economic package then being discussed in Congress and setting the agenda for talks with

Egyptian president Anwar Sadat, who was due in Washington the following week. But he did set aside some time to personally draft a message in case the strike took place. None of his close aides doubted that he would take a tough stand. "He figures this was the first time he had to confront this as president," said a senior adviser. "It's fair to say that he was aware he was setting an example."

The message was delivered over television and radio the following day. It was at the same time calm and defiant. The President noted that earlier both sides had agreed to the $40 million package, but now the union was demanding seventeen times what had previously been accepted. In what the public would soon recognize as a typical Reagan touch, he related the story of a controller who had resigned from the union and returned to work. "How can I ask my kids to obey the law if I don't?" the worker asked rhetorically, to which Reagan appended, "This is a great tribute to America."

After noting that as a union leader he had led the screen actors in a strike, Reagan stated his opposition to strikes by government workers. Government "has to provide without interruption the protective services which are government's reason for being." He concluded by saying that the workers had forty-eight hours to return to work. Otherwise, they would be terminated.

Reagan met with reporters after the talk, and one of them suggested he might have taken a less severe approach. The President bristled at this. "What lesser action can there be? The law is very explicit. They are violating the law." But he added that he believed some of the strikers hadn't considered the consequences of breaking their oaths. While Reagan intended to be firm and unbending in denying the right of the controllers to strike, he was prepared to treat those who returned to their jobs leniently. This gave them an out but also indicated that he meant to follow through on his warning.

A White House spokesman then disclosed that the President originally had wanted to give the strikers twenty-four hours to return, but he was persuaded to make it forty-eight hours. On several occasions in the next few days, Lewis told the press that the government would be willing to rehire any controllers who claimed to have been coerced into leaving their posts. "We will be sympathetic to these claims," he said. In this way, the government portrayed itself at the same time as fair and forgiving.

A back-to-work order was immediately filed, and that night a federal judge found the union in contempt of court for disobeying it. Unless the workers returned by Wednesday, the union could face fines of up to $1 million a day. Poli himself was declared in contempt of court, and would be fined $1,000 a day unless the strike was ended by eight o'clock that night. The union remained obdurate. "This battle is not going to be won in the courts," said the union's general counsel. "It's going to be won on the picket lines."

While there was confusion at the airports and a race by disappointed travelers to trains and buses, the strikers didn't close down the airline system as they had hoped to do. Sufficient controllers remained on the job to keep the system operating, and, bolstered by supervisors and military controllers, more than 70 percent of the flights took place more or less on time.

Support from the rest of organized labor was spotty. United Auto Workers president Douglas Frazer said his members would boycott air travel for the duration of the strike, but also warned that the illegal strike "could do massive damage to the labor movement." Edward Karalis, who headed the 60,000-member American Federation of Government Employees, asked his members to join the picket lines and help raise money for the strike fund. Harry Van Ardsdale, who led the New York Central Labor Council, did not ask his members to take action, but told the press that Reagan's response "brings to mind that fellow in Germany who crushed the whole labor movement in that country. His name was Adolf." But Michael Harpold, who was attempting to organize workers at the Immigration and Naturalization Service, hopped a plane heading to the Southwest. "I've got my own job action to organize," he said.

Recognizing that the public opposed the strike, American Federation of Labor–Congress of Industrial Organizations president Lane Kirkland waffled, noting that the strike was unpopular. "Respect the law," he said shortly after the walkout. "But when working people feel a deep sense of grievance, they will exercise what I think is a basic human right, the right to withdraw their services, not to work under conditions they no longer find tolerable." The AFL-CIO reluctantly went on record as supporting PATCO, and Kirkland briefly marched with the PATCO strikers in Chicago. But he would go no farther than that, refusing to advocate sympathy strikes. "It's all very well to be midnight-gin militant," he told a *Newsweek* reporter. "I am not going to make that appraisal." In fact, PATCO received stronger support from European unions than from the American. The International Federation of Air Traffic Controllers asked its sixty member groups to deny clearance to aircraft flying to the United States, but nothing came of this threat.

Outside observers thought Reagan had played his cards skillfully while Poli had committed one blunder after another. The President's stand, said Roger Dahl, director of the labor-management relations service of the U.S. Conference of Mayors, "will reinforce the resolve of local elected officials to play it tough with unions." Columbia University professor David Lewin said the administration provided a model for other elected officials for how they could "seize control of labor relations, instead of merely reacting to union demands."

Poli rejected any and all compromises, giving the appearance of being convinced, even in the face of contrary evidence, that ultimately the government would have to bow. But behind the scenes he contacted Lewis, probing for a face-saving means of ending the strike.

Lewis ignored this overture, and continued to appeal for a return to the towers. "For the good of the country and themselves, I ask all controllers to come back to work," he said, adding that if they didn't, they would be "barred from federal government hiring forever." As for Reagan, he said there would be no amnesty. True to his word, dismissal notices went out, and orders were obtained for the jailing of five controllers, while felony charges were filed against sixty-five strike leaders. Signaling its determination, on August 5 the FAA announced the hiring of trainees to fill the vacated posts. There were many more applicants than positions. Indeed, there was a back list of 7,500 who wanted to undergo the year-and-a-half training program to become controllers. Lewis said applicants had to have a high school diploma and three years of work experience, news that might have surprised some who had been sympathetic to the strike, not knowing the rather low job requirements.

The government's action received widespread support from a press that had been critical of Reagan earlier. Wrote the *Washington Post*, "The air traffic controllers' strike is a wildly misconceived venture that deserves the government's extraordinary response. A strike against an essential public service is always wrong in principle. In this case it is also illegal, and the controllers' attempt to demolish the law by massive violation is doubly wrong." The *New York Times* was somewhat more circumspect. "Popular support for the President's hard line is holding firm," it wrote after the first week. "And for good reason: an illegal strike by key Government workers is simply not tolerable." Unsurprisingly, the conservative *U.S. News & World Report* editorialized that "back of this latest strike lies a strange and disturbing conviction, growing over the last few years, that it is fair to violate the law if you disagree with it. This is a false idea, dangerous to the perpetrators themselves as members of the whole."

By then the first polls on the strike had appeared, confirming suspicions and evidence that the public supported the Reagan stand. A *Newsweek* poll indicated that 60 percent of the public approved of the President's actions, while 25 percent disapproved. Support for the President's position outweighed that for the union by almost 2 to 1. Even so, there was a close to even split as to whether or not to permit the strikers to return to their posts.

By the end of the week, 5,100 controllers had received their dismissal notices, and PATCO's $3.5 million strike fund had been frozen by the courts. The union was effectively bankrupt. After the initial confusion of the first and second day, the airlines were reporting close to normal operations; the on-time performance on Thursday was 83 percent. While there were some reports of near collisions, these were exaggerated, in the hope that the public outcry would oblige the President to reconsider his actions. There was no chance of this happening. By August 8, it was clear that Reagan had won his gamble.

Moe Biller called for amnesty for the strikers. "There are compassionate ways to end this strike," he said. "This is a strong nation, and compassion and understanding should have a place in public policy." There was no forgiveness, only justice as Reagan saw it. Those strikers who had refused the initial chance to return would not have the opportunity to regain their jobs, at least while Reagan was in office.

On August 13 the President signed into law his sweeping budget and tax cut proposals, telling the audience that the bills represented "a turnabout of almost a half a century of a course this country has been on." The legislation was the highlight of his first year in office, but the PATCO strike was Reagan's defining moment.

"Ronald Reagan is tougher, bolder, and more dogmatic than I expected," wrote TRB in the *New Republic* of August 15. In the same issue another writer said, "Reagan's swift, unequivocal retaliation against the illegal strike and the union was a shrewd political gamble of the kind that has brought him one triumph after another in his confrontations with Congress. The President won public support by posing the issue in stark terms of moral right and wrong." Lou Cannon, who had followed Reagan since his California days, wrote admiringly of him in the *Washington Post* as "The Master Politician," saying, "Reagan has demonstrated once again in these first months of his presidency that it is always dangerous to underestimate him. This is not some Hollywood cowboy who has settled in the White House for early retirement, but a dedicated and serious politician who knows how to grasp the levers of power in the age of television."

In the end, the controllers were replaced, and did not regain their jobs when the strike was over. While the fairness and appropriateness of the government's reaction continued to be debated, Reagan's popularity grew.

An important aspect of the post–World War II labor market had changed. At one time the acquisition of skills, the attainment of a union card, and friends or relatives on the job enabled ambitious high school graduates to achieve well-paid, respected work. This was a central aspect of life in the American economy for thousands of those returned World War II GIs—and for their children as well. The home in the upscale suburb, the two cars in the garage, the summer vacation in Europe, the children preparing for entrance into a fine private university, and all else that went into making the good life in the more than four decades after the end of the war were at risk. The grandchildren of the World War II generation would have to play by a new set of rules.

At the same time, polls and other evidence indicated that the baby boomers had a different attitude toward their children than their parents had toward them. For the GI generation, the children who started appearing in the late 1940s were to be provided all that it took for them to be successful. Middle-class parents of the 1950s and early 1960s considered an unwillingness to sacrifice for one's children to be bordering on immorality. This was one trait they did not pass on to their children, who, after all, were raised in an entirely different kind of environment. Polls taken in the 1970s found that more than 2 out of 3 parents rejected the notion that parents should stay together for the sake of the children. And a like percentage did not believe they had the obligation to save money in order to leave a large inheritance to their children.

6

THE END OF THE POSTWAR PERIOD

There is no question as to which car is most like the U.S. cars—it is the Datsun, with its familiar arrangement of components, its comparatively quiet running, its relatively soft ride, full equipment, and a level of quality that would put many American cars to shame. It is, in fact, a gentleman's or a lady's compact—compact, far from ignominious in behavior or appearance, economical, and pleasant to drive, with every appearance of being well put together. Like any other imported car, it should not be bought in the absence of relatively accessible service. The Datsun is covered against "defects in materials and workmanship" for 12 months or 12,000 miles.

—*Consumer Reports*, August 1965

The intent of the Marshall Plan and other programs geared to promote European and Asian recovery had been to enable the people there to enjoy a measure of prosperity. It was generally believed that this would harden them against the temptations of communism, which in the immediate postwar period was one of Washington's priorities. The irony of attempting to "sell" the people of the liberated countries on the attractions of free enterprise at a time when the American government was busily pursuing programs in housing and related areas did not seem to have struck the government as strange. That these massive government inputs, which, in addition to meeting real needs, would create jobs for those who feared a return to the harsh days of the Great Depression was never far from the thoughts of those who sponsored and ran these programs.

The Rest of the World Recovers

American bureaucrats welcomed each sign of recovery in Europe and Asia. In the early 1950s, European textiles, steel, and other materials not only were able to find customers in Europe, but they were being exported to the United States as well. That European companies were recovering in the 1950s did not come as a surprise, since they had been strong competitors prior to the war. The real surprise came in the form of imports from Asia, Japan in particular.

During the 1950s and early 1960s, the United States exported far more than it had imported, but the imports were rising. In 1964 the trade surplus was $6.7 billion, the highest since 1947, and imports from the Orient were increasing. By concentrating on Europe in the immediate postwar period, American manufacturers tended to ignore the greater threat forming in Japan. Already, in the late 1940s and early 1950s, Japanese textiles and other products produced with low labor costs were taking large shares of the American market.

In 1968 the American GNP rose from $794 billion to

$864 billion. On that score, at least, it had been a good year economically. Yet there were perceived weaknesses amid the strengths of the overall economy, and one of these seemed to be in the area of foreign trade, especially in the automobile industry. This might have surprised analysts a decade earlier. At that time the appearance on American roads of German Volkswagens and Opals, French Renaults and Peugeots, and English Morrises and Hillmans did not cause much comment, though they did draw stares and questions from interested bystanders. Most of these vehicles were brought home by American servicemen who had purchased them while on active duty in Europe. Detroit's executives thought that once the novelty impact of these automobiles wore off, the discharged servicemen would turn to the familiar Chevrolets, Fords, and Plymouths. In 1968, Americans purchased more than $1 billion worth of foreign cars, with the best seller being the Volkswagen. Even when it became evident that the oddly shaped and technologically unusual VW had found a market niche in the United States, the American manufacturers did not appear troubled. The party line in Detroit was that there always would be some eccentrics on the Atlantic and Pacific coasts and among intellectuals throughout the country who would form a market for such small cars. These individuals had railed against American cars during the postwar period, and they would look upon the VW as a sign of their aversion to "the gas-guzzling dinosaurs." But how many of this breed were there? Detroit was prepared to concede the university campuses to the imports, along with a few pockets in seaport cities like Los Angeles and New York. A Ford executive on a business trip to New York would not have been troubled by spying a VW outside of a restaurant in Greenwich Village. Seeing the same car in a Kansas City suburb was another matter entirely.

Fortune wrote of this phenomenon—foreign competition in capital goods and some consumer goods—in June 1965, noting that American firms were losing the competition in industrial goods, "the very area of economic life where we thought we had special competitive strength." The United States was running a trade deficit due to imports of petroleum, copper, and steel, and a deficit in the overall balance of payments resulting from the Marshall Plan. At the time this was attributed to the Japanese ability to compete in inexpensive products that required low labor costs. By the mid-1950s, however, Japanese consumer electronics started to appear in American stores, where they sold for prices that were approximately two-thirds of those for RCAs, Magnavoxes, Zeniths, and other American-made products. They weren't particularly well received, since in this period the label "Made in Japan" still signified inferior workmanship. American veterans who found jobs at domestic electronics companies were not overly concerned about their employment, even when customers started purchasing more Japanese radios and television receivers.

The Japanese Ministry of International Trade and Industry (MITI) responded by bringing together such major manufacturers as Sony, Toshiba, Matsushita, and Hitachi into consortia known as the Television Export Council and the Television Export Examination Committee. These organizations encouraged members to sell their television receivers at low prices in the American market in order to gain market share, force the American companies to the wall, and, this done, only then raise prices so as to realize profits. The Japanese made a major breakthrough in 1963, when Sanyo offered to sell its receivers to Sears Roebuck. In the deal, the retailer was permitted to place its name on the sets and they would be produced to Sears' specifications. From 1963 to 1977, Sears purchased 6.5 million receivers from Sanyo and, later on, Toshiba, worth more than $700 million.

In addition, RCA licensed many of its patents to several Japanese manufacturers. In one agreement, finalized in 1970, RCA licensed 236 patents, all in the area of consumer products. As James Abegglen, one of the eminent Americans studying the Japanese economy, put it, "RCA licenses made Japanese color television possible." This may have been an overstatement, since by then Japanese quality and advanced technology had become quite evident to consumers, who were willing to pay higher prices for Sony television receivers than for their American counterparts. The Japanese invasion was quite real, and it hurt the U.S. consumer electronics companies—and resulted in job losses for the highly paid technicians who had worked for them. By 1974 Japanese companies accounted for more than 20 percent of receiver sales. Echoing Abegglen, in 1985, C. J. van der Klugt, chairman of the Dutch firm Philips, said the American firms had "forged the bullets used to shoot them."

If the loss of markets in consumer electronics was troublesome, that in automobiles was truly frightening; critics charged that American jobs were being transferred to Japanese factories. Perhaps so. Each Toyota or Datsun sold in this period had been manufactured in a Japanese factory by Japanese workers, and most of the price paid by the American customer went to those companies. In addition, scores of Japanese support companies benefited, as did Japanese middlemen, insurers, shippers, and the like.

This Alfred Eisentaedt photo, taken in Times Square on V-J Day (August 15, 1945), has become a symbol for the end of World War II and the start of America's prosperity.

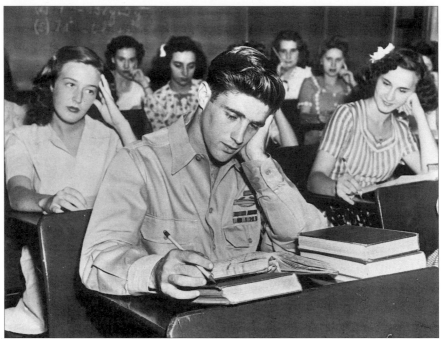

Thanks to the inception of the G.I. Bill, many veterans attended colleges and universities.

During the 1950s, veterans starting families moved out of cities and into affordable suburban housing such as William Levitt's Levittown in Long Island, New York.

During the gas crisis of the 1970s, signs like these were frequently seen in towns across America.

Americans were also purchasing affordable family cars like the Ford Taurus. Seen here are Ford Motor Company Chairman Henry Ford II (right) and Lee Iacocca in 1974.

Architect Frank Lloyd Wright leaning against a model of the Guggenheim Museum, 1945.

These airflow trailers were popular in the 1950s as American families traveled the expanded highways system on vacations.

Founder Kemmons Wilson's children at the ribbon cutting of the first Holiday Inn, Memphis, Tennessee, 1952.

Ray Kroc was fifty-two when he first met Dick and Mac McDonald at their hamburger restaurant in California in 1954. The brothers sold him the chain for $2.7 million in 1961. By 1963, McDonald's had sold its billionth hamburger.

Peter F. Drucker, now ninety, has written many books since his *The Practice of Management* (1954). He continues to be read widely by corporate leaders in the U.S. and abroad.

A 1960s portrait of IBM CEO Thomas J. Watson Jr. in front of IBM data processor 702.

Joseph McCarthy, U.S. senator from Wisconsin (1947–57), achieved notoriety and power with his unsubstantiated accusations against U.S. officials he termed Communists. After the Senate condemned him in 1954, his influence declined.

Martin Luther King Jr. delivering his famous "I Have a Dream" speech at the Lincoln Memorial for the March on Washington, Washington, D.C., 1963.

AP/Wide World Photos

In response to his implication in the Watergate scandal, President Richard M. Nixon announces his resignation on television, August 8, 1974.

Beat poet Allen Ginsberg standing next to a poster of Jack Kerouac, September 22, 1982.

David Cupp/New York Times/Archive Photos

President Jimmy Carter and Soviet President Leonid Brezhnev at the Vienna Imperial Hofburg Palace after the signing of the SALT II Treaty, June 18, 1979.

During a two-week tour of the United States, former Soviet President Mikhail Gorbachev meets with former President Ronald Reagan at Rancho del Cielo, May 2, 1992.

Fred Smith,
founder of FedEx.

Charles Smith,
Directing Partner, Merrill Lynch,
Pierce, Fenner &Beane.

Sam Walton,
founder of WalMart.

Charles R. Schwab.

President Bill Clinton signs the North American Free Trade Agreement (NAFTA), Tuesday, September 14, 1993. Joining the president are (from left): former President Ford, House Speaker Thomas Foley, Senate Majority Leader George Mitchell, former President Carter, Senate Minority Leader Bob Dole, former President Bush, House Minority Leader Bob Michel, and Vice President Al Gore.

Traders at the New York Stock Exchange cheer at the end of day's trading as the Dow Jones Industrial Average hits a record close of 9997.2, Thursday, March 18, 1999.

Later, Japanese management experts declared that none of their insights had made this boom possible. Rather, many of the ideas they utilized had been imported from the United States, in the form of books written by American scholars and management consultants and their visits to Japan to spread their gospels. Among the more important of these were W. Edwards Deming, Joseph Juran, and A. V. Feigenbaum, all of whose ideas regarding zero defects and total quality control were translated into products that "worked right the first time" and did not have to be returned to the dealer for repairs after only a few hundred miles on the road, as seemed to be the case with many American cars.

Juran went to Japan to deliver numerous lectures on these and related subjects. On one occasion he told his audiences that "every member of the production team has to become involved in maintaining high standards and not merely act as supervisors." Such notions had long been familiar to American manufacturers but had not been put into effect. The traditional American view was that when it came to manufacturing and selling consumer goods, it was preferable to accept some rejects in order to realize economies of scale. If the costs of achieving a low ratio of rejects to production were too high, such a policy would be changed. Why should the customer be troubled by this approach? He could always bring the radio or the car back for repair or replacement. After all, that was the purpose of the guarantee. And American customers had become accustomed to finding flaws in their consumer goods, cars in particular. Why change a system that had been working so well?

But now the Japanese manufacturers were reeducating the American customers, putting forth the idea that there need not be any reason for returns for corrections of defects that should have been caught in the factory by assembly-line workers who were as dedicated to customer satisfaction as were the salesmen, or even more so. Pride in workmanship, which had been stressed by the early U.S. manufacturers of higher-priced cars, was now promoted by the Japanese producers of Toyotas, Datsuns, and other low-priced imports. By applying such notions, the Japanese were able to sell their cars to an increasingly satisfied market and, in the process, to transfer many American jobs to the home islands. By the 1980s, Juran was talking with reporters about what he called "the century of productivity" ushered in by the Japanese challenge: "While our consumers loved Japanese imports, our manufacturers did not," he said in 1988. "We lost God knows how many millions of jobs; our trade balance was shattered. We were forced to undertake a counter-revolution. Competition in quality intensified enormously."

However, while the Japanese automobile invasion resulted in declines in the number of domestic workers needed to assemble cars in the 1960s and 1970s, some American jobs were created as well; among the more important were for those individuals who obtained franchises to sell and service the Japanese imports. Moreover, the cars were insured by American companies, and in other ways their sales favorably affected the American workforce. It was the beginning of a phenomenon little noted in the American press or covered by academics: the positive impact of imports on American businesspeople and laborers.

In the process, as early as the 1970s, American companies, having thrown off the belief that they could learn nothing from their Japanese counterparts, dispatched their technicians, executives, and other relevant personnel to Japan to learn the "secrets" of firms like Toyota and

Nissan. The result was an eventual invigoration and restructuring of the American automobile industry, which in the long run made it stronger and more competitive than it had been prior to the Japanese challenge.

The Petrocrises

One major fear of the post–World War II generation had been a new depression, the handmaiden of which was deflation, in which prices of items from rents to clothing to foodstuffs declined, the obverse of which was that the value of money rose. There was no deflation in the late 1940s, the 1950s, and the early 1960s. Rather, consumer prices increased by half in the period from the end of the war to the 1970s, in an inflationary spiral. Inflation was troublesome, but that generation, which considered a depression the alternative, was not unduly worried by the rising level of prices. The Census Bureau estimated that the median family income for 1972 was $11,000, and predicted an increase to $15,000 by 1985. These figures were not adjusted for inflation—in this period such modifications were not routinely made. Rather, Americans celebrated the increase, which they identified with the rising standard of living. "Never before has the average citizen commanded such a high standard of living or been able to spend his money on so wide a variety of goods," wrote Howard Tuckman in his 1973 book, *The Economics of Wealth*, a celebration of the new economy. "Economics textbooks proclaim the message for all to hear: 'The King is dead, long live the consumer!' " Though not quite. Even then, there remained residual fears of a new depression.

Recall that middle-aged Americans at that time had grown up in an atmosphere of falling prices. While this sounded attractive to consumers whose memories were of unemployment and trying to get by on less money each month, their lack of experience with inflation failed to prepare them for that phenomenon.

The inflationary virus had been introduced by the shortages of the postwar period, and then fueled by the imbalance of demand over supply. Government policies also played their role. Government proclivities toward spending more than was being taken in became an important factor, as was the balance of trade problem. Then came the Johnson Administration's decision to finance the Vietnam War through borrowing rather than taxation, while at the same time continuing the President's "war on poverty." The classic remedy for inflation caused by shortfalls in supply had been to produce more, thus creating demands for workers and raw materials. The academic economists saw nothing threatening in this. But inflation resulting from lower demand was another matter entirely. Economists trained during the New Deal era knew how to deal with this too: take measures, from lowering taxes to raising credit bars, to setting a higher minimum wage—all to spur consumption.

However, consider the increase in the price of oil during the 1970s and its impact on the creation of wealth. In the early 1970s, a barrel of oil cost less than $3. In 1973, during another of the series of Arab-Israeli wars, the Organization of Petroleum Exporting Countries (OPEC) embargoed oil deliveries to the United States and raised its price; in January 1974 the price of oil was $11.65, and the United States was tumbling into its worst depression since the 1930s, accompanied by soaring inflation.

As the price of petroleum rose, several government agencies attempted, without success, to fashion a national energy policy, which included rationing at gasoline stations. In time, worried drivers had to line up to top off their tanks. This marked the beginning of the end of an aspect of the postwar love affair Americans had with their large, gas-guzzling cars. Since the early 1960s, a segment of the population had been drawn to foreign compacts that featured excellent gasoline mileage. Now many more sought these cars. Much in favor in the period had been the Honda Civic, with its CVCC engine, which did not require anti-pollution devices mandated by the Environmental Protection Agency. Other Japanese cars also were popular, as Americans who once swore they never would purchase foreign cars were swayed toward Toyotas and Datsuns as well as the Hondas.

American manufacturers experimented with electric and steam-driven cars, and even some powered by solar batteries. Had they been successful, doubtless the marketers of such vehicles would have realized financial bonanzas.

Some free market–oriented entrepreneurs engaged in imaginative practices. The anti-pollution devices mandated by the government, which affected performance negatively and provided a lower level of fuel economy, might be removed by a skilled mechanic not troubled by violations of law. The new cars had to use unleaded gasoline, and the nozzles on gas pumps were altered so the leaded-gas nozzle could not be inserted into the tanks. A small plastic device that cost little to manufacture but sold for more than $10 and attached to the tank's opening rectified this situation. Several enterprising mechanics in various parts of the country purchased used VW Beetles, refurbished them, and retrofitted them with much larger gas tanks, so that the car could hold more than twenty-five gallons, enough for 500 miles and more between fill-ups. During one of the periods of shortage, one fuel company imported Belgian-refined gasoline, which was not affected by the price ceiling, and sold it at premium prices. Several wealthy Americans purchased their own gasoline stations to assure themselves and their friends of a steady supply.

As the higher price of petroleum was passed on to customers, several unlikely ventures appeared, started by entrepreneurs every bit as imaginative as and more realistic than those who attempted to alter automobile engines to improve mileage. Franklin stoves, hardly used in the postwar period, suddenly became very popular, as suburban homeowners had them installed and burned scrap wood to keep warm in winter. Sales of insulation soared, as did those of storm windows, as builders throughout the Northeast, the Midwest, and the West booked record orders. Natural-gas prices did not rise as much as that of fuel oil, prompting homeowners to switch from oil to gas.

With all of this, the economy moved ahead, though not for long. The poverty rate had declined by half from the end of World War II to the early 1960s, and by half again from the early 1960s to the early 1970s. But that was the end of this advance. Why? Certainly the increase in the price of oil played a role, but the aforementioned business revivals of Europe and Asia, which had been taking place throughout the 1950s and 1960s, were also important. American labor, well remunerated throughout the postwar period in part due to the lack of competition from abroad, now had to face foreign competition in some areas.

Sociologists pointed to other aspects of American life as prime causes of the poverty that by then had become an important component of public debate: the economic problems of single-parent families and the drug predicament present in minority communities. By the early 1990s, sociologists focused on what came to be called "the culture of poverty," indicating that a component of poverty may be passed from generation to generation.

While the controversy continued, so did the increase in the importation of Japanese automobiles. In 1963, when the American companies manufactured 5.5 million cars, the Japanese figure was 1.9 million. In 1969 the American companies produced 8.2 million cars, and the Japanese 2.6 million, placing that country third behind West Germany and ahead of France, which was in fourth place. The Germans and the French sold most of their cars domestically, but by then the Japanese companies sold more outside the country than within the home islands. Insofar as the American market was concerned, in 1969 Detroit-based companies sold almost all their cars domestically, while Japanese sales to Americans came to 260,000 and were rising fast. In 1971, 703,000 Japanese cars were sold to Americans, more than all those of German, English, and French companies combined.

All of this continued to have impact on blue-collar workers in American factories, who now had to compete with foreign workers being paid a fraction of their remuneration while working at newer machines constructed after the war, often based on American patents. By the early 1970s, the job loss had spread to high technology. At that time, half the population of India was illiterate, but the country's universities produced some 2 million graduates annually, most of whom had some facility in English. Workers in technology and accounting were paid a third of what their American counterparts received, and, given the revolution in telecommunications, it made sense to outsource work there. So it was done. Much of Wall

Street's and corporate America's back-office work could be done in India by Indians and in other Southeast Asian countries. What began as a drift gathered steam during the late 1970s, and became quite common in the 1980s and 1990s. McKinsey, the large American consulting company, set up a major facility in India, and predicted that by 2010 this kind of business would earn some $50 billion annually for the foreign suppliers.

Newspapers had begun to carry stories regarding the loss of well-paid jobs in the automobile and other industries, noting that the workers had been obliged to shift into lower-paid occupations, the favorite example being that of a hamburger flipper at McDonald's. As it turned out, such analysis was simplistic and overstated.

While it was true that tens of thousands of American workers lost their jobs in automobile manufacture and other areas as well, and that back-office work was indeed being outsourced, this did not mean that the American economy was being deindustrialized or, in the jargon of the times, "hollowed out." Far more jobs were created elsewhere in the economy—and in the country. In addition, job loss was a regional phenomenon. There was a massive increase of jobs in the South and West, and a decline in the Northeast and Midwest. But not in those areas where the need for highly paid service workers existed. One might import an automobile, but not a salesperson in the local department store, a cleaning person, or, for that matter, the person who would sell the owner of the Toyota a replacement battery or repair a stuck valve. From 1953 to 1986, New York City lost more than 600,000 manufacturing jobs, and nearly 200,000 of these were in the wholesale and retail areas; but in the same period service jobs in the white-collar category increased by more than 800,000. By the 1980s, financial services provided an important fraction of the jobs for New Yorkers—but only for those with educations and experience. There had been a time when graduates or dropouts from vocational high schools could hope for work in the city. Such jobs, leading to careers and not only a weekly paycheck that would not increase by much over the years, were now hard to find.

Nor was this situation limited to New York. From 1982 to 1989, more than 7.6 million managerial/professional jobs were added to the American economy, with 1989 median earnings of $32,873. But the manufacturing jobs diminished. In the two decades of the 1960s and 1970s, America's share of world-manufactured exports fell from 25 percent to less than 17 percent. Nor was this a one-time phenomenon. More American jobs were lost to Mexico than to the United Kingdom or West Germany, as firms relocated their factories south of the border to capitalize on lower labor and transportation costs. California and other western locales became the mecca for high-technology firms. Between 1975 and 1990, Silicon Valley firms created 150,000 new high-technology jobs—triple the number for Route 128 companies—and by then that area had become a backwater for electronics firms, quite a change from the situation that had existed during the previous generation. In the early 1990s, Silicon Valley could claim thirty-nine of the nation's fastest-growing high-technology companies, while Route 128 had only four of them. By then Texas as well as California had passed Massachusetts in terms of high-technology companies.

California suffered along with the rest of the country during the recession of 1992, but added close to another million new jobs during the recovery that continued into the millennium. A quarter of this came in the Silicon Valley, and the rest in other parts of the state. As before, the big money—in salaries and stock options—was made in the high-technology area, where some 3,500 firms were organized annually, and the average yearly pay per worker came to close to $50,000.

The balance of trade deficit with the Japanese in 1980 came to more than $10 billion. Automobiles were the leading Japanese export to the United States, followed by steel plates, truck and tractor chassis, radios, motorcycles, and audio and video tape recorders. In this interval, American exports to Japan in terms of dollar value were led by soybeans, followed by corn, fir and hemlock logs, coal, wheat, and cotton. Thus, insofar as the Japanese trade was concerned, Japan was the exporter of goods requiring high levels of skills, while the United States exported raw materials. Armed with figures such as these, critics of the way America was managing its economy seemed justified in their claims that the nation was being "hollowed out."

The Problem with Statistics

But these statistics could be deceiving. In 1954, by which time most of the postwar generation had graduated from high schools and colleges and found jobs, the total civilian employment came to 60.1 million, which was 55.5 percent of the civilian population. In 1974 employment came to 86.8 million, which was 57.8 percent of the civilian population. But it did not stop there. In 1984 employment was 105 million, 59.5 percent of the population. Nor were the employed mostly in low-paid jobs.

Measuring employment created problems. For example, were workers at Ford dedicated to manufacturing or were they in the services sector? One might be tempted to reply that since Ford produced automobiles, they were involved with manufacture. What about a designer, or an accountant, or a specialist in distribution? They clearly were service workers. Yet just how they are categorized depends on the knowledge of the people performing the task of creating the statistics, and their sophistication.

According to the Commerce Department, during the past half century, total manufacturing employment had been a stable 18 to 22 percent of total employment. Yet the Bureau of Labor Statistics, which produced the figures used in the *Economic Reports of the President*, came to different conclusions. According to the bureau's counting, there were 41,650,000 employed Americans in 1946, of whom 17,248,000, or 41 percent, were employed in "goods-producing" work, while 24,404,000, or 59 percent, were in "service-producing labor." Thus, at the end of World War II, a majority of workers already were involved in the service sector. By 1975, the goods-producing sector had risen to 22,600,000, but the advance was not as rapid as that of the labor force, so the share had declined to 28 percent. That year, 54,345,000 Americans, 71 percent, were in the service sector. These figures suggest that someone can always be found who may be quoted in order to "prove" a point. What does seem evident, however, is that as a result of economic forces such as comparative advantage and relatively free trade, fewer American workers, as a percentage of the total, worked at creating goods during the postwar period than in providing services. Moreover, the trend continued. By the late 1990s, 4 out of 5 American workers were in the service sector, according to the Bureau of Labor Statistics.

The Dollar Crisis and Gold

The impact of the trade deficit was not as difficult to analyze. One result was a growing stack of dollars in the coffers of foreign banks, which returned to the United States in the form of investments, either direct or indirect. Some of the most popular forms were Treasury bills, notes, and bonds. And, for a while, gold. Foreign leaders, led by President Charles de Gaulle of France, urged Americans either to cut back on commitments or devalue the dollar, the latter being a code term for returning to the gold standard. The link between the dollar and gold, at $35 an ounce, established as one of the foundations of the postwar international financial structure, was abandoned in 1971. On January 1, 1975, Americans were permitted to own gold, which by then was selling for more than $135 an ounce on the European and Asian markets.

In December 1967, the Treasury sent $900 million in gold overseas, a record, and President Johnson was obliged to issue guidelines limiting American investments overseas and tourist expenditures. The impact was felt on Wall Street when, on December 3, the Dow reached 993 and then began a long decline, bottoming at 627 on May 26, 1971, before mounting a short recovery. The market would zigzag irregularly until the early 1980s. In retrospect, it is easy to see that the great postwar bull market ended in 1968, and resumed in the early 1980s.

There were other, more compelling events that, while not directly connected with the economy and the ability of Americans to increase their financial holdings, did much to alter the atmosphere that made this possible. This was a period of assassination (Martin Luther King, Jr. and Robert Kennedy), riots, a growing antipathy toward the Vietnam War, and the withdrawal of Lyndon B. Johnson from the 1968 presidential race. But there were signs of economic change as well, though few bothered to read them. Throughout the Western world there were declines in productivity. For the United States, productivity averaged from 2.5 percent to 3 percent annually until 1973, when it fell to around 1 percent. At the time, this was taken by some as a sign of a coming stagnation, but later it was seen as an inevitable development after the unusual growth of the postwar period. Which is to say that in the late 1960s and early 1970s, the postwar period came to an end. The end was ascribed, largely, to the sharp increase in the price of oil. With the passage of time, the interpretation that this decline had been caused by the impact of the "oil shocks" has been discounted in favor of the cyclical approach to the falloff.

Some analysts have attributed the last part of the decline to demographic changes. The period from the end of World War II to the mid-1960s was marked by labor shortages. There were fewer veterans entering the labor force after the mid-1960s, and their children were still in the nursery or schools. There was little immigration in this period.

Equally important but incapable of being quantified, as are so many other factors, were the changes in marriage, birth rates, and the middle-class view of just what constituted the proper social conditions for the accumulation of status and wealth. In the 1950s, 19 out of every 20 women who reached the age of twenty got married, and most of them bore children. By 1956 the median marriage age for women was little more than twenty, an all-time low, after which it started to advance. By 1970, 1 in 9 women in the age-twenty-to-twenty-five bracket was unmarried, and this figure rose to close to 1 in 3 by 1991.

In this same period, the number of divorces, which was 485,000 in 1945, declined to 377,000 by 1955, and did not rise to the 400,000 level again until the 1960s, after which it continued to climb. In 1970 there were close to 2 million divorced males and 3 million divorced females (the difference accounted for by remarriages). By the 1990s the concept of serial polygamy—and even legitimacy in some quarters—had gained favor.

The End of the Baby Boom

The birth situation also changed. After the baby boom of the 1950s there followed the inevitable decline. Although statistics by themselves cannot convey the sentiment that accompanied the slowdown in births or the psychological forces that caused it, some demographers calculate that the baby boom came to an end in 1964, when the birth rate fell below 20 per 1,000 population for the first time since 1946, and ushered in the period of the "baby bust" that lasted through 1976, when a pickup occurred as the babies born during the baby boom started having babies themselves—with a difference. Births to women over the age of thirty doubled from 1970 to 1992. Fewer marriages, more divorces, more older parents—clearly the expectations and hopes of parents in such situations were bound to differ from those of the postwar generation, which is to say that the image of the nuclear family presented in the TV situation comedies was altered.

Out-of-wedlock births accelerated. By the mid-1980s, single-parent families were forming at twenty times the rate of two-parent families. Children with divorced or unwed mothers in this period were more than five times as likely to be poor as children from two-parent families. *Father Knows Best* was a good title for a program in the baby boom, but not in the 1980s and 1990s, when single parents ruled the roost on television. Of course, there was an upside to all of this, both economically and socially. The women's liberation movement and other factors resulted in the increase of the labor force and wealth creation by women, one of the major changes of the post-postwar period.

Barely noted at the time but of major importance for the future, not only of the baby boomers but of the nation as a whole, was the demise of the concept that the nuclear family represented the norm for the American middle class, and, for that matter, those who strove to rise on the social and economic ladder. By the 1960s, the evidence that this would no longer be the case in the future was compelling. It was reflected in many ways—in housing patterns, for example. There was a shortage of apartments and, for a while, an oversupply of large suburban houses.

There was yet another change. During the late 1960s, Lyndon B. Johnson's Great Society turned to the problems posed by that large demographic bulge in the population. A baby born at the start of the boom would have been nineteen years old in 1965, about to enter the workforce or college. But while there were those who worried about the immediate impact on the economy, in Washington concerns about that baby's old age had surfaced. That was the year Medicare legislation was enacted, as the nation prepared for the medical problems of older Americans that would become a dominant issue in the 1990s, when the boomers would be considering retirement. Then, in 1978, the federal government raised the age at which companies could force their workers to retire, from sixty-five to seventy, and soon after abolished mandatory retirement for most federal employees. In 1986 President Reagan signed into law a measure that would bar most private employers from setting mandatory retirement ages. Such actions drew mixed reactions. On the one hand, it seemed sensible to permit productive workers, willing and able to work, to continue on. Such action would enable the economy (and, more important, businesses) to perform better. It would also provide those workers with a measure of freedom that previously had been lacking. Finally, at a time when concerns had surfaced about the viability of Social Security, it would put off the date when benefits would be paid, at least until age $70^{1/2}$ when full-time workers could receive full benefits.

On the other hand, those superannuated workers would block the way for young workers by holding jobs that otherwise might have been available to them. As it happened, these changes did not have a major effect on blue-collar workers, or even on many white-collar workers, where early retirement to a life devoted to other pursuits had become a popular option. But as it turned out, tens of thousands of workers stayed on the job, in such professions as college teaching, creating a situation that few seemed willing to address. In areas where shortages existed, such as engineering, this was not a problem. In others, like teaching English literature, it posed difficulties.

The American Malaise?

All of this is to suggest that the American economy experienced a change and even a slowdown in the 1970s, which continued into the 1980s. It did not occur at once, it had multiple causes, and it did not affect all parts of the economy in the same way. The workforce was affected by the pressures, as was the ability to earn high returns from investments. However, there were major areas of growth in this decade and after, especially in the business of what came to be known as "high technology." For the MIT engineering graduate, this was a golden age. It was not so for the steel worker in the Pittsburgh area, who lost his well-paid job and would never regain it. As has been seen, during the two decades following the end of World War II, the American economy had averaged per annum economic growth of some 3 to 4 percent. As a result, the "average" family, assuming there was such a thing, enjoyed a major increase in its standard of living. In contrast, during the 1970s the rate of GNP actually fell into negative figures early in the decade, then recovered in 1975, after which it grew around 5 percent for the remainder of the decade. Finally, during the 1960s and 1970s, the American people were torn asunder by political and cultural forces not foreseen by the veterans who were on the campuses in the late 1940s and 1950s.

The quest for wealth and other aspects of material success was quite apparent in the activities and statements of members of the generation that came out of World War II. But there was more than a dollop of idealism as well—a determination never again to permit such a conflagration to occur, a resolution not to allow the country to fall back into a depression, and, most evident, a willingness to sacrifice to make certain the next generation would be spared war and depression. Moreover, there was a love of country that had been honed by the bad times and the war.

There was yet more to it than that. The dissonance

between the high ideals voiced during the war and the realities of American life was troublesome to some. The quest for social justice that was part of the New Deal had not died. The treatment of black servicemen, considered second-class citizens in the armed forces, was at odds with the avowed goals of the war: democracy and freedom. The same was true for the secondary role played by women in society prior to the war, which seemed unfair given the sacrifices demanded of them during the fighting. The social consciences of some servicemen returning from areas destroyed by war had been aroused. Even so, one of the defining aspects of the differences between the generations was that the parents had been molded by depression and a popular war, while their children had been the product of affluence and an unpopular war.

There were signs of this during the 1940s and 1950s, but they had been masked by the desire for economic and financial success and the coming of the Cold War, the former concentrating on individual accomplishment rather than group action, the latter casting a pall over most calls for social justice. Those veterans who joined organizations that called for social reform and criticized aspects of American life that seemed at odds with the country's democratic objectives ran the risk of being branded communist sympathizers at best and, at worst, "pinkos" or "fellow travelers." This was changed during the 1960s, largely the result of several developments. One was the eclipse of Senator Joseph McCarthy, who had come to epitomize the anti-communist crusade; more important was the appearance of a new civil rights movement and opposition to the Vietnam War, both of which energized student activists on campuses throughout the country. But other factors went into the mix.

The Vietnam War was perhaps the most obvious dividing line between the generations. Older people tended to support the war more than younger ones. Were this all there was to it, perhaps the generational division that developed could have been papered over. What particularly riled the World War II servicemen was the apparent anti-Americanism of some of the more visible demonstrators. Veterans were astonished by the flag burners and cries of "Ho, Ho, Ho Chi Minh, the Viet Cong Are Going to Win." To them this was not only treasonous, but it flew in the face of everything they had fought for in their war. The fault in this probably belonged more to the protestors than to their parents' generation. Opposing America's role in the war was in the American tradition. Cheering opponents who were killing American servicemen was another matter. It was something the older Americans were not prepared to accept, and it created a gulf between the generations that remained long after.

There was more to the protests of the period than the Vietnam War. There was the reinvigoration of the women's rights movement, and the emergence of left-wing regimes in Africa and South America, especially Fidel Castro in Cuba, that found support among old and young American radicals. Not the least in importance was the familiar generational clash in which young people reacted against the values they felt were being forced upon them.

As has been seen, just as their parents wanted to provide their families with homes in suburbia and all that went with it, so some of their children reacted to this by attempting to return to their roots in the cities. Their parents generally accepted the ground rules of American life. They believed that if they worked hard and achieved success in school and on the job, they would be rewarded by participating in the good life they had seen around them and in the motion pictures of the prewar and wartime periods.

The Coming of the Generational Revolution

Even during the early postwar period, there were elements in American society that rejected a good deal of the culture they had found. Perhaps the most important were those who soon came to be known as the New Left, the members of which called themselves "new" to distinguish themselves from the "old" left. The latter group accepted and indeed to a degree epitomized the power structure in western Europe and the United States after the war, which was closer to a continuation of the New Deal ideology than anything else. To the New Left, the Cold War was not the result of Soviet challenges to the West, but rather evolved out of flaws in both the Soviet and American "empires." Ralph Schoenman, secretary to Bertrand Russell, the English philosopher who was one of the major spokesmen for the New Left, put it this way:

> I believe that in fundamental ways the Cold War has served as a Metternich programme on the part of the West, designed to create the climate and the ideological myths necessary to prevent serious challenge to the power of the vast corporations whose control over planetary resources is mentioned as the expense of the agony and starvation of its population at large.

In Schoenman's view, and that of the New Left as a whole, the Cold War was the inevitable result of control of political institutions by those who were interested in power and their own wealth, to be obtained and maintained at the expense of the general population. The very success of postwar capitalism in the United States was taken as a sign of this.

> It is as true of Britain as it is of the United States or the Soviet Union. In these countries individuals find vast impersonal institutions in which they are absorbed like ciphers. More depressingly these institutions feed and breed men for quiescence. The efficient operation of a highly ordered institution, whether private or public, rests on a man who does not question ends, make demands, or display the characteristics of one not disposed to guide his manner to the dictates of the organization he inhabits or of its bureaucracy.

Which, if one puts the most negative interpretation on the ambitions and behavior of those seeking success in postwar America, might seem a fair interpretation. But it did not take into account the issues many of the individuals allied with the New Left in America embraced.

Finally, associated with the New Left, though not as tightly structured as that group, were those for whom such considerations as money and status were not particularly important. They would include those who in the 1950s were fascinated by the poets and others who constituted the Beat Generation, whose centers were Greenwich Village in New York and Haight-Ashbury in San Francisco. Calling themselves *beatniks*, the term derived from "beatific," they rejected the middle-class values embraced by the World War II veterans who "bought into" them. Their leaders were the likes of writer Jack Kerouac and poet Allen Ginsberg. Their rejection of patriotism, financial achievement, and even cleanliness disturbed the "straights" with whom they came into contact. Their philosophical wellsprings were not the Bible and the great documents of American history, but rather the texts of Hinduism and Buddhism, which could be seen in *The Dharma Bums*, Kerouac's manifesto, and the works of Alan Watts, especially *Zen and the Beat Way*. One of the terms encountered often in their works was *alienation*, and in point of fact, in order to understand the Beats, one must first appreciate that they abjured those middle-class values accepted by most Americans, and called upon their listeners to do so as well. "Do your own thing" was one of their battle cries, although much of the time just what that happened to be was not carefully delineated. Indeed, the Beats were more conformist in their separate ways than the middle class they excoriated.

Another key element in the mix was the civil rights movement. The roots of the black revolution were in the 1950s, most particularly in the Supreme Court decision in the case of *Brown v. Board of Education* (1954); the confrontation between the forces of Governor Orval Faubus, who opposed the integration of Central High School in Little Rock, and federal troops, leading to the passage of the 1957 Civil Rights Act, which protected the rights of voters; and the dispatching of "freedom riders" to the South to register blacks to vote. The movement did not come to a head until the 1960s, with attempts to desegregate separate eating and rest-room facilities in the South, which was important in the passage of another Civil Rights Act in 1960 to buttress the 1957 Act. The 1963 March on Washington, led by Martin Luther King, Jr., who by then had organized the Southern Christian Leadership Conference, was an important marker on the road to equal rights. At the same time, black militants split with King, who believed in integration, to form a movement, initially spearheaded by young radicals such as Stokely Carmichael and H. Rap Brown of the Student Nonviolent Coordinating Committee (SNCC), later known as Black Power, which advocated racial separation and in time would be epitomized by the work and words of Malcolm X and the Black Muslims.

Some of this surfaced in 1963, and it developed rapidly in the years that followed, as it became increasingly evident that the struggle for equality was drawing strong opposition. In August 1965, riots erupted in the Watts district of Los Angeles, which resulted in the calling out of the National Guard and thirty-four deaths. Other riots followed—in 1967 it was the turn of Chicago, Tampa, Cincinnati, Atlanta, Detroit, and Newark. White and black moderates alike were dismayed, while advocates of Black Power contended that this was the first step in a revolution. Dr. King, who remained committed to nonviolence, was obliged to take note of what had happened and referred to the Black Power movement as a "call to manhood." The dream of integration was replaced by demands for permanent racial separation, and Carmichael, Malcolm X, and others spoke of the impossibility of peace between the races without a revival of the Back to Africa movement identified with Marcus Garvey, who had formulated the idea in the 1920s. King opposed this change in strategy. "There is no salvation for the Negro through isolation," he said. "The black man needs the white man and the white man needs the black man."

This created a strange variety of dualism in the economy. It was a period when racial barriers were coming down. Colleges that previously would not consider applications from black students were now instructing their recruiters to seek them out, not only because failure to do so might be considered a violation of federal law, but also because some white students were putting pressure on the schools to act. The same was true of employers. The changes came slowly, and not at the same rate at all companies, but by the late 1960s some corporate recruiters were starting to seek black candidates. Change was in the air. But at the same time, those black students who had been attracted by the rhetoric of leaders like Malcolm X and Stokely Carmichael were starting to avoid the "white" colleges and seeking places at schools that were historically black, and taking courses in black history rather than engineering and business administration.

In this same period, the movement for women's rights, energized by the publication of Betty Friedan's *The Feminine Mystique* (1963) and other works, became front-page news. Along with the black students, some women, who earlier had campaigned for admission into the liberal arts and professional programs and equal treatment in the job market, turned to majors in women's studies, annealing their alienation from the larger society. Just as black students were protesting the absence of black faculty members, so activists noted that while women accounted for half the population, only 30 percent of student bodies were female, while as late as 1970 only 9 percent of full professors were female, women were less than 3 percent of all lawyers, and fewer than 8 percent of medical doctors. That year the average earnings of women with college degrees were less than those of male high school graduates. Some attempted to explain this by noting that the sins of the past were being corrected, and that when women obtained the necessary credentials, their status and pay would rise. Few of the activists were willing to accept this. In the process they were sending a message to the World War II generation: equality did not exist, and the economic and social goals of the 1940s no longer sufficed in the 1960s.

The assassination in 1963 of John F. Kennedy, who had been a hero to many of the discontented young people, and the succession of Lyndon B. Johnson to the presidency, was an important symbolic change for these people, despite Kennedy's Vietnam policies. Under Kennedy, the United States had escalated its assistance to the South Vietnam regime, and it would later be learned that the CIA had been implicated in the assassination of unpopular South Vietnamese dictator Ngo Dinh Diem and his replacement by a cabal of Buddhist generals. At the time Kennedy announced that there would be a slow withdrawal of American troops. Kennedy confided to Senate Majority Leader Mike Mansfield that his goal was the total evacuation of American troops, "but I can't do it until 1965—after I'm reelected." When this news was released after the assassination, the American people did not note the cynicism of the statement—the willingness to sacrifice American and Vietnamese lives to win an election victory—but rather that had Kennedy lived, the United States would have left Vietnam. As it was, under Kennedy's successor, Lyndon B. Johnson, the American commitment was expanded, and the escalation of what was becoming an unpopular war added to the dissatisfaction of young people with the society in which they were raised.

This was not apparent during the 1964 election, when

Johnson, who had proved a genuine reformer in the FDR tradition, and his vice-presidential running mate, Senator Hubert Humphrey, who was even more a product of the old political left, ran against conservative Republican senator Barry Goldwater, after a campaign in which Johnson portrayed himself as a "dove" while Goldwater was painted as a "hawk." Millions of people voted for Johnson in the belief that such action was the way to express opposition to the war. Johnson won in a landslide, but the American commitment to Vietnam was increased. There would be no pullout. This, too, reenergized the movement of many young Americans.

Johnson's support of federal aid to education and medical care for the aged (Medicare and Medicaid), his institution of the National Foundation on the Arts and Humanities, his creation of a federal Department of Housing and Urban Affairs and the Office of Economic Opportunity—all part of his Great Society program—did little to win the young dissidents to his side. As a result, the nation was faced with the aberration of seeing individuals and groups that proclaimed themselves concerned with societal reform opposing the president who more than any since Franklin D. Roosevelt stood for change. So this was not merely an attack upon the status quo by a segment of the young. Rather, it was part of a major challenge to the values of the prior generation—the one that had dreamed of obtaining educations, decent housing, and good jobs, who wanted to marry and have families, raise their children in ways that would give them many of the amenities they had not enjoyed, and see them, in the American tradition, achieve even greater success.

By the 1960s many older people had become aware of just how much they had benefited from the colossal boom of the post–World War II period. Now they wanted more of the same for their children. The problem was that some of those children—not all, to be sure, but a sizable number—rejected that heritage. This rejection was one of the most difficult things the veterans of the D-Day landings, the battle of Iwo Jima, and others had to confront in their postwar lives.

The Anatomy of the Counterculture

Ironically enough, the generational revolt was encouraged in large part by the very people against whom the revolt was mounted. The post–World War II generation had spoken and written of the need for racial and gender equality, and Johnson, Humphrey, and other prominent Democratic figures of the late 1960s were if anything more, not less, liberal than the Kennedy entourage. Moreover, the center of their protests was the university, arguably the most liberal and liberated part of American life. In its Port Huron Statement, issued in 1962, the Students for a Democratic Society (SDS), a beacon for the disaffected youths, railed against an older generation that in its view had created huge bureaucracies in government and business that stifled freedom and originality.

The SDS called for "participatory democracy," and warned their elders that they did not intend to be "bent, folded, spindled, or mutilated," referring to the then ubiquitous IBM cards. In the view of the SDS leaders, the university, which the post–World War II generation had seen as the major force in liberating the poor and minorities from poverty and second-class citizenship, was an instrument geared to enslave them. In what was perhaps the most quoted section of the Port Huron Statement, the authors drew the distinction between their generation and that of their parents in stark terms:

> We are people of this generation, bred in at least modest comfort, housed now in universities, looking uncomfortably at the world we inherit. When we were kids the United States was the wealthiest and strongest country in the world . . . many of us began maturing in complacency. As we grew, however, our comfort was penetrated by events too troubling to dismiss. First the permeating and victimizing fact of human degradation, symbolized by the Southern struggle against racial bigotry, compelled most of us from silence to activism. Second, the enclosing fact of the Cold War, symbolized by the presence of the Bomb, brought awareness that we ourselves, and our friends, and millions of abstract "others" we knew more directly because of our common peril, might die at any time.

As noted, enrollment in the colleges and universities was on the increase, rising from 3.8 million in 1960 to 8.5 million in 1970. Encouraged by radical leaders, some students indicated that they, not the administrations and faculties, were the proper judges of what they should learn. At some schools, several considered among the best in the country, student radicals would present the administrations and faculties with "non-negotiable demands," the first of which invariably was amnesty for any actions they committed that, as a result of the rules they had broken, called for punishment.

Because of this situation, some colleges, for a while at

least, had divided student bodies—and faculties as well. For some of the students, probably a large majority not involved in the protests, college was the recruiting group for corporate America and the entry point for the professions, both of which were applauded and supported. For others, college was a gathering place for those who opposed the power structure. In January 1966, Daniel Yankelovich conducted a poll for *Fortune* to determine why students were attending college. He found that there were three groups, one of which didn't want to attend at all. Of those who wanted to be there, one of two statements explained their choice:

1. "For me, college is mainly a practical matter. With a college education I can earn more money, have a more interesting career, and enjoy a better position in society."
2. "I'm not really concerned with the practical benefits of college. I suppose I take them for granted. College for me means something more intangible, perhaps the opportunity to change things rather than make out well within the existing system."

Yankelovich called those who preferred the first statement "practical minded." Many came from blue-collar families, and more than half were enrolled in business, engineering, and science programs. They were similar in this regard to the generation that arrived in the colleges after the war. The second group, which he called "the forerunners," were in the arts and humanities, and only a quarter of them came from blue-collar families. Most of the former group were "hawks" on Vietnam, while the "doves" came from the second group. It would appear, then, that success bred defiance of the status quo, while those who had not made it up the ladder were prepared to play by the rules in order to do so.

Yankelovich also found significant differences among the groups in their support or opposition to the Vietnam War. All three groups expressed sympathy for the soldiers, but there were far more hawks among the high school graduates and more doves in the group that went on to college. Few high school grads expressed sympathy for the SDS, whose members came almost exclusively from the college attendees.

In 1967 the SDS announced that "we are working to build a guerrilla force in an urban environment," which came to be called the Weathermen. Members of this group believed that revolution was necessary to deal with what they considered a repressive society that would not respond to anything less than violence. In 1968–1969, some 4,000 students were arrested countrywide for having violated campus rules, and in 1970 violence erupted at Kent State, where federalized National Guardsmen fired on students, killing four and wounding ten.

While the campus riots and other disruptions bothered older people, they might have reflected that the radicals had not given up on classical American values, but rather were attempting to mold them to their own conceptions of reality. Their goal remained the B.A. and professional degrees, although they hoped to take different paths to achieve them.

Other alienated students reacted to perceived faults in society by "dropping out," and they proved more troublesome. The media labeled them the "counterculture," indicating that they not only rejected the values and goals of the dominant culture, but were also involved in creating a different version of it. At the base of the counterculture were drugs, sexual freedom, and, as with their campus counterparts, disdain for authority. The cultural centers were the Haight-Ashbury district of San Francisco and the East Village in Manhattan. Some of these individuals fashioned themselves "flower children," after their supposed love of the simple life and their practice of pelting police and soldiers with flowers when challenged. Some joined together to form communes, and by 1970 there were some 50,000 young people living in such places either full time or part time. They urged others, as did the Beats, to "do your own thing," which for them included "dropping out" and "turning on," the latter referring to the use of drugs, which was very much a part of the counterculture. Music played an important role in the counterculture, some of whose members became "groupies" for one band or another.

All of which was confusing for their elders, who had difficulty distinguishing between those who called for reforms and others who wanted nothing less than a revolution, a drastic change in the rules that, accepted and followed by the older generation, had enabled so many of them to achieve economic success.

For most of the baby boomers, now adults, the situation was not so cut and dried. Recall Ray Myers, discussed in Whyte's book, *The Organization Man*, who left the army after World War II, attended Harvard Law School, and, instead of opening a practice or joining a firm, took a position at the Continental Illinois Bank servicing the accounts of wealthy Americans. By the 1950s he and his family had relocated to Colorado, and their son, Randy, born in 1948, observed conflicts between the locals and the newcomers. "When I got out of high school, Vietnam was cooking up hot and heavy," recalled Randy. "So you had your basic choice of whether you should go to college or go to Vietnam. And of course, as an organization man's son, college is what you did.

"I grew up with a basic contradiction. I was taught that corporate men were bad guys. And bankers were as bad as anyone you could find. Yet, I loved my dad and do to this day—very, very much. I respect him. He's brilliant, hard-working, scrupulous—you name it—he's got the positive attributes you'd look for in a person. As the same time, I'm being told that these guys are bad and nasty. They kick little old widows out of their houses."

Divided, Randy did not return to college after his first year. In so doing, he knew he was turning his back on what had been his father's ambitions—at least for the time being. "When I told my parents that I wasn't going back to college, they were greatly disappointed, but also a bit relieved, I think. They knew I wasn't going anywhere in school and I think that they thought if I got out for a few years and worked, then I would go back and get the M.B.A. that my dad wanted me to get so badly and become a corporate giant. But I don't think that corporate giantism is in my horoscope." Ray Myers also left college, only to return and earn that law degree, and then go to work at the bank. Could he have thought his son was doing the same?

This is not the place to analyze the counterculture, nor is it the primary purpose of this book. This brief discussion, as well as the one dealing with those who remained on the campuses to protest the culture into which they had been born, has been included to indicate that a significant and vocal number of children of the World War II generation rejected the values of their parents. We are concerned here with the methods by which Americans of the post–World War period achieved economic success and wealth. Clearly, few of the radicals hoped for either—at least at that stage of their lives. In time, some of them would drop out of the revolutionary movements and come to accept the more traditional methods of measuring and achieving success. But for the time being, in the 1960s and 1970s they were more than willing to trade economic success for participation in what they considered a moral cause. While these dissenters received widespread coverage in the press, which at times made it appear as though the social fabric was unraveling and that a new society was in the process of being born, it never involved more than a minority of the post–World War II generation.

Part of this change was the erosion of support for the labor movement. Unions had been a centerpiece of the New Deal, and after World War II they stood in the forefront of the progressive movements geared at raising living standards for their members and providing social insurance for all Americans. But evidence of union corruption, a failure of some locals to support measures aimed at ending racial and gender inequities, and a generalized resistance to movements that would reduce their members to ciphers were also important. Moreover, as the nation became more concerned with services than manufacturing, unions proved less capable of organizing white-collar workers than they had the blue collars. By the 1960s, then, some considered unions to be relics of a past era, while others believed they were a good idea in the hands of bad people, or at least not those who reflected the values of the New Left members.

That the denizens of the counterculture would oppose the re-election of Lyndon B. Johnson, who epitomized the culture and values of postwar America, became obvious. As a result, many of the young dissidents rallied to the cause of Senator Eugene McCarthy, who early in 1968 challenged Johnson for the Democratic presidential nomination, and then many of them switched to the side of Senator Robert Kennedy, who actively sought the nomination after Johnson announced he would not run again. The assassinations that year of King and Kennedy only added to the alienation of this segment of the young. The nomination of Hubert Humphrey was greeted with dismay, as many of the McCarthy and Kennedy supporters vowed to stay home on Election Day. In fact, McCarthy encouraged them to do so, though he changed his mind shortly before that date. Even so, the turnout was poor, and was one of the major reasons for the Humphrey defeat.

The Republicans had responded by nominating Richard Nixon, who, much as Goldwater four years earlier, epitomized everything those young people opposed. To complicate matters further, George Wallace, who had challenged every gesture in the direction of racial harmony, ran on a third party ticket. During the campaign, Nixon appealed to what he called "the silent majority," and when the results were tabulated it appeared that he had provided that anti-counterculture youth with a proper label. In his nomination acceptance speech, whose cadences appeared to have been lifted from the more memorable Martin Luther King, Jr. "I Have a Dream" speech, Nixon provided a coda for the World War II generation, of which he was one product:

> I see another child tonight.
> He hears a train go by at night and he dreams of
>   faraway places where he'd like to go.
> It seems like an impossible dream.
> But he is helped on his journey through life.

A father who had to go to work before he
   finished the sixth grade sacrificed everything
   he had so his sons could go to college.
A gentle, Quaker mother, with a passionate
   concern for peace, quietly wept when he went
   to war but she understood why he had to go.
A great teacher, a remarkable football coach, an
   inspirational minister encouraged him on his
   way.
A courageous wife and loyal children stood by
   him in victory and also defeat.
And in his chosen profession of politics, there
   were the scores, then hundreds, then
   thousands, and finally millions who worked
   for his success.
And tonight he stands before you—nominated
   for President of the United States of America.

Nixon received 32 percent of the popular vote, and when the Wallace votes were added, the anti-Humphrey votes were 57 percent of the total. Nixon was elected nonetheless. But the Democrats retained control of both houses of Congress. Obviously Nixon, while elected by a majority of the electoral college, had not received a clear mandate for any of his programs.

Under Nixon the war was expanded, but at the same time American troops were withdrawn and the military draft eliminated. More so than Johnson, Nixon attempted to deal with an economy in which flaws and problems had surfaced. The most important of these, at least so it appeared at the time, was inflation. Johnson's attempts to pay for the war while at the same time funding his ambitious social programs had resulted in deficits, which forced an increase of the national debt. This continued under Nixon. From January 1969, when he was inaugurated, to August 1971, the cost-of-living index increased by close to 15 percent. Nixon responded with a wage-price freeze and, most important, by taking the American dollar off its gold cover. In addition, surprising those who considered him a reactionary, he increased the spending on social programs. As had been the case with Johnson, such dedication to classic liberal programs and goals did not win for him the support of the dissidents. In 1972, after four years of good economic performance, Nixon ran for re-election against Senator George McGovern, who had campaigned for years against the American intervention in Vietnam.

Without Nixon's knowledge, members of his administration became involved in a break-in of Democratic headquarters in the Watergate building, and the White House soon was implicated in a cover-up of the illegal act. As a result, an impeachment action was initiated, which ended only when Nixon resigned from the presidency. Since Vice President Spiro Agnew had earlier resigned owing to his malfeasance and had been replaced by Gerald Ford, Ford now became president and served out the remainder of the Nixon term.

By themselves, these political developments should not have affected the methods by which young people could achieve success. They remained the same as they had been for their parents; given the proper combination of native intelligence, the desire and ability to work hard and attain the appropriate education and training, dedication, and acceptance of the rules of life, they might expect success. But this too had changed.

By 1974, inflation appeared both serious and permanent. Americans in the aggregate were wealthier than ever, if one is to measure such things by savings and incomes, but when adjusted for inflation it appeared the real value of savings and assets had actually declined. Articles were published offering advice to readers for whom this was a new phenomenon. News stories stressed the inability of retired people, whose savings, pensions, and holdings were not indexed for inflation, to maintain their standards of living. These were accompanied by forecasts of a stock market collapse, which would hurt the savings of those who had counted on this source of wealth for their subsistence. Market analysts urged their readers to sell their depreciating assets and buy gold, which was bound to rise in price. What this indicated, besides an obvious loss of nerve, was a lack of confidence in the future of capitalism, which had sustained the spirits of Americans since the end of the war and dictated their actions in their work, spending habits, savings, and plans. What inflation inferred was that playing by the rules might not pay after all. If the great lesson of the 1920s was that one must save to prepare for the future, the lesson of the early 1970s was that even the savers would suffer in an economy that seemed to be out of control.

7

ALTERNATE MEANS TO WEALTH

It often seems that the poor are drawn to risk-taking more than the comfortable middle class. Threadbare men with fedora hats and cigar stumps populate the dog tracks, clutching racing forms in anticipation of the main chance. Lottery outlets do the briskest business in poorer neighborhoods, and each year millions of elderly people on fixed incomes flock to Atlantic City casinos from New Jersey and New York. Their $1, $2, and $5 bets are for them substantial, yet seem like good investments, because for those struggling against real or near poverty, there is so much to gain, however slim the odds.

The more typical American of the postwar generation, as we have seen, enjoyed a far more comfortable existence. Most looked down on gambling, having been admonished by their parents to stay out of pool halls, gambling rooms, and other stomping grounds for "hustlers." Even so, after World War II millions of middle-class and upper-middle class families would participate in one or more forms of speculation, from lottery tickets to gold, from thoroughbred horses to artwork, from real estate to real estate investment trusts. Some dabbled in these less conventional investments as a hobby, while others plunged in headfirst, building companies that occasionally grew into business empires. Together, these investments proved to be great sources of income for many in the postwar period—unconventional paths to wealth that helped drive the boom economy.

Lotteries

Lotteries were not alien to postwar America. They dated back to colonial times, when revenues from them were used to pay for bridges and roads. The American Revolution received support from lotteries, as did leading institutions of higher education, such as Yale, Princeton, and Harvard. By 1790, some 2,000 lotteries were in operation in the United States, with ticket sales in New York and Philadelphia alone exceeding $4 million per year. During the nineteenth century, securities brokers on Wall Street did more business in lottery tickets than in stocks and bonds. Without a series of lotteries, it would have been difficult to build the nation's capital.

Although most of the lotteries in this period were sponsored by institutions seeking to raise funds for civic, educational, and related purposes, private lotteries flourished despite reports of fraud. There were regular stories of delayed drawings, defaults, rigged operations, and the adding of more blanks than had been advertised. Bogus tickets, always a problem, became even more prevalent. By the early 1860s, only Delaware, Missouri, and Kentucky permitted government-sponsored lotteries. Even so, the public's demand for lotteries remained strong, further encouraging the creation of additional private operations.

The anti-lottery forces continued to grow as well, and in 1895 Congress passed legislation outlawing the drawings. A quarter of a century before alcohol prohibition, America experimented with denying consenting adults a pleasure they sought. As was to be the case with Prohibition, those Americans who enjoyed participating in lotteries found ways to get around the law. The most common methods were playing church-sponsored bingo and participating in raffles organized by recognized charities, both of which were legal. Attendance at racetracks escalated. Wagering on sporting events was illegal, yet the newspapers printed the odds on the sports pages and, during the first half of the twentieth century, everyone knew that hundreds of millions, if not billions, of dollars annually were wagered on the outcome of games and prize fights.

In 1932, a postal official lamented that "the country seems to have gone lottery mad," and incoming President Franklin D. Roosevelt, already on record as favoring Prohibition repeal, called for a national lottery on the model of the Irish Sweepstakes to benefit charities. One 1938 survey indicated that 13 percent of American adults had purchased a sweepstakes ticket, while another poll, in 1944, showed that a quarter of all adults purchased tickets in church-sponsored raffles and 7 percent played the numbers. By the late 1940s, more than half the nation engaged in some form of gambling.

During World War II, there was talk in Washington of starting a national lottery that offered war bonds as prizes. After the war, the agitation continued, with New York congressman Paul Fino introducing measures for national lotteries annually from 1953 to 1960:

A lottery carefully supervised and controlled would provide a harmless release for man's gambling instinct and collect desperately needed funds for useful public welfare activities. These words may shock a good many conscientious and sincere Americans, because they have developed an automatic reaction against gambling. In our modern life with security built in, opportunities for daring are limited. Routine characterizes most of our lives. Buying a lottery ticket is an avenue of escape from routine and boredom.

All the while, lottery opponents criticized the developing groundswell for lotteries. Their arguments were quite familiar, for all had been heard during the previous century and before. Some opposed lotteries on religious grounds, claiming biblical injunctions against gambling. Even so, one of the more common methods by which churches raised money was by running bingo games, and these not only had been going on for generations, but they were also sanctioned by states where other forms of gambling were prohibited.

There was one reason for banning lotteries that resonated among many well-thinking individuals. Lotteries would target lower-income people, they said, since there was little incentive for the wealthy to purchase tickets in a game where the chances for a windfall were so small. To this, the lottery supporters replied that there was no way to learn whether or not this was the case, but even were it so, if the purchase of a $1 ticket provided a poor person with the chance to engaged in harmless fantasies for a week or so before the drawing took place, the price might well be worthwhile to that individual.

This debate would appear whenever a state considered lotteries. In time, however, some of the doubters were silenced by polls conducted regularly by independent agencies, almost all of which demonstrated that lotteries appealed to people in all income and wealth brackets, from the very poor to the extremely wealthy, to all age groups, both genders, and individuals of all races. The "typical" lottery player, if there were such a person, was a middle-class American, not a poor one. A 1999 poll indicated that 59 percent of lottery participants lived in households with annual incomes between $25,000 and $75,000, and the most frequent players were in the 45 to 54 age bracket. In many states, 75 percent of the adult population had at least tried the lottery once; one-third were regular players, meaning they played once a month or more.

All of these arguments surfaced in 1954 as the New Hampshire legislature debated a measure to create a lottery. The state did not have an income tax or a sales tax; more than half the state's revenues derived from excise taxes on tobacco products, alcohol, and horse racing. New Hampshire's educational system was starved for funds, with local municipalities bearing practically all of the burden, and less than 6 percent of the operating expenses were provided by the state. The lottery seemed an "easy, pleasant way" to raise funds, and the state got its lottery in 1964. The New Hampshire legislature tied the lottery to

horse racing—as had been the case with the Irish Sweepstakes—and tickets, which cost $3 each, would be sold
only at the racetracks and dispensing desks at the state's
fifty-one liquor stores, with two drawings a year to start
things going.

In the initial New Hampshire lottery, the purchaser
would put down his money and get a pre-numbered
ticket, on which he would write his name and address,
hand it over to the clerk, and then he would receive a
receipt, or "acknowledgment," while the ticket was sent
to lottery headquarters and placed in a drum along with
the others. The form retained by the customer, however,
had no value and need not be surrendered if the number
won. Rather, it was considered proof that the purchase
had been made for that specific ticket. This was done for
the purported purpose of preventing out-of-staters from
purchasing tickets, but this stratagem was not enforced,
since New Hampshire hoped that residents from nearby
states that did not have lotteries would become patrons.
Indeed, from the first, runners from Massachusetts were
sent to the New Hampshire liquor stores to purchase large
numbers of tickets for resale.

Then, with the press in attendance, an operator
would spin the drum, stop it, and draw the winning numbers. The tickets drawn were matched with a parallel
drawing of horses selected for the horse race involved.
The owners of tickets on the winning horse received a
prize of $100,000 in 1964 and 1965, while the place and
show tickets won $50,000 and $25,000 respectively. The
total take was modest by past and future standards. The
1964 gross came to $5.7 million, which provided $2.8 million for the schools. But then sales dropped off, for once
the novelty of the sweepstakes was gone, so were the
casual customers, leaving hard-core bettors. Besides, $3

was a considerable amount of money in the mid-1960s, around $12 in 1999 dollars, and one thought twice before making the purchase. Finally, the lotteries proved to have little effect on the numbers and policy rackets since, as it turned out, most habitual players were not attracted to the state lottery. Such individuals preferred to pick their own numbers and not have them selected by the lottery personnel through the preprinted tickets that were sold. On the other hand, the business from nearby states, Massachusetts in particular, remained strong.

In 1973 the first "instant" lottery was introduced in Massachusetts. Purchasers received tickets with the winning numbers or symbols masked by an opaque covering, which could be rubbed off with a coin or key, revealing what was beneath. The ticket holder, if a winner, could collect his or her prize from the vendor on the spot. A specified number of the tickets also were entered into a special drawing, which offered grand prizes of up to $1 million. These games appealed to those who chafed at the idea of waiting until the drawing was held, and became very successful.

The New Hampshire experience was monitored carefully by lottery advocates in other states. New York became the second state to have a lottery. Governor Nelson Rockefeller recently had embarked on the most ambitious state construction program since the New Deal. He was financing turnpikes and highways, pouring massive amounts of money into the state university system, and remaking the state capital in Albany. While publicly opposed to lotteries for political reasons, Rockefeller had indicated to key legislators that he would accept one for the state should an enabling measure pass the legislature.

Encouraged by Rockefeller, New York legislators considered a lottery bill that, like the New Hampshire measure, would be tied to horse racing. It passed, and the lottery went into effect in 1966. Although based on the New Hampshire Sweepstakes, it had points of difference. For one, tickets cost $1. New Hampshire had charged $3 to avoid accusations that its lottery was intended for the poor, but this consideration did not trouble the New Yorkers. The tickets were "pull-aparts," with the purchaser retaining the section with the number while the other part, with his name and address written in, was to be given to the lottery agent. Winners were determined by a complicated arrangement that confused both players and lottery personnel. The post positions were assigned to ticket numbers. Those who won had to go through a second stage, a drawing based on the results of races already held. Prizes ran from $100,000 to a series of smaller awards that ranged down to $150. The drawings were held monthly, and there was one annual drawing for $250,000, to be paid out in ten annual installments of $25,000.

According to the plan, 55 percent of the earnings were to go to education, 5 percent were earmarked for commissions, and 30 percent for prizes, while administrative costs would account for the remaining 10 percent.

At first, the New York Lottery did better than anticipated, with sales running at a $66 million per drawing. But then, as had been the case with New Hampshire, interest started to decline. Just as a number of purchasers in New Hampshire had been attracted by the novelty and then stopped buying tickets, so the same phenomenon occurred in New York. Even so, purchases by residents of nearby states continued strong, with the bulk of them coming from New Jersey. Clearly, residents of that state, like those in Massachusetts who patronized the New Hampshire Sweepstakes, were helping to fund New York's schools. As a result, legislators in New Jersey began talking about lotteries. By that time a dozen other states were considering their introduction. In all cases, lottery proponents emphasized the fact that most of the proceeds would go to education. They considered this a crucial aspect for those who were wary of the introduction of gambling, much less state-sponsored gambling. They also stressed their intention to ensure that unsavory elements and racketeers would be unable to influence decisions by following the New Hampshire practice of hiring former FBI men, policemen, and other law enforcement personnel as the lottery directors and their staff. The public response was good. As always, Americans did not like paying taxes and sought ways of lowering them. In some states the plans were for the lottery earnings to be remitted to individual localities. Sometimes simple economic stringency was the reason for the inception of a lottery. In Oregon, for example, a nationwide decline in housing construction hurt the important lumber industry, causing widespread distress, which led to the introduction of a lottery there.

Other states followed, until it got to the point where the pressures on legislators made rejection of lotteries politically difficult. There were some states, such as Utah, where religious sentiments worked against instituting lotteries, but in time they would fall into line. Each state had its own version. In most states, the concept of making direct grants to school districts and the like gained favor.

By 1996, North American lottery sales were $40.9 billion and were returning more than $12 billion to the states, and, as had been the case from the start, the money was used for education. While this practice helped still the lingering opposition to lotteries, citizens whose taxes had been lowered years earlier seemed to have forgotten the source of those funds that improved education. Within the industry, some directors thought about how to bring this matter home to taxpayers. Georgia hit upon a novel method of doing so, bypassing the counties and cities and giving direct educational assistance to individuals. This gave Georgians, even those who had never purchased a ticket, special reasons to support the lottery. The lottery commission in that state developed the HOPE (Help Outstanding Pupils Educationally) scholarship, which was initiated in 1993, when it was dubbed the GI Bill for Georgia. Under terms of the HOPE program, students whose high school averages were above a specified level were guaranteed admission to a state college, while others at a lower level could count on admission to a junior college and not be charged tuition. Another part of the program provided nursery school care for preschoolers. To Georgians, HOPE indicated that it was possible to do good even when participating in a practice that was not considered necessarily uplifting.

By 1997, ten states had allocated all of their lottery-generated funds to education, while twelve put the revenues into their general reserves. Fifteen more lottery states divided the revenues among several recipients. But the success of the Georgia HOPE plan shook up the industry, sparking debates as to the distributions.

The Revival of Gold

In the late 1960s, as the American balance of trade turned increasingly negative, dollars piled up in foreign banks, and toward the end of the decade more and more foreigners opted to turn them in for gold. The old standard of $35 an ounce, established as an international norm after World War II, could not stand this pressure as the price of gold advanced on foreign exchanges. In August 1971, President Richard Nixon took the United States off the gold bullion standard, which had been in effect since the 1930s. The price fluctuated between $44 and $70 in 1972, and the following year saw a rise to $127 on rumors that soon Americans would be permitted to own gold. That news came in late 1974. Starting right after New Year's Day 1975, Americans would be permitted to own gold for the first time since 1933. Almost immediately, plans to deal in gold futures contracts were announced at the Chicago Board of Trade and the New York Mercantile Exchange, but this was not the initial domestic exposure to such dealings. American gold traders had been dealing in 400-ounce contracts on the Winnipeg market for several years. The Pacific Coast Coin Exchange, started in 1972, saw business quadruple the following year, and transacted $273 million in business in 1974. Stock market traders, who until then had attempted to make their fortunes in shares, now switched to gold. As it happened, this was not a particularly propitious time for making money by buying and holding gold, and, to a lesser extent, silver. The first petroleum shock had been absorbed, and for a while inflation abated somewhat. In addition, rumors were floated that the government intended to sell the metal from its holdings, and indeed, a few days after legalization the Treasury announced plans to sell 2 million ounces of gold. The price of gold came close to $200 in 1974, but at times that year sold for as low as $115, and the decline continued into 1975 and 1976, with the price falling to $103 in the latter year, when 25 million ounces were sold by governments and banks.

In this period, some average middle-class individuals, who had never considered precious metals investments, became involved in the trading, and, perhaps more importantly, began to accumulate gold and silver coins, which fell into two categories: numismatic and bullion. The former had been accumulated and traded in for centuries, and included British Sovereigns, American twenty-dollar gold pieces and one-dollar silver "cartwheels," Austrian Kroners, and the like, while the latter were coined for those interested in owning gold, and started with South African Krugerrands, and then spread to the new coins of other countries eager to get in on the mania. It was also possible to buy and sell gold bars, and gold in other forms.

During the second oil shock, set off by the Iranian Revolution, the high for gold came on January 21, 1980, when gold futures prices went to $960. By then, interest in gold-mining shares, and just about everything connected with that metal, had replaced discussions of stocks in the conversations on commuter trains throughout America. Gold, which had not been a significant factor in wealth creation in America since the 1930s, was now an important trading vehicle, for a while on par with common stocks.

Collectibles

During periods of inflation, when the money supply increases at a rapid pace, investors seek assets whose supply is certain to remain constant—thus, the mania for such collectibles as stamps, numismatic coins, works of art, and the like. Of course, there always had been collectors, but now the game was being played not by art lovers, but by individuals who earlier had sought securities in order to achieve profits. Christie's, Sotheby's, and other auction houses became the new arenas for speculation, dealing in such items as English and Spanish porcelain, Chinese snuff boxes, American pewter, antique maps, and old masters and nineteenth-century prints. But almost anything that was considered collectible found markets among investors eager to buy low and then sell high. For those with little knowledge and time, the investments of choice were autographs, first editions, stamps, and coins. They weren't printing any more of the commemorative stamps issued in the 1920s, which, buyers were assured, were "bound to rise in price." Everywhere there seemed to be a search for the next hot collectible.

This was found in an area serious collectors and connoisseurs hadn't considered: items whose value derived from nostalgia, rather than from artistic merit. The players in this arena were those of the GI generation who recalled the icons of the 1920s and 1930s, which they owned or admired, or that in some way held memories to which they clung. Women in their fifties recalled the Shirley Temple dolls they might have owned, or wanted to but could not have due to restricted economic circumstances. Unable to purchase them at $8 during the Depression, in the 1970s these people joyfully paid several hundred dollars for a doll in good condition. Nostalgic items were purchased at fairs organized by entrepreneurs who were aware of the growing markets. Reading of these prices, thousands of Americans searched for the items in their attics and basements. The tale of the middle-aged man whose mother, when he was a boy, had obliged him to get rid of a cache of comic books that in 1975 might have fetched thousands of dollars was told and retold. An autographed picture of a favorite film star might change hands at $100 or so. A Little Orphan Annie decoder ring, obtainable in the 1930s by sending in a portion of an Ovaltine box, or a trinket packaged in a box of Wheaties could be sold for hundreds of dollars to a person who had memories of what these objects connoted in the heady days before World War II.

Likewise, a boom began in used cars of the period. A La Salle or a De Soto in good repair might fetch upward of $10,000, while Packards, Lincolns, and Maxwells had higher price tags. Those who purchased Depression glassware and World War II memorabilia did well for themselves, along with collectors of 1930s-era comic books. Enterprising entrepreneurs spent a great deal of time trying to guess what would be the next fad. Some of them concluded that it would be the "cels" from which the animated motion pictures of the 1930s were created, and Walt Disney and Warner Brothers reaped large profits from selling them wholesale to these individuals, who peddled them retail. For a while framed cels of Snow White and Bugs Bunny signified that their owners were individuals who not only appreciated a formerly overlooked area of art, but who were also shrewd investors. Not so enterprising individuals were convinced that manual and electric typewriters would make the grade.

Feeding on the mania for collectibles were companies like the Franklin Mint, which produced items guaranteed to be in limited editions, such as commemorative plates, coins, and figurines. The aftermarket for these was covered in magazines devoted to the subject.

What was behind this mania for collectibles? Even now, psychologists and others debate the matter. At the heart of it was the belief that Americans would pay a price for an artifact that reminded them of their youth, but surely part of the attraction was based on the idea that the mania would continue, and those comic books, automo-

biles, and decoder rings were bound to rise in price—
unlike shares in General Motors, government bonds, or
new issues. It was a vote for the past against the present.
But the baby boomers and their children derived a different lesson from all of this. They had old recordings of the
Big Bopper, Chubby Checker, and other early rock-and-
roll singers. They put these away in safe places, convinced
perhaps that their stash would attract outstanding prices
by the year 2000. Somewhere in America there were
hopeful collectors in whose attics and basements were
some early computers, such as Commodores, Osbornes,
and Kaypros, next to which were boxes of program disks.
Would these prove interesting to their grandchildren? Or
perhaps to their contemporaries, seeking refuge in the
artifacts of a happier and simpler time, the 1970s?

The stagflation of the period, which led to the quest
for investments whose value would rise faster than that of
the general price level, led to a widespread search for
items in which increases in demand could not easily be
met by increases in supply. Of course, this couldn't be
managed in rare coins and real estate, but it was possible
in fine art. Auctions, once the province of serious collectors, now became the haunts of investors, and the prices
of old masters (and new ones too) rose sharply. The craze
filtered its way down to the middle class, and it began
early in the bull market. At the beginning of the 1960s,
adult education classes dealing with investments in art
and nostalgia were filled with would-be investors.

The Sport of Kings?

The art market was not the only one once reserved for the
blue bloods that now opened to the parvenue. Thorough-

bred horses enjoyed a bonanza period, thanks to the search for investments, the pleasure of racing, and the nature of the tax laws. At one time, owners derived most of their earnings and gratification from racing itself. Now races were held to determine which stallions and mares had the best breeding potential.

In 1973 there were 149 thoroughbred breeding farms in New York alone, and by 1990, 535. Only 214 foals were born there in 1973; by 1990, the figure was close to 2,000. Due to a boom in breeding fees, the large stables prospered. At a time when the tracks were suffering and the country was experiencing a negative balance of trade, horse sales brought fresh funds from abroad and enriched breeders.

This occurred in tandem with the appearance of new players in the sport and the business. The greatest generators of wealth in the world during this decade were the Japanese and the Arabs. Electronics and petroleum bred a generation of multi-millionaires eager to work—and play—among the aristocrats, and in sports this meant thoroughbreds. The way to enter the field was to build stables, which involved the purchase of fine horses capable of proving themselves at the tracks. Just as professional baseball requires the minor leagues to provide players for the majors, so thoroughbred racing demanded the breeding of stallions and mares. The supply of outstanding horses could not keep up with the demand, and prices soared.

So the locus of the sport shifted in the 1970s. Track revenues were not as important as stud fees and yearling sales. In 1972 Secretariat, who had not yet won the Triple Crown, was syndicated as a two-year-old for $6.08 million. The shares went for $190,000 apiece. Ten yearlings sired by Secretariat, offered at the Keeneland auctions in

Saratoga, brought $2.61 million, and three more were sold for $1 million. There was one million-dollar sale in 1978, and by 1983 there had been twenty-eight. Within two years, a yearling was sold for $13.1 million.

Production increased throughout the 1970s and continued into the early 1980s. By then, the progeny of highly successful and visible horses whose earlier yearlings did well still drew high prices. This made such stallions as Seattle Slew, Northern Dancer, and Nijinsky all the more valuable, as were their foals. In 1980 the July sales at Keeneland fetched around $60 million; in 1984 the figure was close to $180 million.

This recognition of breeding as a source of wealth came as the market started to be glutted with horses. One of the basic axioms of economics is that an increase in demand results in higher prices, which in turn brings additional product to market, which prompts a decline in prices. This is precisely what happened with thoroughbreds in the second half of the 1980s. The supply of yearlings increased, the demand for them did not, and so prices fell.

Other factors besides increased production adversely affected the business. One was a change in the tax laws regarding thoroughbreds. Until tax reform, the IRS viewed the horse's cost, operating expenses, and profits received from sales as business expenses and profits and losses. Under provisions of accelerated cost recovery, the owner could depreciate the purchase price, and subtract it from his or her taxes during a three-to-five-year period. After this initial interval, the owner could subtract expenses as they occurred, and a shrewd accountant might save the owner large sums by arranging this in the most beneficial fashion. Moreover, profits from sales were counted as long-term capital gains. Thus, the sport of kings was also the tax haven of the affluent. Under terms of the Tax Reform Act of 1986, the government closed many loopholes that favored the wealthy. In this case, it took away most of the tax advantages of horse ownership. With the end of these benefits came sharp declines in the prices of horses.

To this was added the slump in petroleum and the collapse of the Tokyo Stock Exchange, which prompted Middle East and Japanese multi-millionaires to cut back. The peak for thoroughbred prices was in 1984–1985, when the best yearlings fetched $500,000. By the end of the decade, the price had fallen by more than half. At the Saratoga auctions, second only to Keeneland, 200 top yearlings fetched an average of around $250,000 each. By 1986, the price dropped to less than $187,000.

Real Estate

Real estate has been one of the classic hedges against inflation. Higher prices make land, a finite commodity, more attractive. The replacement values of homes, factories, stores, malls, and all other structures cause their current values to rise as well. For many, real estate was a far safer investment and offered better chances for profit than gold, silver, and collectibles. The prices of the latter depended on supply and demand and paid no interest or dividends. Houses and factories might be leased, and they had superb tax advantages. A factory could be depreciated. An investment of $1 million in such a facility could be written off in twenty years under the tax code, but in inflationary times its true worth—in terms of resale value—could be many times $1 million, and all the while it would be bringing in rent, which itself would be boosted with each new lease. All of which enabled more Americans to become wealthy.

The higher prices for homes of all kinds could not help but be noticed. This phenomenon, and the higher mortgage rates of the period, made owning a home highly profitable, and in this atmosphere Americans who earlier had played the stock market were attracted to the real estate field. California was the locale for some of the leading speculations in such properties. It was not unusual for a speculator to purchase an interest in two apartments in a condominium being planned, for $200,000 each, with down payments of $20,000, for a total of $40,000. Then, when the apartments were completed, he might sell one for as much as $400,000, and so have the other free and clear, along with a cash profit of $160,000. Stories like this whetted the financial appetites of thousands of speculators throughout the country.

Those sharply fluctuating mortgage rates troubled the lenders as well as the borrowers. In the 1950s an S&L might offer a thirty-year fixed-rate mortgage (there were only fixed-rate mortgages in this period) at 6 percent, secure in the belief that rates would not diverge much from that level over the life of the mortgage. This was no longer so in the mid-1970s, and so the S&Ls sought means to extract higher rates from borrowers.

There was another way to deal with this situation, which would provide investors with the means to achieve higher returns with less risk. If the S&Ls could sell them the mortgages, the debts could be taken off their books and put on the accounts of the new owners. The means to do this arrived in December 1970, when the first Ginnie Mae (named for the Government National Mortgage Association) was put together. This was a bundle of insured mortgages divided into securities sold to investors.

The payments from the homeowner would be passed through to the owner, along with his share of any proceeds from mortgages that were paid off. The instrument resembled a bond, but had no final maturity date. To offset this uncertainty, the Ginnie Maes paid a somewhat higher rate than government bonds.

Wealth from REITs

Finally, Wall Street discovered a way to combine real estate with stocks. Imaginative packagers created real estate investment trusts, more commonly known as REITs, by taking properties they already owned or going into the market and buying some promising properties, putting them together in packages, and then taking them public, as they might a common stock offering. Investors could purchase units, which resembled participation in the closed-end trusts that had been popular in the 1920s and were becoming favored in the late 1960s, and became more popular in the 1970s in the form of funds that invested in particular industries or countries. By then the REITs took on some of the attributes of scams. A large real estate developer might own some properties he could not sell. The solution was simple: form a REIT, into which those properties would be placed, and then market it through a marginal investment bank.

It was not a new idea. Real estate trusts had existed in the nineteenth century. The Real Estate Investment Trust of America (REITA), organized in 1886, was the best known of these, but it was not particularly well known. Most of these had been assembled by estate attorneys seeking proper investments for trust accounts, and the benefits of diversification, and they continued into the twentieth century. The investing public still knew little or nothing of such vehicles, and few of them were traded publicly. Those that were did so on the over-the-counter market, where they attracted little attention. The REITA was the exception. It was listed on the American Stock Exchange, where it often traded above its net asset value. One might have thought this would lead promoters to organize similar trusts, but such was not the case until the 1960s.

At that time legislation was passed and signed into law by outgoing President Eisenhower, and was later called the Magna Carta of real estate trusts. According to the law, the trusts, which were largely invested in real estate and distributed at least 90 percent of earnings in the year they were owned to the owners, were exempted from income taxes. In addition, the trusts were enabled to include accelerated depreciation, and so to increase their earnings in this fashion. These earnings too might be distributed. The result was that the REITs formed in the aftermath of the law were able to make large payouts to investors, which made them very attractive to those who sought earnings.

By 1968 there was more than $1 billion in REITs outstanding, and by 1970, they had in excess of $20 billion in assets. At that point the bubble collapsed, and many REITs, whose prices had been bid up far beyond their asset values, declined sharply, to the point where they were below their breakup net worths, a feature that would attract raiders in the 1980s and would enable them to realize large profits.

Money as an Investment

One of the problems that plagued the banks and S&Ls in this period was something the general public learned about when the industry was under siege: disintermediation. In September 1969, interest rates on short-term Treasury bills stood at a record 8 percent, at a time when savings accounts paid $4^{1}/_{2}$ percent and could not be raised higher due to Regulation Q. Passed in 1933, this law was meant to protect the institutions against competition that might lead to their paying higher rates that could result in their demise. Depositors realized that they could withdraw their savings and purchase those T-bills, in the process increasing their returns substantially. Through newspaper articles they learned that this was precisely what the banks and S&Ls were doing. At first few went to the trouble of doing so, but increasingly, as the word got around, more and more took this route. Thus, they got rid of the intermediary between them and the Treasury— hence, disintermediation.

The savings institutions tried to get around this by offering bonuses to depositors, in the form of irons, radios, TVs, and other incentives to open accounts. In 1972, however, Bruce Bent and Henry Brown received permission to start the Reserve Fund, while James Benham opened the Capital Preservation Fund, which offered a better alternative. These funds would purchase short-term Treasuries and sell what seemed to be mutual fund shares to the public. These shares were to sell for $1, and not vary. But each day some of the T-bills in the portfolio would mature, and the money received would be used to purchase others. Thus, the interest rate edged higher or lower each day, depending upon the rates.

The initial organizers of such funds thought they would appeal to institutions seeking places to park their short-term investments, but in time the word got out to those small savers, and as interest rates went higher, they too were attracted to the "money market funds." To top things off, the funds had begun to feature check-writing privileges for share owners, though at stated minimums per check. By 1981, when yield averaged around 16 percent and went as high as 20 percent, these funds had assets of more than $215 billion and accounted for half the total assets of all mutual funds.

The money market funds revolutionized the way Americans saved. At one time middle-class savers had two accounts at their banks: savings and checking. The former paid interest, the latter did not. Now an increasing number moved all of their money from banks to money market mutuals, which, while not insured, were invested in perfectly safe paper. Even when the money market funds went into other, less secure instruments, they appeared quite safe. On several occasions when some of the investments went sour, the management companies made up the difference so as to keep the asset value of the shares at $1. The banks retaliated by lobbying successfully for the elimination of Regulation Q and permission to offer certificates of deposit—in effect short-term debt instruments at competitive rates—that were fully insured. Now the saver had the option of purchasing a three-month to five-year note from the bank at a fixed rate, or of going to the money market funds, where rates varied day to day. Did the saver believe rates were headed higher? Then the money market fund was the preferred vehicle. Were they going lower? In such case a five-year note might be appropriate. American savers who a few years earlier didn't give much thought to such matters, and had little interest in the securities markets, were now faced with such choices. For a nation interested in accumulating wealth, this was no small matter. At one time the financial pages of newspapers attracted small readerships. Now they expanded, and new magazines appeared to satisfy such interests. A more important factor affecting the structure of the brokerage community—and the attitude of customers toward it—was the change in the commissions schedule. Here was an end to the period when brokers were key figures, at least as far as investors were concerned, and investors were obliged to pay the same commissions no matter which broker they used.

After a long struggle, on May 1, 1975, known as "Mayday," commissions were deregulated. Almost immediately discount brokerages appeared, and soon after that the traditional houses were obliged to discount their commissions as well. Investors who once frequented the large, prestigious wire houses now opened accounts at Charles Schwab, Quick & Reilly, Waterhouse Securities, Muriel Siebert, and other discounters, who employed glorified clerks and then automated trading systems rather than registered representatives. By 1985, the discounters had more than 20 percent of the retail brokerage business.

The traditional brokerages, whose positions had been enriched by Merrill and those who had followed his lead, were now reduced in status, and they had to try to meet the discounters' fees. The most severe impact was in institutional trades. Since they now could pit one brokerage against another, they negotiated sharply lowered fees. Commissions for institutions had averaged twenty-six cents a share before Mayday; by 1980, they were down to ten cents.

As equities lost some of their fascination and bond investors underwent much pain in the face of rising inflation and lower bond prices, new markets were organized to serve new clients and customers. These appeared in great abundance and bewildering variety. In 1973, the Chicago Board Options Exchange opened, which transformed put and call options (a security known for close to a century) from an instrument utilized by sophisticated hedgers and speculators into one that, as investors became more familiar with them, became a powerful new investment tool. Listed stock options, a marriage between equities and commodity techniques, were soon to revolutionize the equities market. In time, there would be index options, options on indexes, and other new instruments.

The fluctuating currencies provided another market, currency trading and options on currencies, and the Chicago Mercantile and Philadelphia exchanges entered the field and flourished. Small, efficient trading operations, such as the Arizona Stock Exchange, which accumulated orders from institutions and executed them by matching prices once a day, made their appearances. The Cincinnati Stock Exchange, which didn't reside in that city but rather in an electronic market, was organized. So in the markets, as well as in all other aspects of the investment banking industry, change had become the rule. All of which lowered transaction costs and made investments in securities more complicated than they had been for generations. At the same time, however, the changes enriched a new generation of workers in the financial field, as well as those who were able to adjust to the new dispensation.

The End of the Great Deflation and the Coming of the New Era

The Gerald Ford administration and then the Jimmy Carter administration tried mightily to contain inflation through the use of fiscal policy and deregulation, but the problems continued into the summer of 1979. The old bugaboo of stagflation haunted the Carter people, along with the political frustrations attendant upon the Iranian hostage crisis and the increase in the petroleum price from slightly below $15 a barrel to slightly less than $40—the nation's drivers were once more plagued by shortages. On the first summer weekend of 1979, half the nation's filling stations were closed.

Paul Volcker, who became chairman of the Federal Reserve Board on August 6, was prepared to use other, more drastic methods. At a press conference on Saturday, October 6, Volcker announced a full 1 percent increase in the discount rate, bringing it to a record 12 percent. There would be stiff new reserve requirements on some bank accounts, which would discourage banks from making loans, and there would be new credit controls. Even more important, Volcker announced that the money supply would increase at a slow, steady rate. Interest rates would be permitted to fluctuate. Economically literate people who listened to this knew what it meant. Volcker intended for interest rates to rise sharply, to levels where they would choke off economic activity and smash inflation and inflationary expectations. In this way, the Fed became the central player in the anti-inflation wars.

As anticipated, both stocks and bonds fell the next session, with the Dow going from 898 to 884 and averaging below 800 within a month. But then it recovered, and started to rise, passing the 900 level in mid-February 1980. By December the Dow was once again flirting with 1000. But interest rates had risen sharply, and the bond market was savaged. From the time of the Volcker announcement to December 1980, little more than a year, bonds had fallen from 77 to 61. Not since 1932 had that market been so critically injured.

Even so, inflation was abating. In 1979, the Consumer Price Index had risen by 13.3 percent. The figure for 1980 was 12.5 percent, and for 1981, 8.9 percent. It would decline to 3.8 percent in 1982, and remain at that level for three more years until going to 1.1 percent in 1986. Early in the decade, most Wall Street pundits thought the decline was temporary, and indeed bond prices actually fell for a while. By mid-decade, however, the ranks of those who expected renewed inflation had lessened, though the widening of the budget deficit was cause for fears of higher prices. These did not materialize.

The reason, of course, was the Volcker medicine. In 1979 the average Federal Funds Rate—the rate at which banks borrowed from one another—came to 11.2 percent. It would go to 13.4 percent in 1980 and to 16.1 percent in 1981, peaking at a shade below 20 percent in June. The consequence was a short, brutal recession in 1980, followed by a recovery, after which there was another recession that lasted through the early years of the Ronald Reagan administration. For the first time since the 1930s, the nation experienced double-digit unemployment.

Then, in August 1982, the Fed cut the discount rate and the mood started to change. The Dow, which had fallen below 800 early in the month, started to rise. Investors noted that corporate earnings were good, the economy was recovering, and the prices of stocks were low historically, and they started to buy. Indeed, for those with long memories, the situation in the late 1970s appeared not too different from that of the late 1940s. In the period from 1978 to 1981, the average P/E ratio for the Dow was below 10. Soon after, analysts concluded that the bear market had ended, though they weren't certain a bull market had begun. As it turned out, it was the beginning of the market upswing that continued, with some interruptions and one major correction in 1987, into the 1990s, and perhaps beyond. Investors who had purchased real estate, gold, and collectibles now returned to stocks, attracted by those low P/E ratios. As will be seen, those who ventured into this securities market after the long period of drought did quite well, but the really big money was made in takeovers, the mania that engulfed Wall Street in the 1980s and created more wealth for a new group of players, known to some as the leveraged buyout commandos, than had been imaginable earlier. Finally, the economic recovery and the rise in stock prices benefited the wealthy, and those aspiring to that status, as did many aspects of the Reagan tax policy.

If one looks at the period as a whole, it becomes clear that on the average the American standard of living declined. From 1972 to 1987, the median American income rose 153 percent, but in the same period the value of the dollar declined appreciably. The cost of a new house rose by almost $83,000, or 294 percent, and the average monthly mortgage payment went from $152 to $581, rising 282 percent. Federal income taxes rose 175 percent, and payroll taxes, due to changes in the Social Security laws, increased from $468 to $2,018, or 331 percent, while state and local taxes also rose. So did the cost of consumer goods. A 1972 Chevrolet Impala cost $3,700, while a 1983 Impala went for $11,800. College tuitions also rose—at Bennington College, for example, by more than 250 percent. In the same period Social Security benefits rose 205 percent, but, as can be seen, this did not make up for the boosts in the cost of living for senior citizens.

The LBO Commandos Restructure American Business

Two categories of wheeler-dealers came to the fore in the 1970s; the leveraged buyout (LBO) commandos and the venture capitalists represented the downside and upside of American business, respectively, in the 1970s and afterwards. The LBO commandos produced critics who argued that all the banks were doing was shuffling the cards in the same deck. When a restructuring was completed, the companies that existed prior to the changes were still there. A few might have been shuffled, and some closed. But in the end, productivity was not changed markedly and few new jobs were created in an economy where this had become an important consideration. In contrast, the venture capitalists were in the business of helping to create new companies, industries, and jobs, as well. Both groups had one thing in common. They were creating new wealth, the LBO commandos for those involved in the restructuring, and the venture capitalists for the innovators, entrepreneurs, and businesspeople whose companies they helped finance. The distinction was considered significant by students of the American economy. To those concerned with the liberation of the entrepreneurial juices, it was deemed important to encourage the innovators. Wall Street did not accomplish this, they argued. As Herbert Stein, who was close to Eisenhower, put it when discussing the LBO movement, "The financial markets are still in the grip of inflationary psychology. By that I mean people with money are bidding up the prices of existing assets—stocks and bonds—instead of lending their money to create new assets."

The generalized lack of interest in equities that marked the stagflation era of post-1973 Wall Street continued into the early 1980s. But there were definite signs of a turnaround by the summer of 1982. There were several reasons for this change. Corporate profits were rising, and there were indications of what had been unimaginable only a few years earlier: an oil glut that might force prices downward. The popularity of Ronald Reagan, who had won election in a landslide in 1980 and took office the following year, also had something to do with it. When the public became convinced that the market advance was no fluke, more of those who earlier had been disillusioned with stocks started nibbling at them.

Of major importance in causing this turnabout was the beginning of a major wave of corporate takeovers that sparked interest in potential candidates for tender offers. As had been the case in the earlier movements, this one brought wealth to buyers, sellers, those who arranged deals, and bystanders who may have thought they had no stake in the outcomes of contests.

The takeover movement of the 1980s was born in those dismal markets of the 1970s, during which earnings rose while stocks declined. In 1975, the earnings per share for the Dow was $75.70, which rose to $121.90 in 1980, while in the same period stock prices actually fell. Then they took off, propelled in large part by those takeover bids, as imaginative "raiders" sought companies whose net asset values were far below their breakup values. Which is to say, the raider might acquire a company for $100 a share in cash or stock, and then sell off the parts for $150. In 1966 the value of corporate assets for the Dow was around half the price of their shares, and it actually fell somewhat by the end of the decade. As stock prices declined and assets rose, the direction was reversed. At the beginning of the 1980s, the Dow's book value was 90 percent of market value. For some sectors the spread was much larger. In July 1984, the rating firm of Standard & Poor's estimated that nearly 30 percent of all industrial stocks listed on the NYSE were selling below tangible book value. This is to suggest that someone might purchase all of the shares, and assuming this was done at market value, would own a company whose treasury had more cash than was expended in the takeover.

Added to all of this was a feature of the 1981 Economic Recovery Tax Act (ERTA) that made debt financing by corporations more attractive. Hoping to encourage greater capital investment by corporations, the government permitted them to accelerate their depreciation of equipment. This resulted in larger cash flows and higher earnings.

With all of this, the average American who benefited from the upward movement of stocks did so more through mutual and pension funds than through individual purchases. In 1981 there had been 665 funds; by 1984 the number had increased to 1,246. Within a decade there would be more mutual funds than NYSE-listed stocks.

Perhaps the most acclaimed person in equities during this period was Peter Lynch, the manager of the Fidelity Group's Magellan Fund, who turned in an outstanding record before retiring in 1990. That Lynch was so celebrated was due in large part to the fact the public had become wary of individual stocks, and started taking refuge in the diversification and professional management offered by mutual funds. This time they shunned the go-go funds, concentrating instead on those whose managers seemed able to perceive value in small capitalization and undervalued stocks.

In its early months, the new bull market was driven by the decline of inflation and the normal period of catching up after a long stretch of falling share prices. But after the initial recovery, rumors of takeovers became the engine that drove stocks. What was known as the leveraged buyout movement pushed stocks of potential takeover candidates to new heights, while shrinking the equity base. The term referred to the way the purchases were financed, which will appear quite familiar to anyone who has bought a home with the help of a mortgage. The buyer may be obligated to pay $100,000 for the house, putting down $20,000 and raising the other $80,000 by taking out a mortgage. Then, over a specified period, the buyer would pay off the mortgage. The difference between the two transactions is that the LBO buyer often raised the money to repay the debt by selling off the portions of the company.

If the raider who sought control of a targeted company had to pay cash for the stock needed to take over the company, he would raise it from short-term borrowings and then make a tender offer. Assume the price of the stock at the time was $30 a share. The offer might be for $45, whereupon management often would argue this was a "lowball bid," that the company was worth far more than that. The raider would ask why the market price didn't reflect what management asserted was the true value. His claim would be that it was due to the failure of the old management to realize the value of its assets. With a new management in place, the market price would rise. In other words, his takeover, in addition to benefiting him and those he had assembled in his "buying group," would promote the interests of all shareholders. The buyer's actions might attract the attention of rival groups, whereupon a bidding war would develop. Or management might decide to mount a takeover campaign of its own, or seek a "white knight," a friendly company interested in taking over, which usually pledged to retain the existing management, or give them a "golden parachute" or "golden handshake," a financial arrangement that would ease the pain of departure. The raider then would proceed with the buyout, making payments from a fund raised through banks. At this point, he would arrange for permanent financing, the placement of bonds with a selected roster of customers. Because the bond ratings for so large an issue with assets of questionable value would be low, they were known as "junk bonds," and the prime investment bank for such deals was Drexel Burnham Lambert, where Michael Milken held sway with his list of customers prepared to take much of what he had to offer.

Now in control of the company, the raider might take the next step. He could dismember the company, sell the parts, and make a large profit in this fashion. Doing this would not be too difficult, since so many of the firms were those conglomerates discussed earlier, that had been cobbled together in the 1960s and 1970s without regard to the fit of the component parts. Or the raider might bring in a new management and attempt to turn the company around. Should he succeed, earnings and cash flow would increase, enabling him to pay interest on those bonds and even retire a portion of them. If this succeeded, the company's net worth would increase. In time the raider might want to make a new public offering of the stock, in the process enriching himself and his group.

Takeovers and potential takeovers became the subject at gatherings of wealthy and middle-class investors, and the topic at conferences costing audiences hundreds of dollars a day at which they would hear from experts in the field and then rush out to telephones to place orders for shares in companies they thought about to be "put into play."

During the 1980s more than a third of the Fortune 500 were taken over, merged, or taken private. Mergers and acquisitions were done at a $1.5 trillion clip. Bankers and their allies took in some $60 billion in fees. The Dow Industrials tripled, and so enriched shareholders. Academics who decried the movement as causing unemployment and making billions of dollars for the "raiders" often did not reflect that as participants in their Teachers Insurance and Annuity/College Retirement Equities Fund (TIAA/CREF), they were among the greatest beneficiaries of the movement.

According to one study, during the peak year of 1986 there were 331 leveraged buyouts, which was only a quarter of the total mergers and acquisitions for the year. For the 1983–1988 period as a whole, close to 3 out of 4 LBOs were friendly, and another 11 percent were unsolicited. The remaining had their origins in unfriendly approaches. Of these, 12 percent were done by white knights called in to defend the target against a raider. Some 2 percent of hostile takeovers ended on an amicable note. And only 1 percent of all LBOs began and ended in an unfriendly fashion.

While each foray was different, initially most of the targets shared several characteristics. They were large, multi-divisional firms that easily could be dissected and sold to others. Often they were to be found in unglamorous industries with profitable but mundane products, which meant that their stocks merited low P/E ratios. Their businesses may have been competitive but not cyclical, so that owners could expect a reliable cash flow. Such firms required little by way of research and development. Raiders sought firms with swollen bureaucracies and wasteful methods of allocating funds, which meant that once in control they could introduce efficiencies. It would be helpful if management didn't have much by way of ownership.

Later on, critics of takeovers would charge that fears of raiders led companies to neglect long-term planning in favor of faster profits, so as to maintain the prices of their stocks and thereby avoid raids. As Household International CEO Donald Clark put it in 1988, the typical investor no longer cared about the company of which he was a part owner. "He is now a speculator on a piece of paper and has lost the long-term interest of the company. His driving force is a short-term turnover." Clark suggested that managers merely filled the gap left by shareholder disinterest. Revlon CEO Donald Drapkin disagreed. "If today's raiders were around during the days when the steel business was going under, the industry would be in a prosperous state. There are some raiders who go too far, but you cannot let corporate bureaucracy go unchecked."

In 1982 former Secretary of the Treasury William Simon led an amicable LBO of Gibson Greetings, Inc., paying RCA $80 million for that unwanted operation. Simon and his group turned the company around, and a year and a half later took it public for $290 million. There were many such stories, and each whetted the appetites of LBO practitioners.

One of the earlier and most lucrative LBOs was the one that Drexel arranged for Metromedia in 1984, done at the behest of the company's CEO, John Kluge. This was not the first publicly offered LBO, but it was the largest to date, and its complexity and size intrigued and troubled Wall Street. Metromedia was a large, diverse company, which owned television and radio stations, outdoor advertising, and other non-related businesses such as the Ice Capades and the Harlem Globetrotters. During the past four years, Kluge had bought or sold thirteen television stations, purchased depreciation rights to $100 million of New York City buses and subway cars, invested $300 million in the mobile telephone industry, and expended $400 million in a stock repurchase program. Part of the money came from transforming the outdoor advertising business into a tax shelter and financing arranged by Drexel. Kluge had borrowed heavily throughout—Metromedia had $550 million in long-term bonds outstanding—and as a result its debt-to-equity ratio in the spring of 1984 was 3 to 1.

Drexel's bankers presented Kluge with a plan whereby his former 26 percent stake in the company would become 75.5 percent through the transformation of equity into debt, much of the money to finance the change coming from Prudential Insurance, which would receive short-term rates plus a fee for initiation.

Drexel first offered shareholders $30 a share in cash, and debentures with a face value of $22.50, but an actual value more on the order of $10. When hit by stockholder suits, Kluge added a half warrant to purchase another debenture plus a 19-cents-per-share dividend prior to the buyout, which brought the package's value to around $41 per share. The shareholders accepted the deal on June 20, at which time Moody's lowered the company's credit rating. "Metromedia's existing businesses remain sound and are strong cash-flow generators," it said. But "over the next few years, protection for fixed (interest) charges will be significantly reduced by the magnitude of new debt and associated interest expenses."

The next step for Drexel was to arrange permanent financing. This was a key—and questionable—part of the deal. Metromedia's prior-year cash flow would not cover interest on the debt, and its net worth of debt was negligible. But Milken and Kluge knew the company's intangibles were quite valuable and could be disposed of easily for high prices.

The financing would come in the form of a $1.9 billion offering, quite complex and the largest for a non-financial corporation at the time. There would be $960 million in six tranches of zero-coupon bonds maturing from 1988 to 1993, $335 million in senior exchangeable variable-rate debentures due in 1996, $225 million of 15 $5/8$ percent senior subordinated debentures of 1999, and $400 million adjustable-rate participating subordinated debentures of 2002 offered at a discount, with interest payments to rise starting in 1988 should there be a specified amount of earnings from the radio and TV stations. Almost all of the buyers were lined up by the Milken team prior to the offering, which sold out in less than two hours.

In May 1985, Kluge sold Metromedia's TV stations to Rupert Murdoch for $2 billion plus $650 million in debt. Other sales followed, and by early 1987 Metromedia had raised close to $6 billion through asset sales. Kluge made more than $3 billion and became one of the nation's wealthiest men, and the Drexel-Milken reputation was burnished, helping to make it the bank of choice for future LBOs.

Leslie Fay was bought out for $58 million, and four years later taken to market, fetching $360 million. The investment bank of Kohlberg Kravis Roberts (KKR) purchased Fred Meyer for $420 million, and five years later took it public for more than $900 million. Better management, divestiture of undervalued assets, and some imagination—plus a compliant bank like Drexel—seemed to be all it required. Borg-Warner sold its financial operations, and Revlon its medical business and all others unrelated to cosmetics. Hanson PLC purchased SCM for $930 million, and proceeded to sell divisions—Glidden Paint, Allied Paper, Durkee Foods, and more—for a total of $1.1 billion, retaining companies that in 1989 threw off more than $50 million in profits. In time the raiders would turn to the shares of REITs that had been battered down by the malaise that affected the entire group, and virtually any stock whose price was far below its net asset value. When the raiders were criticized for their actions, they noted that well-managed companies generally had stock prices in excess of their breakup values. Only the poorly managed ones were worth more dead than alive. The former group had nothing to fear from raiders, while the latter, who were not serving their shareholders well, merited their worries.

The losers in such deals, everyone agreed, were the old managements, who lost their jobs. The winners included the stockholders, who received higher prices for their shares; the new bondholders, who received high-yield paper, which had the implicit guarantee of the issuer; and—in the case of asset sales and redeployment—the new owners.

Beatrice, a food company that became a conglomerate in the 1960s, was one of the more dramatic LBOs. That it attracted KKR came as no surprise. After protracted negotiations, KKR took it over in 1986, through a $6.2 billion LBO, with Drexel handling the banking end. Out went Avis ($250 million), Coca-Cola bottlers ($1 billion), and Max Factor ($1.3 billion), and scores of other companies, all of which more than repaid the purchase price, leaving Beatrice a profitable operation in foods. The new management did quite well for itself. CEO Donald Kelly made more than $400 million on an investment of $5 million.

While some of the hostile takeovers worked out poorly, most did result in greater economies, and there wasn't a single case in which shareholder values didn't rise on news that a campaign was being mounted. Eugene Fama, professor of finance at the University of Chicago and one of the foremost authorities in the field, remarked that "the empirical evidence is clear. In mergers, tender offers, and proxy fights, stockholders of the attacked company almost always profit."

After the collapse of OPEC, many petroleum companies shared those attributes perceived in Beatrice and Metromedia. The elevated petroleum prices of the 1970s had encouraged the petroleum companies to seek additional reserves in areas previously neglected due to the high costs of recovery. This worked well with petroleum at $30 or $40 a barrel, but not when prices were falling steadily. When the price of petroleum fell under $25, exploration became a losing game for most. It later would be learned that during the first half of the 1980s each dollar spent on exploration returned 58 cents in reserves.

Few companies made big finds, or had success at adding to their reserves. The majors still had large cash flows, which some used to purchase oil assets. The industry's hard times and unwise takeovers caused the prices of oil stocks to decline. Raiders eyed these companies. All they had to do was to take the reserves of any petroleum company, divide it by the price of the stock, and find out how many barrels were behind each share. The next step was to multiply the number of barrels per share by the price of oil. When this was done one would have discovered that the companies' shares were underpriced in relation to assets, and many in cases, sharply so. In the summer of 1981, *Newsweek* estimated that Getty, then selling at $72 a share, had assets of $250 a share. Marathon, with $210 a share in assets, sold for $68. Cities Service had $130 per share in reserves, and went for $56. In time all would disappear, taken over by the raiders.

Why seek oil in the Gulf of Mexico, or anywhere else for that matter, when, if everything worked out, it would cost $12 to $15 a barrel and might be sold for little or no profit, if the same amount of oil could be purchased at $3 or $4 a barrel by taking over a large company? Why indeed? In mid-decade raiders liked to say that the cheapest place to locate oil was on the floor of the NYSE. This was certainly so. And if such were the case, it made abundant sense to purchase reserves from other companies—by taking them over—rather than spending money on exploration.

The takeover mania within the petroleum industry was kicked off in 1979 when Shell purchased Belridge Oil for $3.6 billion, and continued with Du Pont acquiring Conoco in 1981 for $7.4 billion in cash and stocks, followed by the $6.5 billion purchase of Marathon by United States Steel (half cash and half notes), both in 1981. All of these were friendly and, despite their size, conventional. Consider the position of investors in this period. Knowing not only that the oil companies were selling for fractions of their net worths but also that raiders would soon appear with attractive tenders, they plunged into the market and awaited the bonanzas. The stage had been set for the next round in the decade's corporate raids, which would center around the petroleum industry.

Some of the deals of this period demonstrated that raiders could win even when they lost. They might enter into a bidding war with a competitor, only to see the prize fall to him. In such a case, however, the original raider might sell his shares to the eventual winner at a large premium, and then go on to the next contest with an enhanced war chest.

Such was the situation when T. Boone Pickens, one of the more original and colorful raiders, took off after Gulf Oil, which was selling at a huge discount to assets and at a price of 2.2 times cash flow. In 1983 Gulf had sales of $29 billion, and few thought anyone could muster the kind of financing needed for a takeover. Through his major holding, Mesa Petroleum, Pickens started accumulating Gulf shares in August 1983 and within two months had 2.7 million shares, which were transferred to Pickens' new entity, Gulf Investors Group (GIG), led by Mesa but including a large group of investors, and eventually accumulated 13.5 million shares at a cost of $6.5 billion. For his part, Gulf chairman James Lee formed a group of his own—38 banks that provided him with credit lines of up to $4 billion—and started open-market purchases of Gulf shares. Needing additional capital, Pickens met with a group of Drexel bankers, headed by Milken, who committed themselves to raising $1.7 billion by selling senior preferred stock in Newco, a shell company into which the Gulf shares would be deposited, and $450 million on low-rated junk bonds. With this kind of backing, Pickens was able to best another bid, from Atlantic Richfield, which offered $65 a share and extended that offer to Pickens himself, whose group stood to make a great deal of money if he accepted. But Pickens rejected the offer, whereupon Atlantic Richfield CEO Robert Anderson came up with a $70 offer to shareholders. Soon after, Lee offered to purchase GIG's shares at a price that would have given the group a profit of $500 million, which was rejected. By then it had become evident that no matter what happened, owners of Gulf shares, especially those who had purchased them before the contest had begun in earnest, would reap large profits.

The contest continued into February, with each side boosting its offer on a fairly regular basis. Matters came to a climax in March, when Atlantic Richfield came up with an offer of $72 a share and a newcomer, Chevron, was invited to make bids by the Gulf management. On the periphery was a team comprised of Gulf managers planning to make an offer of its own. Chevron ultimately won the battle on March 5, with $80 a share in cash, or $13 billion. Thus, GIG, which tendered its shares into the offer, had a profit of $6.5 billion, which is to say, investors doubled their money while coming out on the losing side. Institutional investors, such as pension and mutual funds, owned more than half the shares. TIAA/CREF, which was one of the largest institutional holders of Gulf shares, alone owned 1.7 million shares, enriching college professors, many of whom had no clear idea of what was happening to increase the value of their holdings. Other such contests followed. according to one estimate, during the 1980s more than $100 billion went to shareholders of oil companies that fell to raiders or their opponents through mergers, acquisitions, and recapitalizations.

The beneficiaries of this movement—outside the obvious ones, namely the raiders and their bankers and advisers, and the stockholders—were the major institutions that held large blocks of stock. Then and later, critics of Ronald Reagan would claim that his was an administration geared to help the rich at the expense of the poor. Such arguments were informed more by sentiment than by a realistic analysis of the administration's actions. As it happened, millions of modestly remunerated taxpayers no longer had tax liabilities. Of the total $34.8 billion reduction in tax liabilities resulting from the 1982 Reagan tax reforms, the largest decreases were for middle-income Americans, while $8 billion went to those with incomes of more than $100,000. By way of comparison, taxpayers with incomes from $20,000 to $30,000 had reductions of $12 billion.

That these recapitalizations and restructurings resulted in the loss of jobs is incontestable. Tens of thousands of middle-level executives were made "redundant." According to the *Wall Street Journal*, from 1980 to 1987 Fortune

500 companies alone fired 3.1 million middle-management personnel, and the American Management Association reported that in 1987, 45 percent of merged
companies cut staff, and in the 1990s even more would be
fired. Middle-management jobs, once considered the
upward path in a corporation, were now viewed as dead
ends. The top executives at the nation's large corporations
were receiving an average take-home pay that was forty-
four times that of factory workers, and so could hardly be
the subject of sympathy. At one time, especially for the
generation that came out of World War II, a bond had
been forged between the corporation and its management.
In the 1980s, that contract was severed. Even so, the top
managements did quite well for themselves. By the late
1990s their average pay was $7.8 million, which was 326
times that of average factory workers. The wealthy were
doing very well indeed, but, judging by government statistics, the poor were standing still economically.

8

THE NEW RULES OF THE GAME ON WALL STREET AND ON THE CAMPUSES

Traditionally, lenders have found the future more risky than the past. Future-oriented lenders, however, have a different perspective. For example, if you were considering buying a bond issue or making a new 25-year loan to the Singer company back in 1974, the fact that they had paid dividends for 100 years would not have been the relevant issue. The only issue would be whether Singer could sell sewing machines or fabrics in the future. Future, not past, performance, after all, was going to pay off the loan. As it turned out, not enough women decided to continue sewing and making their own clothes and Singer lost millions in its fabric stores.

—Michael Milken, 1989

The new round of investments in securities attracted new people, both as customers and service personnel. As we have seen, when the stock market revived after World War II, a goodly number of bright young graduates, almost all of them white and male, arrived to take positions at the investment banks. Many of them became brokers (or, as Charles Merrill preferred to call them, "customers' men"), for with the revival of interest in investment, that seemed to be the place where one could do quite well financially. The situation was different in the late 1970s and 1980s. Investment banking, especially in the area of new issues and takeovers, was by then the prime arena of interest. While the brokers of the 1960s hoped to earn comfortable salaries, the newcomers to the Wall Street of the 1980s aimed for positions in investment banking and trading, and thought in terms of millions of dollars or at least hundreds of thousands simply to sign on, with bonuses alone in the seven figures. The word was spread in the newspapers and on television. More of the top students were attracted to business, and of these, the most ambitious went into finance. In 1948, the nation's graduate schools turned out 2,314 M.B.A.s, and, at the height of the conglomerate movement, the number reached 8,648. This was merely a trickle compared with what was to come.

In 1978 the graduates numbered 50,331, rising to 67,527 in 1985. Many of them aimed at careers in finance. During the 1970s, 1 out of 7 Harvard M.B.A.s became investment bankers, traders, and salesmen, with the first of these occupations being preferred. By 1985 the ratio reached 1 in 4, and those holding B.A.s and B.B.A.s, especially from the elite institutions, also flocked to Wall Street. At one point one-third of Yale's undergraduate class applied for trainee positions at First Boston, where partner Bruce Wasserstein had the reputation of being the hottest player in the merger and acquisition field, a position one of his aides believed was the passport to millionaire status. Starting salaries for unseasoned trainees at major M&A banks were in the high five figures, rising to six in short order.

The New Breed

Many within the Wall Street community were distressed at this turn of events and troubled by the outlook of the new generation, which differed drastically from the views of those who sought positions after World War II—and for good reason. Several surveys of the period indicated that "being very well off financially" was a major career goal, and in one of these studies it was the primary goal for 3 out of 4 participants, nearly twice the number who responded in that fashion in 1970. Those concerned with acquiring a meaningful philosophy of life declined dramatically in the 1980s. As will be seen, this new attitude was to have repercussions in the field of education that would affect an entire generation and that represents one of the most significant alterations in the ways Americans viewed higher education.

The rise of several investment banks, whose leaders differed from those who had gone before, played a role in the change. By the 1980s, Salomon Brothers was among the more prominent of the banks, and attracted those who had a strong desire to be successful, which to them meant joining the ranks of the wealthy. While wealth always had been important, in earlier periods a position at Salomon had not been the goal of anyone who had ambitions to become part of the Wall Street aristocracy.

From its founding before World War I, the Salomon professionals lacked pedigrees. The three founders had not attended college, and the company's CEO during the post–World War II period, Billy Salomon, followed in this family tradition. Its chief bankers and traders in the early years were uneducated by the standards of the Street. "We weren't high school dropouts," boasted one of them, "we were elementary school dropouts." Richard Schmeelk, who arrived at the firm before World War II, returned there after the war, and was in charge of most foreign placements, had barely completed high school. He arrived when the B.A. was not a requirement and, at some banks, was even a drawback. This was a time when Sidney Weinberg, known as "Mr. Wall Street" to his generation, had left school after completing the eighth grade, and George Woods, CEO at First Boston, came to Wall Street as an office boy at Harris, Forbes, after graduating from Brooklyn Commercial High School. So Schmeelk's educational qualifications were not unusual for the time and place. The firm's crack arbitrageur, Richard Rosenthal, had quit high school at the age of fifteen to take a job as a runner. Lew Ranieri, who had helped create the Ginnie Mae, a key security of the period, was a dropout from St. John's University, where he had majored in English. Even those with degrees did not have distinguished academic records. John Gutfreund, who succeeded Billy Salomon as CEO, had majored in English at Oberlin and came to Wall Street after disappointments in his bid to become a theatrical producer. Bill Simon, the firm's top trader, who would later become secretary of the treasury, had attended Lafayette, where, as he told it, he majored in swimming and beer. "I never hired a B-school guy on my desk in my life," Simon told a reporter. "I used to tell my traders, 'If you guys weren't trading bonds, you'd be driving a truck. Don't try to get to get too intellectual in the marketplace. Just trade.' "

The new breed marked a distinct change from their predecessors. At one time, according to Peter Passell of the *New York Times,* newcomers were expected to adjust to the old dispensation. Now this was no longer required. "Sharp elbows and a working knowledge of spreadsheets suddenly counted more than a nose for sherry or membership in Skull and Bones." Prejudice against Jews, Catholics, blacks and women was no longer as evident. Alan "Ace" Greenberg, who had risen to head Bear Stearns, put it this way: "I look for PSD degrees—poor, smart, and a deep desire to be rich." Most of the newcomers, if appearance and impressions counted, were smart and had that desire. But few emerged from actual poverty. Rather, these were middle-class people with aspirations to move up a notch or two. One of Drexel Burham's clients thought it worth noting that the firm, which had many Jews in leadership positions, rose to the top during the LBO period, something that might not have occurred before the war. Connie Bruck, the author of *The Predator's Ball* (1988), a best-selling work on the period, put it this way:

> It used to be that the Jews would go into Manny Hanny, or Morgan Guaranty, and they'd *beg* for money, and they'd be rejected, while the Gentiles would come in and they'd all go out to lunch and smoke cigars. Now it's a shift of power to the Jews. Drexel is making these huge sums of money, and the banks comparatively little.

They certainly were original thinkers, or so ran the conventional wisdom toward the end of the decade, when the commonplace means of valuing securities using fundamental or technical methods seemed positively antique and irrelevant.

The bankers of the period serviced a wide variety of clients, but by then the corporate raiders had emerged as the most lucrative category. Raiders won even when they lost, as bewildered outsiders learned a new vocabulary, which included poison pills, white knights, shark repellents, golden handshakes, and Pac-Man defenses, all thought up by those imaginative young people with six- and seven-figure incomes. Or, to be more precise, they rediscovered the gimmicks, since most were employed in earlier eras by their forebears.

The new class of raiders was best known for financial legerdemain, not managerial skills, and had they limited themselves to raiding one might have been able to make a case for their activities. But some of them intended to take an active role in management. Such was the hubris of the newcomers of the 1980s. The conglomerateurs had assumed that a good manager could lead any company, that the switch from lumber to car rentals to electronics, for example, could be made easily. The raiders of the 1980s took this one step farther: A non-manager could manage any kind of company, they seemed to be saying. Ron Perelman, Carl Icahn, Nelson Peltz, and especially T. Boone Pickens seemed blithely confident of their abilities in this area. In some cases they proved capable enough at their tasks, but for the most part their records were spotty. More than most, Pickens, who specialized in raiding large oil companies, felt he was on a divine mission, serving the interests of the stockholders who had been ignored by the old managements. When the LBO movement was a memory, Pickens set down his thoughts on the matter:

When I first started talking about restructuring in the early 80s, some people called me a radical. They said I was really against traditional values and things like that, that I was fooling around with stuff I had no business talking about. I saw undervalued assets in the public marketplace. My game plan wasn't to take on Big Oil. Hell, that's not my role. My role is to make money for the stockholders. I just saw the Big Oil's management had done a lousy job for the stockholders, leaving an opening to upgrade the value of those assets.

Most of the raiders, Pickens included, felt themselves too strong and capable to be subservient to any banker, and were repelled by the fees the large banks demanded and got during the mid-1980s. For example, Goldman Sachs received $18.5 million for its work in Getty's sale to Texaco, and First Boston's fee for four days of work on that transaction came to $10 million. Even so, the raids could not be financed without their participation, and so the alliances continued.

Ultimately, big business struck back legislatively and in the courts. In August 1989, as the result of a strong effort of lobbying, Congress passed the Financial Institutions Reform, Recovery, and Enforcement Act (FIRREA), which required the S&Ls, where the underwriters had placed many of those junk bonds, to mark them to market, which is to say, carry them on their books at their market value rather than their face value. In addition, the S&Ls would have to sell their junk-bond portfolios by August 1994, which meant that approximately 6 percent of junk would come to the market at the same time. The S&Ls started liquidation procedures almost at once, which riled the market. While this operation was not a major cause of the S&L debacle, it did play a minor role, which was elevated by enemies of the leveraged buyout movement. At the same time, a series of legal cases against some of the manipulators and the banks reflected negatively upon the movement. By the early 1990s the LBO movement was over—but not before those aforementioned individuals and institutions had racked up major gains. So the M.B.A.s and the others who had planned on Wall Street careers went elsewhere to make their fortunes.

Whose Wealth, Whose Jobs?

Before launching into a discourse regarding who were the truly wealthy in America in this period, how these people achieved that position, and why others were not able to do so, it is necessary to reiterate that all aggregate figures pertaining to such matters have to be considered through a series of filters. Some young people require more money than others, and the same is true for older Americans. Married Americans with families have a greater need for money than single ones, and health considerations play a role, as do a myriad of other factors. Simply knowing a person's income and assets does not alone enable us to conclude whether that person is wealthy or not, or whether he or she benefited from the great boom after World War II that continues in different forms to this day.

Take the matter of where the person lived. "Gypsies," the soubriquet applied to scientists who in the 1980s flitted from one position to another, usually in different parts of the country, or college professors offered positions elsewhere, and many others, realized that the salary offered with a job was only one part of the equation—the cost of living had to be taken into consideration. Writing in 1997, economist Andrew Hacker noted just how important such matters can be:

New York's Chenango County deputy sheriffs start at $16,000. A radio news director in Vermont is offered $17,000, while in Albuquerque, New Mexico, airline reservationists make $14,000. The average salary for lay teachers in Chicago's parochial schools is $21,000. In fact, according to a recent census survey, a third of all full-time jobs pay below $20,000. Many who hold these jobs are women supplementing the family budget; but for the first time, men account for almost half the workers at this bottom tier. These are working Americans, not individuals who are unemployed or receiving public assistance. The paychecks just mentioned might suggest that a significant segment of the workforce is falling perilously close to the poverty line. But the $17,000 news director and the $16,000 deputy sheriff will be quick to tell you that they do not view themselves as poor. They may agree that they are just getting by and sometimes feel the pinch. Yet they are aware of the term *poverty* and in no way do they wish to be associated with it. That they can and do feel this way conveys a lot about just how the economy operates.

On the other side of the equation could be the Major League pitcher who receives several million dollars a year for his part-time services and believes his team is getting a bargain. Or the corporation CEO whose salary and bonus place him in the same class. In the post-post–World War II world, such matters have to be considered when estimating just who is "making it" in American society, and the whys and dimensions of the accomplishment.

These factors can be important when calculating the winners and losers in the well-publicized leveraged buyouts of this period, and the degrees and depth of the successes and failures. Invariably, when an LBO was announced, or a major merger disclosed, or an American plant closed and the ground broken for a foreign one, the newspapers would calculate and report just how many American jobs were lost. That such losses occurred was undeniable, and much of this was a continuation of the movement that began in the 1970s. Donald Barlett and James Steele, *Philadelphia Inquirer* reporters who wrote the best-selling *America: What Went Wrong* (1992), voiced the common thought that "caught between the lawmakers in Washington and the dealmakers on Wall Street have been millions of Americans forced to move between jobs that once paid $15 an hour into jobs that now pay $7." As a result of this, they wrote, "the already-rich are richer than ever; there has been an explosion in overnight new rich; life for the working class is deteriorating, and those at the bottom are trapped." This was the popular view of what had happened in the 1980s. But government statistics, compiled by the Bureau of Labor Statistics and the Census Bureau, indicate that such was not the case.

The number of jobs created in the period from January 1982 to December 1989, in the managerial/professional category, whose 1989 median earnings were $32,873, increased by 7.6 million, or one-third. In contrast, service workers increased by 2.2 million, which came to 17 percent, and these had median salaries of $14,858. However, these numbers were skewed by the movement of many part-time workers in low-skilled areas to full-time status. In all, during this period close 20 million new jobs were created, with median earnings of $23,333.

The same misunderstanding existed when it came to measuring household income. Income for the top 5 percent of the population rose from 1977 to 1990 from $117,000 to $139,000, while that of the lowest fifth of workers was virtually unchanged, at $7,000 for both years. In 1969, the wealthiest 5 percent of American families had 15.6 percent of the income, and by 1996 it had 20.3 percent. In contrast, in 1969 the poorest 20 percent of families had 5.6 percent of the income, and only 4.2 percent in 1996. The statistics seemed to bear out the assertions that in this period the rich became richer, and the poor stood still. But the raw numbers did not take into account that in this span some workers moved up the ladder and others down. When this was taken into consideration, calculated Mark Condon of the Urban Institute, the real incomes of those who were at the bottom in 1977 had risen 77 percent by 1986, which was more than fifteen times as much as those who started at the top. In his view, "the rich got a little richer and the poor got much richer." Even so, if the wealthy are defined as those whose income is seven times that of the government's definition of a "poverty line," a questionable assumption at best, according to Census data, in 1949 the poor comprised 40 percent of the population and the wealthy 0.5 percent. In 1979, the poor were a mere 13.1 percent of the population, a two-thirds decline in a thirty-year period, the kind of performance that most countries would believe quite impressive. At the same time, the rich increased to 7.4 percent of the population, a figure that liberal reformers believed indicated this group had achieved that estate through some unfair means. In fact, both statistics were to be applauded.

The United States had become the kind of society those World War II veterans hoped it would be: a place where hard work, education, playing by the rules, and sobriety paid off. As for the other statistics, the liberal reformers might ask, "Must the poor always be with us?" The reply might be that there will always be some who cannot handle capitalism and freedom. In addition, one must discover what proportion of the poor are children, unwed mothers, the elderly whose only source of support is Social Security checks, and other groups. Moreover, these raw figures cannot disclose the reasons for the poverty, or the composition of the cadre of poor. Such information might prove useful in demonstrating that the system is working well, but that some cannot or will not accede to its demands.

What caused this change? Since the 1970s, there had been a shifting need for all kinds of workers. As a result of foreign competition, technological developments, changes in marketing, and other factors, the demands for and opportunities open to unskilled and semi-skilled workers in the United States have declined. At the same time, the need for skilled workers with advanced training has expanded greatly. Whatever the situation, it seemed clear that in spite of widespread concerns about malaise, income for most Americans had risen in the 1970s, though not equally, and certainly not for skilled workers in those industries affected by job losses who were unable to find comparable work elsewhere. As indicated, the gap between the rich and the poor was becoming evident in the early 1970s. By the late 1990s, it had become what seemed to be a feature of American life, that nothing could alter. Throughout this period scholars and journalists attempted to uncover why this was so. The facts were compelling. According to government figures, the average earnings of the top fifth of the male population rose 4 percent between 1979 and 1996, while those of the bottom fifth fell by 44 percent. Some blamed this on the new technologies that were replacing unskilled workers, while others thought it was due to the loss of jobs to new immigrants.

Gary Burtless of the Brookings Institute came up with a novel notion. The main reason, he thought, was the changing pattern of marriages. In 1957, 57 percent of the poorest fifth of men were married, and this statistic fell to 43 percent by 1996. In the same period the marriage rate for the wealthiest fifth remained steady. Thus, fewer poor families had two incomes. In the same period more wives of wealthy men entered the labor force, and their salaries rose from $15,800 in 1979 to $27,200 in 1996. This was a different kind of work pattern than existed in the 1940s and 1950s.

It may well have been that the American Dream of the 1940s and 1950s had been revised in the 1970s, that the children born to the World War II generation during the baby boom had a different set of desires and priorities than their parents. But it was still in place and, as will be seen, for some who managed to find places in the new economy, the dream was realized on an even greater scale.

In 1991 Paul Leinberger and Bruce Tucker published *The New Individualists: The Generation After the Organization Man*, which was based on more than 300 interviews over a seven-year period with the children of the World War II veterans, the ones William H. Whyte had interviewed for his landmark book, *The Organization Man*. They concluded that those veterans had become "stout individualists—each in exactly the same way." By this they meant that they were not "rugged individualists," but rather employees who demanded that the organizations for which they worked be "more caring and sensitive." Even so, they did not intend to abandon corporate positions if such changes were not made.

Alternatives in Education and Implications for Wealth Gathering

The newer graduates were different qualitatively. One indication of this might be found in the scores racked up on the Scholastic Aptitude Tests. In 1963, the average for college-bound high school seniors had been 478 verbal and 502 mathematical. In 1979, the scores were 427 and 467. Those grades did not decline all at once. Rather, there was a steady erosion from the early 1960s, when the last of the World War II graduates had departed the campuses but those of the Korean Conflict were still there. For the most part, the Korean Conflict veterans had views similar to those of World War II veterans. Their academic profiles were comparable. This was not surprising. After all, they were the teenagers who went to the war movies at the local theater, listened to war news on the radio, and recalled seeing servicemen on the streets. They also realized that if the war did not end before they came of age, they had a good chance of being drafted, or would volunteer.

So to them the SATs were important predictors of what the future held. Anecdotal evidence regarding the relationship of the SATs to actual accomplishment abounded. When George Washington University initially rejected an applicant with high grades who had been his high school valedictorian but whose SATs were 310 verbal and 280 mathematical, they asked him to take private tests, which verified the SAT results. "My feeling is that a kid like this has been conned," said the dean of admissions. "He thinks he's a real scholar. His parents think he's a real scholar. He's been deluded into thinking he's gotten an education." Yet this type of student was gaining admission to colleges across the country. Given this, it was difficult to argue against the proposition that the colleges had lowered their standards, supposedly in an attempt to make certain that classrooms erected during the boom years of the 1950s were kept filled. None of this would matter in a book dealing with how Americans became wealthy after World War II were it not for the real or supposed link between education and accomplishment. As noted, after the war, especially for the GI Bill generation, the link was taken for granted. By the 1960s and certainly the 1970s, observers were obliged to conclude either that it no longer existed, or that the graduates were in for trouble in the job market. A front-page article in the *New York Times* of March 13, 1972, quoted a University of Wisconsin senior as saying, "No question about it . . . I never go to school anymore and I still get wonderful grades." This statement did not draw protests from the academic community, whose reaction was, "So? What's new? Everyone knows that standards have gone down. We don't need newspaper corroboration of what we know is a fact."

Recall the backgrounds of those baby boomer traders and bankers who arrived at what had been the second-tier Wall Street houses during the 1960s. Compare their aspirations with the dreams of the generation that came out of the Great Depression, fought World War II, and then hoped to earn a chance at the good life in the late

1940s and did so in the 1950s. Bear in mind that many of them had been successful beyond their most ambitious dreams. Their children and younger siblings did get those blue chip educations, along with vacations to Disneyland, homes in the suburbs, and the use of the family car. The baby boomers did well for themselves, and hoped for even more for their children, known as "Generation Xers" or the "Millennium Generation." But at the same time, the boomers were more willing than their parents had been to take chances. They would take quit a well-paying job they felt was uninteresting or unrewarding. They looked upon their parents as conformists, something that to them was not praiseworthy.

Even so, they seemed certain that their children would do well for themselves. The money for their educations and starts in life often was provided by parents and grandparents, and even were this not so, generous government aid packages, scholarships, work-study programs, and more were available. The dream that each generation would do better than its predecessor remained alive in the United States. Along the way, however, something went terribly wrong—for some of the grandchildren of the baby boomers, that is. The rules by which their own parents and they played were changed, and their own ambitions clashed with those of their parents and older brothers and sisters. This had an important impact on those who strove to achieve success toward the end of the twentieth century.

One of the problems was structural. As always, the economy was in a state of flux. Middle-management jobs shrank in the face of the global competition the United States faced in the postwar period. The arrival of more women in the workforce provided another form of competition. As will be seen, the coming of an economy based more on services and electronics than on manufacturing and electricity was another factor, one in which the possession of a union card was a badge of irrelevancy, not class solidarity, which in any case was by then frowned upon. Of course, not all the changes that came after the war had an impact on the young people entering the workforce in the 1980s and 1990s negatively. For example, there was franchising, bigger and more important than ever, particularly for those able to obtain rights to sell Japanese cars. New opportunities in electronics, especially relating to the Internet, were open to those qualified by intelligence, ambition, education and training, and foresight. The problem here was that the traditional means of obtaining the required education and training did not seem to serve all of the needs of the new developing economy.

The crisis was essentially one of education and outlook. Simply stated, the system that had performed so well for the grandparents did not do so for their grandchildren during the 1980s and 1990s, and this became more evident as the nation came closer to the millennium. A century earlier, a young person who lacked the proper contacts and pedigree might graduate from high school prepared for a trainee position at a nearby factory, often obtained through the intercession of a relative or friend who was already there. Then, with the growth of public college education, a number of these graduates might attend colleges, an ambition beyond the reach of their elders, and, with B.A. or B.B.A. in hand, find white-collar jobs that might lead to greater things in terms of remuneration and status, or entry into the professional classes. It seemed to work famously. Prior to World War II, less than 15 percent of high school graduates entered college. By the 1980s, college, junior college, or some other form of continuing education was the goal of most high school graduates, especially in middle-class neighborhoods.

The high schools, an American creation initially geared to serve the needs of those who thought it the last step in the educational ladder, now became the entry point to colleges. As a result, the college population increased sevenfold by the millennium, when fully 15 million students were attending. In 1949–50, when the GI generation graduated, 497,000 bachelor, graduate, and professional degrees were granted. During the 1960s the number doubled. Between 1980 and 1993, college enrollment increased 20 percent. In 2000, the number of graduates had passed the 1.7 million mark. By then it was an article of faith that a college degree was the passport to the good life. Without those magic letters after one's name, college administrators argued, one would find it virtually impossible to achieve the American Dream. Parents were urged to establish college tuition accounts for their children, at birth if possible, and the government cooperated. For those who started individual retirement accounts for the babies, it was possible to make withdrawals to pay for tuition.

The unspoken question in all of this was, what if the students are not college material? Or, for that matter, what if they did not want to go to college? What if a person's ambitions did not require four years on a campus in order to be realized? Finally, what if those students did not accept the concept that college was the key to the good life?

To further complicate the situation, most people seemed to believe that a high school diploma and college degree required the same level of effort and performance and meant the same in the 1980s and afterwards as they did in the 1950s. Such was not the case at many schools and for many students. As pressures for admission to colleges increased and the effects of movements to reform high school education were felt, a lowering of standards took hold. Then, as part of the reaction against institutions that took place in the 1960s, students questioned the need for certain required courses. In their demands for "more relevant subjects," they campaigned to end courses that once were part of the essential curriculum. Those who rejected many aspects of American life viewed these courses as attempts on the part of the "Establishment" to ignore the contributions of non-Western peoples to civilization. They claimed history and literature courses were a "parade of dead white males," not reflective of the nature of society as they saw it and part of a conspiracy to exclude entire categories of people from their educations. This resulted in eliminating or refurbishing English, foreign language, and history requirements in the high schools and then, in the 1960s, the colleges as well. This was not done in an orchestrated fashion, but rather occurred within individual school districts and colleges.

At the same time, these schools started to advocate placement of computers in classrooms, arguing that computer literacy was an important attribute for the workplace of the future. So it was—for some students, but certainly not for all of them. However, such learning need not have been obtained in the classroom. Indeed, experience soon indicated that students gained such knowledge on their own. Access to computers may have been important, but instruction in their workings was not necessarily needed. Rather, the word from employers was quite clear. Send us students who can read and understand and interpret what they read, can write in a clear and comprehensive fashion, and can solve problems.

Their grandparents and parents had honed such skills. But quite a few of the graduates of many urban high schools and some colleges in the 1980s and 1990s could not do so. A 1979 federal study estimated that 13 percent of the nation's seventeen-year-old cohort was functionally illiterate, unable to read newspapers or road maps. In 1983 a report released by the National Commission on Excellence in Education indicated that 1 out of 8 seventeen-year-olds was functionally illiterate, and the same year the Education Commission of the United States reported that a quarter of all mathematics teachers were unqualified. The commission also found that elementary students received only four hours of instruction a week in mathematics and one in science.

Some of the responses that developed were the creation of charter schools (public schools organized and run by local authorities and divorced from the central school system), home schooling, and a drift toward private schools for those who normally would have attended public high schools. For others it took the form of demands for educational vouchers, which, if fully implemented, would have revolutionized American education perhaps to the point of doing away with the public school system. In the mid-1990s, some 90 percent of all pre-college students were being educated in public schools, which included charter schools. By then there was a decided movement to seek some kind of alternative. All of which was opposed by most teacher and administrator organizations, who saw the changes as challenges to their bureaucratic powers and aspersions on their accomplishments.

Unsurprisingly, between 1973 and 1983, the number of undergraduate science majors fell by 15 percent, while the annual number of mathematics graduates fell by half, which was made up in part by the migration of foreign students to the United States.

Notwithstanding all of these problems, the boom and the belief in the ability of higher education to lift those who acquired degrees into the middle class continued unquestioned in the late 1960s and 1970s and early 1980s. But then questions emerged as to whether this was likely to continue. The most obvious signs of this were the reactions of some employers to the kinds of graduates who were applying for positions at their companies. Simply stated, they were not as able as those who had preceded them. Rather, a decline in the quality of American education, especially in the liberal arts, led employers to question the credentials of some of those young people. This did not extend to those graduates who had majored in sciences and engineering, and to some of the business school graduates. As one vice president for personnel at a major corporation indicated, "One and one still equals two, but there is no single way to judge the intrinsic merits of a painting or novel. At one time liberal arts grads could discuss it, and were prepared to defend their conclusions with solid arguments. Now far too many of them lack this facility." The reasons for this change were many and loudly debated. Some attributed it to television, others to the drug culture, more than a few blamed the faculties for having given in to student "demands." Some noted that the excellent female high school teachers of earlier periods were not being replaced by individuals with the same qualifications and abilities; bright, ambitious females no longer aspired to posts as teachers. Now that other doors were open to them they wanted to attend law and medical schools, or find places at corporations. Others blamed the Vietnam War and the reactions it had elicited, along with the general mood of protest in the 1960s.

Finally, there was a statistical measure most people at the time ignored. The graduates of the 1960s were for the most part a segment of the baby boom generation. From 1960 to 1975, the fifteen- to twenty-nine-year-old cohort had increased from 35 million to 57 million. The 1964 group of eighteen-year-olds was 1 million larger than the one that came of age in 1963, and the number increased in the years that followed. The number of new jobs created in the 1960s could not keep up with the number of young people entering the job market. As a result, while the general unemployment rate did not rise substantially, the rate for young people—who were entering the job market at the rate of 240,000 annually—increased. In retrospect, one can see that the babies born during the Great Depression, when the birth rate was low, would be in short supply for the rest of their lives, while those born during the baby boom would face problems relating to the size of the group from the time of their birth.

They would also be affected by the differences between their backgrounds and those of their parents. The baby boomers had not experienced the Great Depression and World War II. Some were rich, others were poor, but insofar as the generational experience was concerned, theirs was not as difficult as that of their parents. To them the possibilities of failure were not as excruciating, the promise of success not as alluring. Moreover, they did not seem as ambitious or as fearful of failure.

Throughout American history, the surfacing of problems would bring forth entrepreneurs eager to solve them, usually by setting up alternative mechanisms through which solutions might be realized. It was no different with education in the 1970s and beyond. Mention has been made of the use of vouchers and the establishment of charter schools, both of which have continued to grow in the late twentieth century, with charter schools becoming more popular as time went on. By 1999 there were more than 1,200 such schools that enrolled more than 300,000 students. Other, more ambitious alternatives also developed, with the goal of totally replacing the existing public school systems.

In 1991 Christopher Whittle, who had made a fortune by starting media companies and taking them public, joined with former Yale president Benno Schmidt to found what they called the Edison Project, which was to have been a chain of 1,000 for-profit schools. The structure resembled a combination of McDonald's and health maintenance organizations more than any existing school system. It seemed a promising field, as this happened at a time when there were more than 1,000 charter schools in operation, and they were proving popular with parents of gifted students.

The project foundered, however, largely due to inferior management, and the company turned to the more promising area of managing public schools. By the year 2000 it had more than fifty schools under its control, and costs were lowered and results were good. Others appeared soon after, such as Nobel Learning Communities, which had more than 150 schools under its banner and even better results at lower costs. There were attempts to purchase existing private schools, which proved difficult since many of them were owned by charitable boards or religious bodies. Other entrepreneurs entered the field of supplemental training, coaching students to enable them to score higher grades on such tests as the SATs. One of these, Sylvan Learning, was so successful that it ventured into the field of running public school systems on a fee basis, specializing in schools in areas where the majority of students were poor, and by the year 2000 was running

347

more than fifty of them in seventeen states, with generally good results.

Problems in the area of public education attracted some surprising individuals, including several investment bankers, who brought to the field expertise gained on Wall Street a decade earlier. In 1997 the investment banking firm of Kohlberg Kravis Roberts agreed to restructure the financially ailing Kinder Care, introducing a new curriculum geared to treat each student as an individual, which had initial successes. Michael Milken, the former junk-bond king, joined with the likes of Larry Ellison, the CEO of software giant Oracle, to organize Knowledge Universe, convinced that the "human-capital" market was prepared for radical changes in education. Knowledge Universe started a chain of day-care centers and a toy company, and also took minority interests in several school projects, and by the year 2000 had revenues well in excess of $1 billion.

Black parents in New York City who were unhappy with their public schools opted for home schooling in the 1960s, but in 1971 organized the Cash Campus Schools, which charged low tuitions, and whose results were markedly better. By the 1970s colleges had expanded their facilities, in the process incurring large debt obligations. College costs have escalated more rapidly than any other in our society, except perhaps health expenditures, while the contents of college educations have been watered down sharply. Students and their parents are paying more for less. As with all such matters, the causes are complex, the remedies uncertain; perhaps there are no solutions to the problems. But there are several actions that might cure at least some of them. Unsurprisingly, they involve the two central components on a campus: the faculty and the students.

At every university, the college faculties have four tiers: the superstars, the large body of the professorate, the adjuncts, and the teaching assistants. The superstars could justify their remuneration, the adjuncts and the T.A.s were paid very badly, while the professorate, on the whole, received compensation that defied the verities of economics. This does not mean that all these teachers were overcompensated. An old saying was that while a good teacher is priceless, a bad one is worthless, and it was as true in the 1990s as it ever was. It's just that colleges could get fine teachers, willing to accept adjunct positions, at lower wages.

This situation resulted in a paradox. Excellent faculty members, who had managed to find full-time positions in this Darwinian academic environment, were teaching more than a few poorly motivated, unprepared students, and this led to some ugly consequences. Those fortunate young professors observed the adjuncts slaving away, knowing that such a fate might yet be theirs, since they could easily be replaced. Poor students avoided demanding professors, whose registrations suffered as a result. Given this situation, tenure might be out of the question. So they lowered their standards in bids for popularity, and published drivel to have a record in this area that would please their chairpersons. The result was poorly taught graduates and worthless scholarship.

Faculty salaries are one of the reasons why tuition and fees at public colleges rose so sharply. Tuition and fees averaged $800 a year in 1980 and by the late 1990s they were more than $2,700, while average private college tuition had gone from $3,600 to $12,000 in the same period. Some colleges were in the $30,000 neighborhood. Total expenditures on higher education in 1980 were $25 billion; by the millennium it was $230 billion.

Some of this money was used to fatten endowments, but by far the larger portion went to running the colleges. These schools had to attract additional students to pay the bills, and so standards declined even more. Since the marginal cost of placing another student in a class is close to zero, why not accept a few more of them? Increasing the freshmen class another 100 students at a college that charges $15,000 a year in tuition would return $1.5 million, to which may be added profits from food services, the bookstore, and other places where students spend money.

Some of the professorial superstars received six-digit salaries for six or fewer hours of teaching per week, eight months a year. Because they brought in grants and provided luster for the schools, a case could be made for superstar remuneration, as it could for some rock singers who sell tickets or a hot pitcher who draws fans to ball games. The difference was that these faculty members weren't accessible to ordinary students. Was there a Nobel Prize winner on the faculty? If so, the undergraduate may be fortunate if that person was spotted walking to the library. The leaders of the schools during this period believed that those scholars were on campus to assist the school and help provide it with lucrative government contracts. A goodly number of them taught only graduate students; others, when exposed to the undergraduates, lectured to many hundreds at a time in large halls, some over television hookups. Then teaching assistants—graduate students who are what amount to academic interns—met with the undergraduates in small study groups.

What about the academic equivalent of baseball's .250 hitters, which is to say decent enough scholars who are well suited to teach undergraduates? There is a large oversupply of these aspiring professors. Virtually every department chairperson at adequate but not outstanding colleges knows that an announcement of a faculty opening will bring hundreds of applications, and that the school could have its pick of some very capable people.

For their part, college administrators devoted much effort and money to market research, recruitment, and the creation of "image." They wined and dined high school guidance counselors, dispatched alumni to recruit students, and advertised in the appropriate media. Except for a handful of colleges and universities generally recognized as superior and thus having no need to pay for promotion, the colleges functioned in much the same way as Procter & Gamble, Anheuser-Busch, and General Motors do when selling toothpaste, beer, and cars. Yet parents who shop for these products with care and knowledge of the influences of advertising don't do the same when considering higher education.

Even so, the B.A. soon became a requirement for many jobs that once were filled by high school graduates. The reason was that at one time a high school diploma signified literacy and the ability to perform basic mathematical operations. By the 1980s employers often found that the degradation of the high school diploma was such that this could no longer be taken for granted, and so they hired college graduates, assuming that they possessed these skills—only to be occasionally disappointed. Another response came in 1998, when Virginia, which at the time was spending $25 million annually for remedial courses to bring freshmen in the state colleges up to par, considered a voluntary program under which the state would guarantee the competence of graduates from its public high schools. When some of the educators complained that this cast reservations over all diplomas, others took note of the fact that college freshmen at the public colleges already were taking an average of one remedial course in their first semester. In addition, the program would be voluntary, with participation probably appealing primarily to students who feared that their elevated high school averages did not indicate their true abilities and accomplishments.

The upshot was that the college students of this period were faced with a paradox. The media, their relatives, and even the want ads informed them of a shortage of managerial and technical trainees, while employment officers enlightened them as to the facts of life regarding their preparation for the job market. The sight of a person with a Ph.D. in English or history driving a cab had been unusual in 1960. This changed. In the 1970s, such individuals had to learn to have different expectations than their parents had had, adjust to the job market, or live a life of bitter resignation. Had some of their teachers or others informed them of the changing nature of the economy and had they attempted to find a place in the new economy, such need not have been the case. Among other things, they would have been well served had they known of the franchise boom, and the arrival of employee stock ownership plans (ESOPs).

This is not to suggest that all schools, and all students, reflected these lower standards. The "best schools" continued to turn out well-prepared and educated students, as did many of those viewed as being mid-level. But graduates from the lower-level institutions faced this condition in the job market and in the quest for placement in professional and graduate schools. During the 1990–1996 period, fully half the Americans who entered the job market did so with college degrees, and they were in oversupply. The result on wages was as might have been expected when supply exceeded demand. In aggregate terms, the wage differential between high school and college graduates declined from 60 percent to 54 percent. One of the more important reasons for this was the lack of jobs for the college graduates, who were obliged to compete with high school grads for entry positions. The result was that more than 1 in 5 college grads earned less than the average high school graduate. Further study indicated that the average remuneration for college grads was lifted substantially by the inclusion of newly minted doctors, lawyers, and other professionals, as well as managers and occupants of other posts traditionally reserved for the college educated. For example, 45 percent of graduates who entered such fields as transportation, machine operation, and general labor earned less than the high school graduate median salaries. On the other hand, fewer than 1 in 4 college graduates who became involved with precision production and repair work fell into this category. Much depended on what had been studied and where, a thought that did not enter into the calculations of those who claimed that the B.A. was the key to higher remuneration. By the late 1990s, those graduates who majored in such subjects as education, social science, and general liberal arts reported monthly starting salaries of less than $2,000, at a time when high school graduates with some experience were drawing more than $4,000 as real estate brokers, better than $3,000 as insurance salesmen, and above $2,000 as legal secretaries.

The earnings of college graduates continue to advance faster than those of the general public, but the rate slowed down in the 1980s. By 1991, 16 percent of male and 26 percent of female college graduates between the ages of twenty-five and thirty-four earned less than the poverty line for a family of four, which at that time was pegged by the Census Bureau at $13,924, an improvement over the

1972 figure. Some Reagan Administration officials claimed that this was a temporary situation, which would end once society was freed from the harmful regulations that had held the economy back. But the regulations were changed and there was no improvement.

A 1998 poll by Cannon Counseling Group indicated that some 77 percent of business executives at domestic companies were willing to hire immigrants; they would take anyone with requisite skills, knowing from experience that a college education wasn't what it used to be. As noted, in the 1970s Americans turned away from domestic cars and switched to Japanese products, prompting Detroit to clean up its act. Might similar actions have jolted the schools into action?

The Dissidents

In time, the Beats of the 1950s and the New Left would metamorphose into and identify with the "Woodstock Generation," a catchall term that included Vietnam War protestors, the students for whom drugs were an important part of life, defenders of Third World leaders and peoples, assorted radicals who rejected capitalism and all it stood for, and the usual rebels against parents. At a time when women's studies and black studies were becoming quite popular, those students who elected to major in such areas often belonged in this category. To them college was a meeting ground for similarly inclined individuals, who would agree, in one way or another, that Uncle Sam was "the Great Satan." It was, perhaps, a sign of just how prosperous America had become that they were not only tolerated on the campuses, but found support from faculty members. In time they would discover that many employers would not interview graduates with these interests, proclivities, and training. Some would come to regret their youthful leanings and turn to ideas and individuals they earlier had rejected.

All of this had dawned upon young people during the 1960s and afterwards. One college graduate who had difficulty finding the kind of work he had expected while an undergraduate spoke of this to an interviewer in 1978 and concluded there was something "terribly wrong with the system. Having a college education doesn't mean that in fact you will make more money or even get a job. A guy with a high school diploma can go out and work as a common laborer and make twice the money that a kid with a college education can make." He continued, saying, "The educated individual is not needed as much in our society now. Universities have become factories. They're just grinding out thousands and thousands of college-educated individuals every year. I think a lot of kids and parents are realizing that perhaps college isn't necessary."

Leaders of the educational establishment tended to ignore such talk, and in 1998 they observed that college graduates earned $40,478 annually, which was 77 percent more than high school graduates ($22,895) and high school dropouts ($16,124). But critics of this approach responded that one of the reasons for this situation was that smarter and more ambitious students tended to remain in school, and so this proved an example of self-fulfilling prophecies. Moreover, there was a shortage of some specialists that presented a constant problem. For all the talk of how specialists involved in electronics and related fields might be best created through education on the job, the electronics industry haunted the better schools, seeking their graduates. Toward the end of the 1990s, American colleges and universities were turning out engineers at the rate of 65,000 annually, and most of them had no trouble finding employment. But engineering, especially electronic engineering, is a field in which knowledge quickly becomes obsolete, and the need for constant upgrading has taxed the abilities of many companies to keep up. In any case, engineers who could do the job were in constant demand. Just as Wall Street investment banks offered large bonuses to investment bankers willing to come aboard, electronics firms were prepared to pay bonuses to any employee who located engineers prepared to accept job offers.

All of which is to suggest that the business picture for the grandchildren was more complicated than it had been for their grandparents. However, the potential rewards for those who could meet the demands of the marketplace were greater as well. While some of the grandparents may not have been willing to trade their yesterdays for their grandchildren's tomorrow, others, with more insight into what the new technology implied and awareness of how opportunities would be greater in the new post–Cold War world than at any other time, might well disagree.

9

THE NEW VIEW OF RETIREMENT AND EDUCATION

Strayer Distance Learning, also known as Strayer ONLINE, is a division of Strayer University designed for those students who desire to integrate academic study with their professional lives in order to enhance their careers or to accomplish personal goals. It is beneficial particularly for those students who cannot attend the traditional classroom environment because of demanding work schedules.

—Strayer University Catalog, 1999

The Passing of the GI Generation

Let us return to the veteran who had been born in 1920 and entered the armed forces in 1942, to be discharged in 1946 at the age of twenty-six, at which point he married, attended college, graduated in 1950, found a job, started a family, which eventually included three children, and along the way purchased a suburban house, a four-door sedan to be driven to work, and a station wagon for his wife. He would have moved up the economic ladder in the years that followed, by dint of hard work and playing by the rules, and with the help of a buoyant economy and a strong market. He probably was dismayed by the antics, though not necessarily the political and social goals, of his children and their friends. Such a person would have been sixty-five years old in 1985, and prepared to retire. His children would have left the nest, the last around 1980. Perhaps two had married and had children, and one of them might have divorced on a more or less amicable basis. He would have Social Security income, maybe a pension from the company for which he worked, along with money in an individual retirement account and other savings. But perhaps not.

Retirement did not mean vegetation, however. Many retirees found part-time work, either because they felt the need for additional money or because life without work would lose much of its meaning. Some worked for the social aspects it provided. A large number of retirees used their free time to engage in a variety of hobbies, from gardening to bridge, to carpentry to taking adult education courses. The arrival of the Internet proved timely, and many started spending hours in front of the screen, sending and receiving E-mail messages, buying and selling stock, browsing, or engaging in a cyber version of adult education.

Some had financial problems. By the late 1990s, half of American workers were covered by pension plans. Only two-thirds of those given the opportunity to participate in company-sponsored 401(k) plans (of which there were 200,000, with assets of more than $1 trillion), which became a major source of retirement income, did so. The average account balance was more than $37,000 and the median balance was below $10,000 for the more than 30 million participants. But 50 million workers had no pension plan other than Social Security.

With memories of the Great Depression, World War II veterans would have been troubled by the looming problems of old age, and considered preparing for their futures while still in their fifties. They might sell their homes and move to an area where there were compatible people. Just as William Levitt had erected Levittown, New York, with a specific population in mind—the World War II veterans and their families—so other builders constructed communities in the 1970s and after, with the same populations as their targets, only by then those veterans would be retired, with needs and desires different from those young families of the late 1940s.

While no single builder of retirement housing achieved the fame and significance of Levitt, for some Del Webb came close. In the early 1960s, getting in ahead of the wave, Webb purchased 8,900 acres of cotton fields in Arizona, on which he constructed homes, most of which were just a step or two above those Levitts of the late 1940s. There were 47,000 residents with a median age of sixty-nine, more than a third of whom were over the age of seventy-five. They had a median income of $22,000, a level that at that time was 30 percent higher than that for their cohort, and they had savings. People who filled this template were considered affluent. Soon the West and South were dotted with Sun Cities, Golden Ponds, Leisure Worlds, Sun Centers, and the like. "Gray Power" was a formidable political force in California, Arizona, the Carolinas, and especially Florida.

The houses sold for between $50,000 and $270,000, and most were paid for with cash and no mortgage, the money coming from the sales of the buyers' former homes. In these communities there were more S&Ls than supermarkets, and by the 1980s there were more than $2 billion in deposits. Doctors, dentists, and hospitals were close by. Stock market firms rushed to open offices, and Merrill Lynch reported that the average portfolio was $50,000.

These builders calculated that the retirees would also want low-maintenance homes, sunny weather, recreational facilities (especially golf), and clubhouses where they might play bridge, attend shows, and participate in other activities. There should be access to popularly priced restaurants (which offered "early bird" specials), and few, if any, children, which meant low school taxes and less crime. Just as taking care of the needs of the young veterans and their families helped energize the economy after World War II and was a factor in the growth of franchised businesses, so the new communities would provide stimuli to the local and general economy. The parent-teacher associations had been important to the families of the 1950s, and in like fashion the American Association of Retired People (AARP) was a central force in the lives of the soon-to-be retired. A combination special-interest, lobbying, and marketing organization, the AARP offered its members lower prices on a variety of goods and services, from wheelchairs to insurance to housing to travel. By the 1980s it was deemed one of the most powerful lobbying forces in Washington, ever trying to obtain new and added benefits for its members.

Michael Weiss's *The Clustering of America* (1988) offers a study of this generation in its retirement years. He claims that he can tell a great deal about anyone if told his or her postal zip code. Like people tend to flock together, he says, with justification. He then divides Americans into forty "lifestyle clusters." One of his clusters was the "Golden Ponds," which in the late 1980s accounted for more than 5 percent of the population. These were inhabited by those fifty-five years old and over who had median incomes of $20,140 and a median home value of $51,537. They had high school educations, were likely to belong to civic clubs; drove Dodge Diplomats, AMC Eagles, and Mercury Grand Marquises; watched TV quiz programs and soap operas; and were more interested in local environmental matters than in foreign policy. Their upscale counterparts, whom Weiss categorized as "Pools & Patios," were 3.4 percent of the population, some of whom had graduated from Levittown years earlier; were college graduates with white-collar jobs; and were between the ages of forty-five and sixty-four. Their median household income was $35,895, and the value of their homes $99,702. They read the *Wall Street Journal* and *The New Yorker*, drove Alfa Romeos and BMWs, and their TV fare included *60 Minutes* and *Newhart*. "The Furs and Station Wagon" group, which had done somewhat better, was 3.2 percent of the population, with an income of $50,086 and owned homes worth $132,725. They belonged to country clubs, were on their second marriages, bought imported wine by the case, read *Gourmet* and *Bon Appetit*, favored BMWs and Jaguars, and watched *The Tonight Show* and *60 Minutes*. Those who remained in the Levittowns of America, 3.1 percent of the population, generally were high school grads with white-collar jobs who had median incomes of $28,742 and houses valued at $70,728. They were partial to bowling, drove Yugos and Mercury Marquises, liked instant iced tea and English muffins, and enjoyed the TV program *Lifestyles of the Rich and Famous*. But they also enjoyed ice hockey on TV.

So it went. At least by Michael Weiss's measures.

There were others who did not fit into Wiess's categories due to reasons of health. Instead they went to retirement homes offering "assisted living," meaning that for physical or mental reasons, or a combination of both, the retirees required the assistance of professionally qualified personnel to get about and perform some tasks. In earlier periods, such individuals might have been cared for by relatives, but not in the 1980s, when those familial caregivers tended to have their own lives to consider. So facilities were organized by professionals and others to care for this population. The most striking examples of these were located in the rural and suburban South, much of which had been bypassed by the economic changes of the post–World War II period and had a plentiful supply of unskilled yet responsible labor. Some of them specialized in caring for those stricken by Alzheimer's disease and similar ailments whose relatives preferred them to be in some out-of-the-way location.

Even more pervasive was the growth of nursing homes. Most of these were founded by individuals involved with the health-care industry. But in time many were gobbled by chain operations, such as Beverly Enterprises, which obtained management contracts and in many cases ownership. The best known and largest of these was Hospital Corporation of America, which was co-founded by Jack Massey, who earlier had helped organize Kentucky Fried Chicken. Like KFC, HCP was noted for its economical operations, and for a while its stock was a star on Wall Street. Thus, entrepreneurship entered virtually every aspect of American life.

For wealthy Americans at the turn of the millennium, such places were not unthinkable, especially when a large portion of the cost was paid for by government programs. These "human warehouses" also helped resolve an embarrassing unemployment problem. Parents had encouraged their offspring to seek advanced degrees at a time when the job market in social work and psychology was quite limited, and now the degree holders were able to find employment in this booming area of geriatric caregiving.

Finally, the suburbs became less monochromatic. In 1970, 1 out of 4 blacks lived in areas the Census Bureau defined as suburban, itself a large leap from what had been the situation in the days of William Levitt. By 1990, demographer William Frey of the State University of New York at Albany, examining the census of that year, estimated that 40 percent of blacks were suburbanites, while the Los Angeles suburb of Monterey Park was 60 percent minority—most of them Chinese Americans. Out of this and other studies came a new term, *ethnoburb*, to reflect what had become a new reality.

So we return once more to the question: who or what had been responsible for all of this? There is a tendency in America both to blame and to credit presidents with events that took place during their administrations for which they actually had little responsibility. So it was that Herbert Hoover did not cause the Great Depression and Franklin D. Roosevelt did not take the nation out of it. Harry Truman and Dwight Eisenhower bore little blame or credit for the postwar prosperity, except in that both presidents supported Cold War expenditures, which played such an important role in the development of the military-industrial complex, which, as noted, was really the military-industrial-educational complex. The Cold War came to an end during the administrations of Ronald Reagan and George Bush, but how much credit they deserve for this accomplishment can be debated with no resolution.

Reagan made it clear that educational reforms would

be one of the important parts of his agenda. He also averred that poor educational opportunities were a major reason for the inability of black Americans to achieve the levels of success of their white counterparts. By the late 1990s less than half the nation's public school students could read at their grade levels. Newspapers ran stories comparing performance in largely black charter and private schools to the achievements of students in public schools. By most measures, the public schools were laggards. At the time, the chances for abandonment of public education by blacks as well as whites and an acceptance of what in time could become a voucher system and charter schools looked good, with larger than anticipated numbers of graduates entering and completing college. In this regard, public education, which to the GI generation seemed a cornerstone of the Great Boom, was being disowned.

New Educational Paradigms

One of the more unusual developments in secondary education occurred in the Bronx, New York, where James Monroe High School became a haven for drug and weapon dealers and had to be closed, its students dispersed to other schools in the area. The Board of Education and the Center for Collaborative Education took over, and transformed the building into Wings Academy. Special career programs were developed in conjunction with the State University of New York, Bronx Lebanon Hospital, and Hostos Community College. Starting out with 59 students in 1994, its enrollment soon grew to 380, and test scores increased sharply. Wings and similar schools that have developed since then are openly vocational in tone, which the students seem to appreciate, since they feel they are being prepared for meaningful work, which would be their passport into the middle class.

Community colleges, offering two-year programs and A.A. degrees, were among the winners in this switch to educational alternatives. Not only were classes there scheduled at convenient times for working people, but the faculties seemed to appreciate that their students were interested in usable knowledge, not abstract ideas, no matter how interesting they might be. In addition, costs were lower, and this was a major factor.

With the arrival of the Internet came a plethora of on-line courses, which, while not as acceptable to many employers at first, were beginning to achieve a higher status by the end of the century. In some parts of the country, the stress in this area was on certificates to indicate successful completion of requirements for elementary or secondary school diplomas. In 2000, Michael Saylor, the president of MicroStrategy Inc., pledged $100 million to launch an on-line university.

The movement toward alternatives was not limited to the elementary and secondary schools or to the creation of large-scale Internet programs that initially attracted only a small number of students. In the area of college education, experiments were being carried out in all parts of the country. Some were conducted by individual faculty members, or departments, or, at the most, divisions. But a few affected the basic mission of the school itself. We already have seen how the Vietnam War and civil rights movement caused changes in the schools, motivated by political and humanitarian impulses. There were other changes, deeper and more lasting, that emerged from a questioning of the mission of the college in the new kind of world that seemed to be emerging in the

1980s and afterwards. Most of these were conducted quietly and attracted little attention outside of the schools themselves and academic circles in general. Some of the others became topics of widespread debate.

Savio Chan, who arrived in the United States from Hong Kong in 1985, and worked at an accounting firm during the day and attended college at night, switched from job to job, and wound up as a salesman making $100,000 a year in commissions. Chan dropped out of college, realizing that he was learning more on the job than he was in the classroom. He joined with a friend to found Computer Emporiums. In the late 1980s Chan became friendly with Charles Wang, who had moved from Shanghai to New York, where in time he would form Computer Associates, which became the nation's second largest software firm (after IBM). Chan and Wang were part of the immigrant flow that was invigorating American business. Wang informed Chan about some of the opportunities in the field, which included a shortage of about a quarter of a million computer specialists. The colleges were not doing their jobs, said Wang. A different modality was needed.

Out of these conversations came Technology Training Solutions, which did so well that Microsoft certified it as a training center. Soon word was out that completion of a TTS program was the path to well-remunerated work in the field. By 1998 TTS had two schools, one in New York City, the other on Long Island, and plans were being made for additional ones. Chan envisaged a nationwide chain, for which he would have an initial public offering of stock shortly after the millennium. He made plans to franchise the schools, in this way overcoming his shortage of capital. Chan was providing a route into the middle class for many ambitious would-be computer technicians as well as wealth for himself. It was an old formula, the wedding of demand and supply to produce profits. Schools like TTS would not replace colleges, but they would provide an alternate route to success for an increasing number of students. Toward the end of the 1990s such enterprises were among the fastest-growing segments of the market, and had joined the franchise boom.

Strayer University, founded in 1892 as Baltimore-based Strayer Business College, was one of these new kinds of schools. In 1904, Strayer organized Washington, D.C.'s second business school, but then it remained content to rest on its laurels, as a well-recognized provider of second-level graduates for local businesses. In 1969, Strayer was licensed to grant bachelor of science degrees as Strayer College, and in 1987, the M.A. was added to its quiver.

Strayer was owned by Strayer Education and was accredited by the Middle States Association of Colleges and Schools and other rating agencies. Ultimately it had twelve campuses in Washington, D.C., Maryland, and Virginia, offering classes around the clock, seven days a week. In addition, classes were offered on the Internet. Strayer concentrated on attracting local and foreign students, drawing them from more than fifty countries, to be served by a faculty largely composed of part-timers who held full-time positions in government and industry. The school proved very successful in placing its graduates, who were attracted by its low tuition, flexible hours, programs for part-timers, and reputation for finding jobs for graduates. By the 1990s an ambitious on-line program enabled students to take the courses—exams included—on the Internet. By then the school had several campuses, enrolled more than 10,000 students, and reported that well over half its part-time students were earning more than $30,000 a year, with 14 percent in the $50,000-and-over category. Students seeking training for a vocation (as opposed to a liberal arts education) were attracted by such a record, as were employers. Academic critics protested that this was not truly what education was supposed to be, while defenders responded that today's students were more interested in knowledge that could be applied to contemporary business and technological problems than in the abstract notions that were being discussed at the nation's supposedly elite schools.

Then there was the University of Phoenix, which lacked an established campus as well as conventional students and faculty members. Rather, Phoenix—which by 1999 operated in thirteen states and the District of Columbia—located its classrooms in buildings near freeway exits so as to be convenient for its students and faculty. Its classes used computers extensively, and its student body was comprised in large part of managers and others who needed both the credentials and the knowledge to proceed further with their careers. The school even offered an M.B.A. over the Internet, and its success has led to imitations by conventional schools of higher education, including such prestigious institutions as Duke, Stanford, Penn State, and Ohio State Universities, all of which were motivated, in part at least, by shortages of trained personnel in the new technology. Phoenix aimed to accomplish in a six-week course what usually took ten weeks at a traditional college. Then the work was, in effect, graded twice—once by the instructor, the second time by the company for which the student worked, which often paid a substantial part of the tuition.

Owned by the Apollo Group, like Strayer, Phoenix was unabashedly a for-profit operation, which charged low tuition and paid its faculty members salaries far below those offered by conventional universities. Given the oversupply of Ph.D.s in the 1990s, attracting qualified teachers was not difficult. There is no evidence that Phoenix graduates were any less prepared for entry positions in the job market than were those of second-tier public universities. Moreover, as will soon be seen, the university was in the middle of one of the fastest-growing technological centers in the nation. At one time Columbia and New York University profited greatly from being able to send their liberal arts and professional school graduates to Manhattan's financial centers, law firms, hospitals, and the like. In the late twentieth century it was the turn of universities like Phoenix.

There was opposition to parts of the program from conventional faculty members. "A lot of schools have been trying to get on-line programs through their faculty councils for years, and all they ever do is get ready to get ready," said Robert Tucker, the head of the Phoenix-based research assessment firm InterEd. "Then they end up trying to shoehorn a traditional classroom into a virtual one."

Some conventional colleges reacted by carefully drawing the distinction between what they were offering and the programs of institutions like the University of Phoenix. "Distance learning and for-profit universities are delivering one product," said New York University dean Matthew Santirocco. "Our kind of university is delivering something different, in loco parentis, a model of community with mentoring and classroom interaction." Phoenix claimed to have both, though not as intensively as programs offered by N.Y.U. But Harvard dean Harry Lewis conceded that the programs offered by traditional colleges were geared more to pleasing the parents than the students. "There is something troubling about students working so hard to fulfill the dreams of others. It makes it harder for them to discover something on their own, get excited, and pursue it." Which is the point of it all, and why Phoenix was so appealing to many students. Nor was it the only college engaged in remaking the collegiate experience.

Baker College was another attempt to reinvent the college. Like Phoenix, it lacked a true campus, but rather operated its main facility from a number of formerly abandoned buildings on the outskirts of Flint, Michigan. They abutted a fast-food operation and a gasoline station with an auto parts store nearby—all of which were franchises, thus wedding traditional education and a new form of vocational education. The campus was not the central learning site. In this school a good deal of instruction took place over the Internet.

The main road leading to the campus is called Opportunity Avenue, which offers an idea of the school's goals. It is headed by Edward Kurtz, whose title is CEO, not president or chancellor. The school was founded in 1968, at which time it was operated out of six rooms over a paint store in downtown Flint, its major mission the training of secretaries for employment in the automobile industry. However, Baker soon expanded to offer more academic programs.

By the end of the century, as the result of intense recruiting and constant upgrading, the Flint campus was home to 5,000 students, some of whom were residents, and the school operated nine other campuses in different parts of the state. It offered a regular liberal arts program, but was basically involved in career preparation, especially in health care, technical fields, and business management. According to one student, Baker's program offered the best of resident colleges and on-line instruction. "I get to study here in my room on my own time," she said, "but if I need something, people are right next door."

"We're less concerned with making you a well-rounded individual than we are with making sure you get a good job and do well at it," said Kurtz. Through careful budgeting, Baker kept tuition down to less than $5,300, a fraction of the cost of conventional private colleges. For those who enter with a 3.5 high school average, there is an automatic partial scholarship. Most of the faculty members teach part time, and are employed in the fields in which they offer instruction.

Is this the college of the future? At a time when liberal arts majors with degrees from well-established colleges had difficulties not only finding jobs but even getting interviews, Baker graduates were succeeding in both areas. So were the holders of degrees from Jones International University, which offered all its courses over the Internet. It did not take long for the Jones experience to filter down to the cash-poor public colleges. By 1999 UCLA's administration had recommended that all liberal arts courses have Web sites. This prompted faculty reaction in the form of noncompliance.

The small classes, Internet instruction, and concentration on the needs of the marketplace seemed to be paying off. The baby boomers and their offspring were adapting well to this reinvention of the college. No one seriously thinks such schools as Strayer, Phoenix, and Baker are going to replace the traditional schools, much less the Ivies. But in a new age with new requirements, they certainly have found a niche.

It is too early to come to meaningful conclusions about the new paradigms. Much of the judgment will depend on what students and employers expect of the collegiate experience. Both groups seem to agree that there is more to a college education than what is learned from professors and in classrooms, libraries, and laboratories.

There is an acculturalization process to be considered. The CEOs and COOs of the future will have to possess wide interests and be able to discuss subjects other than those relating to business. Recall the message Henry Kissinger received from a family friend when he considered enrolling at City College of New York to train to become an accountant. Fritz Kramer had told him, "Henry, a gentleman does not go to City College. He goes to Harvard." Kissinger took the advice and attended Harvard. Given the world of the 1940s and 1950s, one may conclude that his career would have been quite different had he become a CCNY-trained accountant. The advice is still good, but not to the extent that it was half a century ago. Today's college graduate knows that the Ivy League cachet is still important, but not as much as it was when Kissinger was a student. Rather, the college graduate realizes that to get ahead it is necessary to be educated in a wide variety of subjects, to be able to speak intelligently about them, and to be prepared to process information and ideas that are not directly related to work if he or she hopes to be more than a technician.

Even so, the colleges have to deal with basic economic considerations. Anyone who has taken Economics 101 learns that an increase in supply with no large increase in demand should result in a lowering of prices. This hasn't happened in higher education, where one of the greatest costs is faculty salaries. In the 1970s, as a result of economic problems of that decade, faculty salaries barely moved, and did not keep up with the cost of living. This changed in the 1980s, when the increases made up for lost time and rose faster than the inflation rate.

In 1980 the college student population was 12 million; by the year 2000 it was over 15 million. More than 1 out of every 5 Americans over the age of twenty-five has completed four years of college. The reason is not a sudden love of learning or a sharp increase in the national intelligence. Rather, parents were told their infants haven't a chance in this world without a college education, and they probably didn't consider that not every eighteen-year-old is what used to be called "college material." Some young people have other interests, some lack maturity and judgment, and some, simply stated, aren't bright enough to benefit from what colleges have to offer. A large number of them have received shoddy high school educations, and so require heavy doses of remedial work. Colleges reported that some 30 percent of entering freshmen had serious problems in reading, writing, and mathematics.

No matter—they attended college anyway. The day after the baby was taken home from the hospital, the proud parents started putting away money every month, often in a mutual fund, targeted for tuition. Less fortunate young men and women took out major loans to pay for college, and then pauperized themselves for many years to pay for an education they may not have truly received. Like the scarecrow in the *Wizard of Oz*, they had a diploma, but it didn't necessarily provide them with the knowledge and skills that meaningful jobs in the workplace demand.

How could this decline of standards and results have happened without leading to an uproar? If an auto company had put out inferior products, it would have lost customers. Indeed, this was what happened in that industry during the 1960s and 1970s. But those parents who were saving for their offsprings' higher education didn't seem to care very much about what was happening at the colleges their children attended, a sin of omission rather than commission. They may have visited the place once or twice when selecting a school, and then not set foot on campus again until graduation.

The result of all of these forces was a generalized lowering of standards, to the point where employers complained that the high school graduates who were applying for positions were unprepared, and so they were obliged to set up remedial programs of their own, and then the same kind of problem appeared among college graduates. In 1981 a bank officer told a *Wall Street Journal* reporter that "half or more of the applicants who we're seeing straight out of [high] school can't write a complete sentence." The loss of literacy had many results. For example, the Internal Revenue Service revised its 1981 forms to conform with ninth-grade reading levels, two full grades below the earlier forms.

If the B.A. degree meant little, perhaps the M.B.A. would take its place as the entry credential. But, as we have seen, not all M.B.A.s were created equal. New programs geared for B.A.s who would take their advanced degrees part time, while working, were developed by the dozens. By the 1990s there were more than 140 such programs, with students who averaged thirty-seven years of age and had approximately seventeen years of work experience. So some positions required more than the four-year degree. Others called for less than that.

Reinforcing the thought that some occupations did not require four years of a college education, high school graduates who became machinists, food-service workers, and lodging and clerical supervisors were doing quite well, with starting salaries higher than those of many college grads. In addition, positions requiring a two-year A.A.S. degree, such as paralegals and nurses, started out at salaries higher than those of B.A.s and B.B.A.s. One sign of this was the appearance of a significant number of college graduates in junior college classes. At a loss to understand this at first, the junior colleges later explained that the B.A.s awarded to such students did not enable them to find jobs, or at the very least a place in society, and so they went to the junior colleges to acquire salable skills.

At the same time, a number of college graduates opted for jobs as police officers and firefighters, positions for which college degrees often were not required. This phenomenon attracted the attention of educators, sociologists, and others interested in such matters. In some cases the graduates indicated that they did not believe there necessarily had to be a relationship between their studies and their work. They attended college to acquire an education, was a common reply, and it had nothing to do with the kind of work they intended to do. One Cornell graduate, when asked about those who questioned his choice of police work in New York City, replied, "They don't understand. They say, 'With that kind of education?' They think you are wasting it. But I don't feel that way. I feel like I'm doing what I want to do." One man who had an M.A. degree in environmental sciences from New York University and was earning $40,000 a year as an insurance investor left that work to enter the police academy, and after graduating earned $23,000. But he rose in the ranks, and by the late 1990s commanded a precinct and was earning $68,000.

The New York Police Department did not release such information, but a spokesman allowed that dozens of graduates of elite universities had joined the force. A private poll conducted in the mid-1990s disclosed that onefifth of the force held college degrees, which came to 7,350 police officers, and that another 535 held advanced and professional degrees. When interviewed, several replied they had been attracted by incentives—hefty pensions, lofty ideals, and adventure—which also would have been familiar to both their grandparents, who were concerned with long-run incentives, and their parents, who asserted their individuality and desire to "do good." "Not to sound corny," said one such officer, "but I always liked helping people and this is a real helping people job."

The America of the immediate post–World War II period seemed a country in which those who were prepared to make sacrifices would be able to join the middle and perhaps the upper class. The change from this attitude did not take place overnight. Rather, over a period of more than a generation, it seemed the country was dividing into a place where there were winners and losers, and the possibilities of passing from one category to the other were becoming more questionable. Yet in the early 1970s none of this was very obvious.

To return to the impact of education on wealth and status, it is worth noting that those graduates who were accepted for franchises also earned more than their classmates. More than one observer commented that the cost of a franchise was less than that of a four-year college degree. Some dropouts realized that these were professors who had ideas formed in a different generation, one with little relevance for the present. One of these was Federal Express founder Fred Smith, who had been informed by his economics professor that his idea for an express service to compete with the U.S. Post Office was unrealistic. Then there were the Internet pioneers, led by college-dropout Bill Gates and followed by literally hundreds of others, who perceived no relationship between what college had to offer and what they wanted to do with their lives. Those who entered college spent more time in the computer labs than in classes, and then, after a year or so, dropped out. Michael Dell was a student at the University of Texas in 1983 who devoted more time to building and selling personal computers in his dormitory room than boning up for exams. When his sales reached $80,000 a month, Dell dropped out, and in the next few years remade the face of the industry. Those who remained to complete their studies included large numbers of indifferent students who were there primarily because their parents and society at large informed them that without college degrees their lives were bound to be dire. Even those who later entered the mainstream of the new economy might reflect that they had suffered financially due to their choice. Christopher Lawson, a 1981 Princeton graduate, was one of those who had been involved with Microsoft from its origins. Bill Gates urged Lawson to leave Princeton and join him, but Lawson opted to remain until graduation, whereupon he took a post at the company. But by delaying his entry, Lawson received far less by way of founders' stock than otherwise would have been the case. Lawson's story and many similar ones instructed hundreds, perhaps thousands, of computer nerds who could not perceive the relationship between what was going on in the classrooms and their interests. Some of their professors attempted to explain the importance of education for the full life, but all these students had to do was look at the majority of their classmates, who were not particularly interested in such matters, and contrast them with the ones who eschewed college for the workplace.

These famous businesspeople were hardly unique. Writer Brigid McMenamin noted that "fifty-eight members of the Forbes 400 either avoided college or ditched it partway through. These fifty-eight—almost 15 percent of the total—have an average net worth of $4.8 billion. This is 167% greater than the average net worth of the 400, which is $1.8 billion. It is more than twice the average net worth of those 400 members who attended Ivy League colleges."

Might it be that the nongrads got such a head start in their careers that the others never caught up? Or are those numbers just a fluke? Either way, there is growing evidence in the country that college diplomas aren't what they are cracked up to be when it comes to obtaining gainful and satisfying employment.

Financial factors had to be taken into consideration, especially when it came to the increasingly important matter of tuition, living expenses, and the forgone income for the students while attending classes. Sean Levatino, an honor student at Albany Academy, was set to enter Worcester Polytechnic Institute, with his parents' blessings. Then they reconsidered. "Are we doing the right thing to push him to get a college degree?" they wondered.

The degree could run Dr. and Mrs. Levatino $120,000. If they were instead to invest that money in municipal bonds paying 5 percent, Sean would have a nest egg of $500,000 by his fiftieth birthday. That's far more than most college grads can hope to accumulate in that time. And the prospective income from that $500,000 is a lot more than the theoretical premium that college grads own over nongrads.

By the mid-1990s, manuals appeared explaining this to those who saw little use for a college education as it was formulated in the 1990s. J. Michael Farr's *America's Top Jobs for People Without College Degrees* (JIST Works) could not have found a publisher in the late 1940s. It became a popular work half a century later.

None of the writers who noted the turning away from college education analyzed the social and economic backgrounds of those who chose paths other than college. Invariably, they were the sons and daughters of first-generation college attendees who had their degrees from public colleges. The Harvard and Yale graduates made whatever sacrifices were needed to be certain their progeny attended their alma maters. Attendance at such prestigious schools did not mean they would be exposed to the renowned members of the faculty listed in the school's catalog. By the 1960s, the most distinguished faculty members were won over by promises that they would not even see an undergraduate unless they bumped into one walking from building to building, and that their classroom exposures would be quite limited. More and more of their time was being spent at those off-campus facilities. Little wonder, then, that some of the brighter students in the sciences came to understand that they could learn more at the plant of some electronics company located near Stanford than as an undergraduate at Stanford itself, especially when the faculty stars were employed at the company and were quite prepared to act as mentors for the younger people there, a role they might have been loath to assume at the university.

The America into which the grandchildren of the World War II veterans had graduated was one where engineers who could resolve problems, handle data, and make the proper presentations could write their own tickets. But it was also a world where those reluctant college students who had been unprepared for difficult work could not find employment. By the end of the 1990s, several technological centers were going still farther by organizing consortia to present candidates in school board elections, supporting charter schools, and making other efforts to raise standards in order to produce the kinds of candidates their companies needed. Some companies went so far as to organize their own charter schools intended primarily for the children of their employees but open to others in the community as well. In recent years these companies have found this to be an attractive fringe benefit.

Consider the major investments made in infrastructure during the 1950s—schools, highways, and even housing. There was little need for new schools by the 1960s, and the highway program was well underway. Infrastructure creation and repair had been well funded and the programs would go on, but there were no major new ones on the horizon. Cold War spending would continue, as would expenditures relating to the space program, the most important new government initiative of the late 1950s.

Even so, the economy did not level off and then fluctuate due to the much-feared recession or depression anticipated during and immediately after the war. Rather, it occurred because of a lowering—and an adjustment—of expectations.

10

"The electric light is very probably a great invention, and . . . let us take it for granted that its future development will be vast. But this, unhappily, cannot be urged as a reason why the pioneers' companies should be prosperous." Time and technology have moved on since 1882, when these words appeared in *The Economist*. But the same sentiments apply to today's great invention, the Internet. Because it is a potent and entirely new medium, the Net will change the way the world works and plays. Even so, today's pioneering Internet companies are unlikely ever to earn the vast profits needed to justify their current share prices. Indeed, future historians may well add Internet shares to the long list of industrial assets—including biotechnology firms in the 1990s, radio companies in the 1920s, electric light companies and railways in the 19th century—that have come spectacularly crashing to earth.

—*The Economist*, February 1999

The creation of technopolises, nerdistans, and the like did not mean that the old ways of urban work, recreation, and education were abandoned. There was to be no wholesale relocation to new centers on the part of those who would live and work there. The older industrial cities were not bound to disappear, or even shrink. After all, in the new world of the Internet, people would still drive automobiles constructed in factories, although those factories might no longer be in the Detroit area but rather scattered throughout the South. By the 1980s, a majority of the "Japanese cars" sold in the United States were not manufactured in Japan. The popular Honda Civics came off assembly lines in Ohio and Ontario; the Nissan Sentras from factories in Tennessee and Aguascalientes, Mexico; and many Toyota Corollas were built in California and Ontario. The Japanese companies located their assembly lines out of the country for several reasons, not the least of which was to overcome protests that Japanese workers had taken well-paying jobs from Americans. By the 1990s, however, despite rhetoric at elections and when it came time to debate the North American Free Trade Agreement (NAFTA), most American buyers didn't seem to give the matter much thought.

Nor did these changes signify the end of the evolution. With the arrival of the World Wide Web came the creation of virtual communities. Members communicated with one another, using bulletin boards and E-mail, exchanging information, buying and selling, hiring and firing, and in most ways behaving as though they were members of a society with its own rules, objectives, and missions. Once more, it is difficult to say just where this will lead—or end—or whether it will not end but rather keep evolving, which seems more likely. A large number of very bright and ambitious people spend many hours each day in front of computer screens, communicating, working out business arrangements, and, most important, sharing information. Stories were told of offices where co-workers, rather than actually talking to each other directly, communicated by means of E-mail. This is one extreme of the new age. At the other are the cities and actual communities so familiar to the grand-parents of those young people, the GIs who came home in 1945. They are not going to abandon the old ways except in peripheral areas, and there is no reason for them to do so.

There certainly is room and a need in the America of the present and future for those older cities. "Deindustri-alization," the mantra of the doomsayers who in the 1970s warned that America's industrial base was being eroded, was disavowed by industrialists in such cities as Youngstown, Detroit, and others when older companies left—but new ones arrived. Originally a center for steel, Pittsburgh transformed itself into one for biotechnology. Houston, a focus for the petroleum industry and once considered a candidate for deindustrialization, was by the end of the 1980s one of the nation's leading cities in terms of population growth, employment, retail sales, residential construction, and office space. Reflecting upon this, in 1978 *U.S. News & World Report* declared that Houston was "bursting out all over":

> Houston is not a city. It's a phenomenon—an explosive, roaring urban juggernaut that's shat-tering traditions as it expands outward and upward with an energy that surprises even its residents . . . Absorbing capital, people, and new corporations like a sponge, Houston is constantly being reshaped—physically by the wrecking ball and new construction and culturally by newcom-ers with fresh ideas and philosophies.

Biotechnology

New industries were appearing regularly. In 1953 biomolecular researchers James Watson and Francis Crick, working out of Cambridge University in England, outlined their hypothesis that the "double helix" was the basic building block of human life. This was the warning shot that a new discipline was aborning. In 1971 Cetus Corp. was organized in California to produce products based on this insight. It had strong sponsorship from Standard Oil (Indiana), National Distillers & Chemical (New York), and Standard Oil (California).

But the hype continued. Genentech excited Wall Street on October 14, 1980, with its initial public offering of stock, in which management sold 13 percent of the shares for $35 a share, in the largest public offering on Wall Street to that date. This led analysts and investors to look up such terms as gene splicing, genetic engineering, interferon, recombinant DNA, and, most important, biotechnology, the last being a catchall term for the new industry. Genentech already had done some important work involving the insertion of a gene for human insulin in bacteria, which had been licensed to Eli Lilly. The stock opened for trading at the IPO price, within twenty minutes was at 89, and spent the rest of the day seesawing, closing at 70. Six months later the company was the subject of a cover story in *Time*.

Genentech was preceded by and followed by the likes of Enzo Biochem, Biogen, Genex, Genetic Systems, Amgen, Applied Biosystems, Immunex, Repligen, and more, most of which had similar backing or were financed by interested banks, large established drug companies, or venture capitalists, many of whom were veterans of Silicon Valley and Route 128. It was not unusual for the "finder" to receive hundreds of thousands of rights for pennies to purchase shares at low prices once the company had gone public. More money was made through stock sales like this than through actual operations. That none of these companies and the many others in the biotechnology field had any products or records of sales and earnings did not seem to bother Wall Street. It was the biggest new industry, as far as investors were concerned, since computers, and it held out the promise of cures for a variety of illnesses from cancer to Alzheimer's disease, to strokes. And this was only one part of the new industry. Others included methods to increase food production and to bring an end to animal diseases; several companies were involved with work to lengthen the human life span. Those who followed the industry often claimed biotechnology had the potential to alter human life to a greater degree than computers or any other development in the twentieth century.

In the 1980s and beyond, biotechnology enriched the new companies, the older ones with which they affiliated, and investors smart or fortunate enough to buy and sell their stocks at the right times. During the next few years there were more than 100 IPOs, attracting some $500 million to the equities markets. It even had a name: biomania. For the rest of the decade the biotechnology stocks would help make fortunes for their originators, and provide fodder for traders and analysts in this warm-up for the Internet craze of the 1990s.

Writing of the mania and the research bonanza it set off in the *Manchester Guardian* in early 1982, John Elkington said:

Think of a moderately high number, feed it into your calculator and multiply it by a million or, if you are feeling bullish, by an American billion. Dress up the resulting figure . . . in some breathless text and publish. If you can find the nerve to charge several thousand dollars or pounds for the resulting report, so much the better. The market for surveys of the developing market for biotechnology products is itself booming. Yet one conclusion which can have escaped few of those who actually read the results is that the forecasts are so wildly different that only a small minority are likely to be near the mark. The problem is identifying which these might be.

In the early 1980s, the total market for biotechnology products, worldwide, came to less than $25 million, but there were thousands of firms in operation by then, and most had not produced their first commercial products. Forecasts, which ran from the hundreds of millions to the tens of billions of dollars by the end of the decade, were easy to come by. But the actual results were not anything like these figures.

The magic-bullet treatments and cures for cancer, AIDS, and other diseases did not emerge from these companies. Most of their accomplishments came through alliances with old-line pharmaceutical companies. Genetic Systems had several such alliances, the most important of which were with Bristol Myers and Syntex. Genetic Systems' common stock was selling for less than 5 by 1984, and in the following year it was taken over by Bristol Myers. In 1984, W. R. Grace came to an understanding with Cetus to form a jointly owned company to be called Agracetus, which was to conduct research into producing genetically engineered rice, wheat, soybeans, and corn that would be able to resist infestation and disease. Cetus would contribute its Cetus Madison Corp., and Grace would provide the cash for funding the research and development.

Agracetus did not produce significant or profitable products and services, but it was doing some very interesting work. It developed a blue, genetically engineered cotton that is herbicide and insect resistant, and a "gene gun" that can fire microscopic particles of gold coated with deoxyribonucleic acid (DNA) into plants or animals that will alter their genetic composition. However, these did not open the way for a financial bonanza for either company. In 1990, badly in need of financial aid, Genentech sold a 60 percent interest to the Swiss company Roche Holdings for $2.1 billion. Other alliances followed. Biogen, one of the research leaders, entered into a series of relationships with Schering Plough, SmithKline Beechman, and Merck, among others. So it went down the line. Genex, Cetus, Centocor, Genetics Systems, and Hybritech all were purchased by larger companies. Biotechnology remained an industry that was very promising but by the end of the century had not fulfilled most expectations. In addition, the dreams of entrepreneurship of the founders tended to end with bows to older, established corporate interests. Even so, by the late 1990s there were more than 350 independent biotechs. By then, however, all of the larger firms had entered the field on their own, by taking over an existing biotech or by forming alliances with one or more of them.

The Mutation of the Military-Industrial-Educational Complex

As has been noted, the postwar period saw an acceleration of the collaboration among agencies of the federal government, business, and the research universities to the point where it became difficult to determine where one ended and another began. Those students who protested American involvement in Vietnam railed against government presence on campus, demanded that professors and schools forgo research grants tied to the military, and called for the end of the presence of the Reserve Officers Training Corps and Military Science programs, and of collaboration on projects relating to the federal government's military and political goals. They also demanded that the universities sever relationships with corporations involved in the war, and attempted to deny them access to campuses for recruiting activities. In some cases they were successful, but most of the time the schools rejected these demands. To acquiesce to any or all of them was deemed a violation of academic freedom and an unwarranted delegation of powers rightly belonging to the schools and the faculties. Moreover, to do so would anger the alumni, many of whom were of the postwar generation that seemed to feel differently about these issues. The debates revolving around university-business-government collaboration served to highlight just how important these associations had become, and how separation would be difficult, if not untenable. To break off the connections would be to shut out important sources of funding and enrage the star faculty whose research projects depended on corporate and government funding.

The debate concluded without resolution when the

Vietnam War came to its end in the mid-1970s. As the nation seemed to become less concerned with such issues, attention turned elsewhere.

These matters did not lend themselves easily to the old categories of liberal and conservative, "left" and "right." By most existing measures, the Johnson administration was one of the most liberal in the sphere of domestic policies in American history. Yet it was opposed, insofar as its foreign policies were concerned at least, by a substantial portion of the liberal community.

At the philosophical heart of the matter was the question as to whether the future could be created through the free will of participants, or was destined to develop in particular ways due to certain aspects of life in the present bound to be extrapolated into the future. Added to the mix was the end of the Cold War, the effective end of the debate between supporters of some forms of socialism or statism on one hand, and free-market capitalism on the other.

By the early 1990s most analysts employed the rubric of free enterprise in their futuristic scenarios. The debates of the ideologues of the past revolved around such topics as free trade, immigration policy, changes in the tax codes, the future of Social Security, and other matters that often involved recourse to basic issues of ideology. Would the world of the future be based on the American or the Soviet template? Such questions were no longer being asked in the late 1990s, when virtually all the scenarios were based on an essentially free enterprise model. One of the more seminal thinkers about such matters was Virginia Postrel, whose *The Future and Its Enemies: The Growing Conflict Over Creativity, Enterprise, and Progress* (1998) became a textbook for "futurologists" of all persuasions.

Postrel believed that the only meaningful debate was between those who believe the future can be created and those who hold that future developments depend a great deal upon competition, in which choices are limited and involve a myriad of individual decisions. However, the information on which these decisions are to be based is more complicated now than at any other recent period.

Consider that the personal choices presented to the World War II veterans were rather simple, and involved such matters as whether to enroll in college and, if so, which one to attend, what subject to major in, when to get married, where to live, when to have that first child, which car to buy, and so forth. Which job offers to accept was a major matter. Life may have been difficult then, but the options were fairly straightforward. Even the choices facing their children, the baby boomers, were not that difficult. Their decisions included what position to take on the Vietnam War and what to do about it, as well as racism, sexism, the environment, and the like. But for the grandchildren, the choices involve the nature of the civilization in which they intended to live and pass down to their children.

The same might be said for their personal aspirations. At one time it was thought that middle-class Americans wanted more than anything else to be able to "keep up with the Joneses." In the immediate postwar period, the Joneses were the people who lived next door in Levittown. Keeping up with them meant having the right car, sending your preschoolers to the right nursery school, taking the right vacations, and wearing the right clothes. There was more to it than that, of course, but the idea was clear enough. Consumption, as much as savings, was a badge of wealth and of having arrived. According to economist Juliet Schor, Americans of the 1980s and 1990s—

the grandchildren of the GI generation—are still interested in keeping up with the Joneses, only the identity of the Joneses has changed. Now they are the affluent yuppies seen on TV shows, such as *Frazier* and *Ally McBeal*. Schor claims that every hour of time watching the television set per week adds around $200 to annual spending. "The likely explanation is that what we see on television inflates our sense of what is normal," she says, adding that "with a few exceptions, TV characters are upper-middle-class, or even rich." Others, including Robert Frank, the author of *Luxury Fever*, assert that the explanation is the ready availability of credit and the wealth effect caused by the stock market rise. In any case, the decline in the savings rate in the 1980s and the rise in spending certainly indicates that today's grandchildren are not quite the same as their grandparents.

The grandparents and parents knew that they would live in Western civilization. This very term meant something different for them. By the end of the century, or, as was popular to say at the time, the end of the millennium, it seemed Western civilization was about to take one of those turns that come every so often—such as the one that accompanied the rise of modern capitalism a century ago, the Industrial Revolution, the Commercial Revolution, and other events that molded the future.

The Birthing of the Internet

The origins of the Internet included the development of the Defense Agency Research Projects Administration, known as DARPA, which itself would not have been possible without several technological developments, including the appearance of the integrated circuit, the personal computer, and various advances in telecommunications. More important, perhaps, was the energization of such programs by the Soviet space launch, which stirred fears that the United States was falling behind in what was perceived to be an important technological battleground in the Cold War.

DARPA, which soon was rechristened ARPA (Advanced Research Projects Agency), created ARPANET, a communications system that came under the control of the Information Processing Techniques Office (IPTO), another of those cooperative ventures between government and business. ARPA had four sites, all on the campuses of the University of California, connecting the computers of government scientists and defense contractors. In the 1980s it gave promise of becoming an important building block in the creation of a new economy, or at least of becoming a mutation that would change the old one markedly. By then it had been renamed the Internet, and by the mid-1980s it spanned the globe. In addition, the Internet was no longer restricted to the Department of Defense; its channels were available for academic communications. Further, consideration was taken of the commercial possibilities of the Internet, and one of the throwoffs was the development of Web sites. In order to differentiate one from another, the suffix ".com" was added for the commercial sites, ".gov" was used for government sites, and ".edu" served for the educational institutions, thus giving us fedex.com, commerce.gov,and mit.edu. Sites outside the United States were given their own acronyms, like missile.uk. With the Web sites in place, it was possible to exchange information, and, in time, communications (E-mail), all subsidized by the government.

From this developed many companies, each hoping to profit from what had become a multi-billion-dollar industry with plenty of opportunities for newcomers, along with the realization that most of them would not be around in a few years. Among the leaders were Internet service providers such as UUNET, NETCOM, PSInet, and BBN; equipment manufacturers like Cisco, Ascend, Silicon Graphics, and Sun Microsystems; software creators that included Netscape, InterVista, Open Market, and Marimba; companies that dispensed search engines like Yahoo!, Lycos, Excite, and InfoSeek; and a host of small firms interested in providing other applications to subscribers, perhaps the best known of which was Organic Online. There were specialists who do not fall into any of these designations, such as CNET, which among other things became concerned with the possible marriage of the Internet with television. Some familiar companies—IBM, Dell, Microsoft, among others—entered the fray, and experienced rebirths. With possibilities such as these and the seeming overlap of functions, and with the many alliances, mergers, and disappearances, along with the lively initial public offerings market on Wall Street, the non-expert might be forgiven for not being able to distinguish among functions and confusing them with one another. What was clear to all concerned was that this was going to be big, and that many fortunes would be made with Internet-related companies.

One of the more important developments of this early period in Internet history was the creation of the World Wide Web. By the late 1980s there were some 80,000 computers on the Internet. It was then that British scientist Tim Berners-Lee, based at the Conseil Européen pour la Recherche Nucléaire (CERN) Center in

Switzerland, came up with the World Wide Web, which was made available to the general public in 1993, when the first Web browser, Mosaic 1.0, was released. Others soon followed. Without these "browsers" it is doubtful that the Internet would have developed as rapidly as it did in the 1990s. In addition, the government's role expanded. Between 1960 and 1990, more than $2 billion in federal funds was routed into IPTO programs, and over time, in cooperation with established firms like IBM and newcomers led by Cisco, the networks were enlarged and perfected.

Not until the 1990s did the general public come to realize the implications of the new technology. The Internet was the end-of-the-century development that capped the Great Boom involving Americans since the end of World War II, and it performed for the grandchildren of the GIs what the wonders of the 1940s and 1950s did for those veterans. When they returned to witness the technological wonders that America was creating in that period, they had a comment that expressed their reactions: "What will they think of next?" That is the kind of question that has been asked, regularly, ever since.

That the Internet was a new glamour area in the stock market could hardly have been doubted by anyone who followed the markets in the late 1990s, a time when Internet-related stocks were selling at stratospheric prices and making their originators overnight multi-millionaires—if only in terms of their stock holdings, some of which were of dubious marketability. Defenders of the boom pointed out that their prices were justified by the promise of the "new economy" they were helping to create, one in which a great deal of retail business would be conducted over the Web and in which E-mail would become the most common means of communication. Critics argued that the mania was just that: a fad, or, in the vernacular of Wall Street, a bubble—that was bound to burst.

The Internet Market

As has been mentioned, the real family incomes for perhaps 80 percent of Americans in the late 1990s had not risen since the early 1970s. These people knew of the Internet phenomenon, and some of them may have participated in the technology. But they lacked the funds to invest in stocks that came to the market as new issues in the late 1990s, or to purchase stocks of older companies that were involved. These investors were in the top 10 percent of the population, although some thought the figure was more like 25 percent. The difference was accounted for by "day traders," who at the keyboards of their computers bought and sold stocks using the services of "on-line brokers." This phenomenon may also have contributed to the imbalance of spending over savings, which began in 1998. In the past, negative savings rates had been associated with depressions—the last time this happened was in 1933. The negative savings rate of the late 1990s was ascribed to the "wealth effect," the fact that some Americans "felt" wealthy as a result of their profits from the stock market. They consumed more—in terms of cars, clothing, vacations, college tuitions, and expensive houses—because they felt they could now afford to do so. The statistics indicated that their behavior was not irrational. Figures for the "average" can be misleading in such a large and complex country. At the same time that the government released numbers indicating the savings rate had declined so sharply, the net worth of the average American household was up by more than 50 percent since the early 1990s.

More Americans were affected by the movements of Internet-related stocks than by the companies themselves. It was a replay, on a large scale, of the biotechnology boom of the early 1980s. Once the novelty value of Amazon.com passed, for example, would book buyers continue to order books over the Net when, with the postage added, prices were quite similar to those in a bookstore? Would the buyer prefer to leaf through the book in the store to make certain he or she really wanted it, and to take possession immediately?

Wall Street was divided as to the meaning of the Internet. For some it marked the next stage of capitalist development, and more wealth would accrue to those in positions to capitalize on the technologies than anything since the franchise boom of the 1950s and 1960s. For others, it was a bubble bound to burst when the investment community came to realize that when the inevitable shakeout took place, Wall Street would be awash in the blood of failed companies. Some of those with experience argued that while this might be so, in the meanwhile it was possible to accumulate a great deal of wealth through day trading. But this required skill, knowledge, fast reflexes, and a taste for risk, which few day traders had in the proper combination. What it does not require are the services of a broker—not even a discount broker. Just as the full-service brokers who were among the most successful figures in the industry during the 1950s and 1960s were savaged by Mayday, after which many customers switched to discounters, so Internet trading had affected the discounters. In effect, day traders have obviated the need for brokers. With all of these changes in techniques, far fewer young people aimed for careers as brokers than since World War II. To be sure, there will always be some customers who require the services and assistance of full-service brokers. But the number of such individuals seems bound to decline.

What all of this indicated was that Americans without the requisite technical knowledge who hoped to cash in on the new technology thought they had found a vehicle through which to do so, and in the process eliminated their need for brokers. Some of the more cautious customers found their own solace in "index funds," which were essentially unmanaged and set up to follow one or another of the popular indices, such as the Standard & Poor's 500. For them there was a measure of comfort in knowing that when the TV announcer proclaimed "the market went up 4 percent today," he or she probably was referring to the S&P index, which meant that the customer's fund had risen that 4 percent. The trouble with this was that there were many sessions in which the high-technology and Internet stocks rose or fell and the broad market went in the opposite direction. The person who owned shares in Lucent, AOL, Dell, or some other Internet or high technology stock was not comforted by the knowledge the market had risen that 4 percent, and he or she would have to await additional reporting before celebrating.

As a result, some investors turned to another device, from an earlier period: the mutual fund. In the late 1990s, mutual funds such as Berkshire Capital Growth & Value, ProFund Ultra OTC, and Grand Prix became the stars of the industry. While not widely advertised, word of the funds was passed from speculator to speculator, and they garnered many new accounts. Their performances were as spectacular as those of their underlying stocks, which is to say their quotations were likely to rise or fall by more than 25 percent on any given session. Internet Fund, for example, came close to tripling from October 1998 to February 1999. To track how the Internet stocks in the aggregate performed, new indices appeared in this period. The Wilshire 5000, one of these, was hardly known outside the professional community prior to 1998. Now it became the preferred index, with several mutual funds replicating its portfolio. In addition, there were the Galaxy II Small Company Index, the Vanguard Extended Market Index, and the Wilshire 4500 (which was the Wilshire 5000 minus the S&P 500). The Vanguard Value Index tracked the lowest-priced companies in the S&P 500 based on their price/earnings ratios.

Another way to invest in Internet companies was through finders or individuals prepared to take positions in the securities before they became public companies. In 1986, David Wetherall organized the leveraged buyout of College Marketing Group, a small company that compiled and rented lists of college professors, which he took public as CMG Information Services, which then took equity positions in Internet companies. In 1998, now renamed CMGI, it became a public company whose fortunes rose and fell as the Internet craze waxed and waned. Quoted at under 8 in January 1999, the stock rose to close to 200 by March, and then fell back to less than 100. Such were the vagaries of Internet stocks and the vehicles that invested in them.

Finally, at around the same time, the NASDAQ 100 Index created a trust that tracked the biggest names on that exchange and its partner, the American Stock Exchange, with high-technology companies accounting for almost all of the holdings. It was an easy and convenient way to hedge on the fortunes of the likes of Microsoft, Intel, Cisco, MCI WorldCom, and Dell.

So much for those investors and would-be wealthy Americans who were not directly involved with the Internet and related technologies. In their attempts to become wealthy, they hitched their stars to the truly successful entrepreneurs, those who had realized the dreams of the GI generation and rose to the top of the economic heap. What were they doing with their wealth? A sizeable number of them took seriously Andrew Carnegie's admonition that "he who dies wealthy dies disgraced," and set about giving away large portions of their fortunes. Bill Gates of Microsoft, according to most accounts the wealthiest man in the world, established the William H. Gates Foundation and the Gates Learning Foundation; in early 1999 the two foundations had assets of more than $5 billion. As it was, the assets of these foundations were greater than those of the Pew Charitable Trusts, the John D. and Catherine T. MacArthur Foundation, and that of the giant of a previous generation, the Andrew W. Mellon Foundation. Other moguls set up their own philanthropies. So it may be that, financially speaking, the impact of the new technologies would be to filter money from consumers and practitioners of the new technologies to their chosen beneficiaries. Great power would be garnered by the managers of such trusts who distributed the assets. If so, power to set public policy might have been bestowed upon unelected individuals and foundations, another of the many problems that remain to be resolved in the early years of the new millennium.

A Bubble or the Real Thing? A Bit of History

Some of those with a sense of history and an awareness of the impact of technology on economies and societies as a whole might have argued that the Internet and the Web were hardly improvements over what already existed, and might prove a chimera. The ability to communicate with others in all parts of the globe was hardly new. It could be done by mail, telegraph, or, if time were important, by telephone. If the individual to be contacted was not there, users of E-mail or fax could leave their messages to be read later. But the telephone answering machine also took care of that. Which is to suggest that while E-mail was less expensive, it was not much of an improvement over the telephone. If large amounts of information had to be transmitted, those involved might use the various forms of express mail that had developed during the past two decades. True enough, some documents and information could be sent instantaneously, but there was not enough of this to result in a radical remaking of an entire society. For all the talk of electronic commerce, Americans will likely still want to shop at stores and malls. History is replete with examples of how new methods of producing and distributing did not eliminate the need for older ones, and in fact may have invigorated them. Indeed, there have been times when progress meant going back, not ahead.

In the nineteenth century, Sears Roebuck and Montgomery Ward pioneered in the field of catalog sales. The farmer would look over his catalog, place his order, and then receive it by mail. If for any reason the product was unsatisfactory, it might be returned. In the 1920s these companies opened retail stores. Wasn't it better for the customer actually to see and feel the product he or she was buying than to have to rely upon pictures in catalogs? Wasn't it more convenient to take possession of the product immediately rather than waiting for it to arrive in the mail? Over time, catalog sales declined, at least for Sears and Ward, which in the 1980s and 1990s, along with other mass retailers, discontinued them. While speciality retailers continued to utilize catalogs, Dell and Gateway and other electronics retailers demonstrated by selling through the mail that catalogs were not about to disappear. But the heyday of the general merchandise catalog had passed.

Given this, was it possible that Internet commerce would supplant retail outlets? Perhaps it might complement the malls of America, but those malls, complete with Kmarts and Wal-Marts that were also supposed to be the shape of the future, were not going to disappear. It seemed just as probable that, once the surprise and novelty of E-mail wore off, the true worth of telephones and mail, which, after all, were faster in the case of the former and more permanent in the case of mail, would reassert themselves.

The coming of age of the Internet, and the developing universality of service for most middle-class Americans, recalled the craze that developed for radio and motion pictures in the 1920s, and the installation of telephones in most middle-class homes in the two decades prior to World War II, while electrification of the homes proceeded apace in this period. In other words, the World War II veterans had seen crazes similar to that of the Internet before. But they were not old enough to recall that the Great Bull Market of the 1920s had been powered by the stocks of companies in these industries, along with aviation securities, even though a majority of Americans had not flown until the 1960s.

There had been no shortage of glamour in the 1920s market—accorded by radio, motion picture, automobile, and aviation securities. Radio stocks, in particular, provided key speculative vehicles. These included Atwater Kent, Crosley, Grebe, Grigsby-Grunow, Freed-Eisenmann, FADA, Philco, Zenith, and CBS.

Radio Corporation of America was the star of the market in 1928. In 1921, RCA, then involved in ship-to-shore transmission with a limited future in view, had a trading range of 3–1. In 1924 RCA had affected a 5-for-1 reverse split, and the adjusted range was 67–19, on earnings of $2.91 per share. On March 3, 1928, RCA sold for 91. On March 12, on rumors that television would soon become available, the stock opened at 120 and closed at 138, and the following day opened at 160 on rumors of a takeover of Photophone. These were the kinds of swings that took place throughout the year, and not only for RCA, which continued to rise as CEO David Sarnoff transformed it into an entertainment conglomerate. In 1929 RCA peaked at 573 on $7.90 in earnings, no dividend, and then split 5 for 1. The range for the new stock was 114–26. From then on the path downward was irregular but quite steady. The 1931 range was 28–6.

The 1920s market rise was not straight up. There were several major corrections along the way—in early 1923, 1925, 1926, and 1928. On these occasions there was no shortage of pundits proclaiming that the party was over.

The American investor of the late 1900s hardly ignored the fact that in the year and a half from March 1928 to September 1929, while RCA rose from 94 to 505, some of the old warhorses did pretty well for themselves. As the bull market developed, scores of magazine and newspaper articles appeared recalling the events of the 1920s, when American Can went from 77 to 182, Anaconda Copper from 54 to 162, Montgomery Ward from 133 to 467, Union Carbide from 145 to 414, and Westinghouse from 92 to 313. So while this was a time when glamour stocks rose due to dreams, in that same period some of the old blue chips advanced as a result of economic performance and the spillover effect. Does it sound familiar? It should, as a perusal of the stock tables virtually any day during the 1990s would disclose. While the glamour issues, led by Internet-related stocks, performed spectacularly, the rest of the market as measured by the Dow Jones Average hardly was a laggard. In March 1999, accompanied by widespread celebration, the Dow crossed the 11,000 mark.

This performance had heartened those who believed strong stocks always came back, despite periodic selloffs. Few considered that RCA's 1938 range was 9–5, and in 1947 it still sold for less than 10. In 1960, with a strong position in TV receiver sales and NBC, RCA had earnings of $1.97 per share and a dividend of $1, and sold in a range of 78–46. So when it had nothing but promise, RCA was a 573 stock (adjusted to 115). When the promise was realized, at one point three decades later, it went for less than half of its 1929 high. In the mid-1980s, prior to its takeover by GE, RCA was in the low 40s.

Such was the situation during several post–World War II bull markets, like the one featuring new electronic stocks, including the likes of Beckman Instruments, Hoffman Electronics, and Varian Associates. The last was founded by two brothers who had invented the klystron tube at Stanford and exchanged half interest in their company for $100 in materials and free use of a laboratory.

One boom followed another in this period—there were the new issues of the early 1960s, which saw Bristol Dynamics, Nytronics, and Polychrome doubled in price in the first day of trading.

All of which is to suggest that the wild Internet market may or may not have been a bubble, and that while Internet stocks had captured a good deal of attention, there was more to the bull market than the Internet. Moreover, some of those stocks may be the blue chips of the future. After all, there was a time when GE, IBM, GM, and other familiar names were new issues.

Which Internet companies will make the grade and will the Internet usher in the next state in human evolution? Who can say? If the purchase of such stocks as Amazon, Cisco, and AOL is not quite the same as was the purchase and holding of a solid blue chip a quarter of a century ago, it is at least better than buying a lottery ticket. Or might a more apt comparison be made with investments in Genentech, Cetus, or the like in the early 1980s?

The Internet has captured the imaginations of many Americans, not only those who followed the Internet stocks on the new issues market. Just as flight had inspired millions of Americans who followed the flight of Charles Lindbergh across the Atlantic in 1927, so the operations of the Internet and related technologies have fired the dreams of Americans who did not own computers. But the GIs, now retired, still remembered the times when new and exciting technologies appeared, and did what they could to make certain their grandchildren could participate in the wonders of the new era. It may be that every generation is destined to experience the euphoria that comes with such developments. Whatever the situation, and however it turns out, the Internet boom has already earned its place in the chronicle of the Great Boom that Americans underwent during the second half of the twentieth century.

The entrepreneurs and scientist-businessmen involved with the Internet became heroes to this generation. As Jeffrey Young, one of the early historians of the technology and industry, wrote in 1998:

> The Internet, in all its glory and tawdriness, owed its exuberance and vigor to the spirit of entrepreneurs of all ages who can see a new, wide open, and limitless vista before them. The Internet is the new frontier. And the only limits to the Internet are those of the human imagination, and the personal will of new entrepreneurs to create business successes. If the experience of the past ten years—or even the fifty years of the digital age—is anything to go by, there's no shortage of either of those things in the world. If anything, the supply of both is increasing.

The arrival of the Internet was only one of the major shocks that had to be absorbed in the second half of the 1990s. In much of this period the front-page news was not good: problems in the emerging economies of Southeast Asia, Russia, and Latin America; wars in eastern Europe; political chaos elsewhere; questions surrounding the introduction of the euro in Europe; uncertainties regarding what might happen to the world's computers as the year 2000 dawned; and, as though to add some spice to the mix, the Bill Clinton impeachment "crisis."

What must their grandparents have thought? In the midst of all of this, in the autumn of 1998 came the release of a book, *The Greatest Generation*, by TV newsman

Tom Brokaw, a celebration of the people who survived the Great Depression and World War II, and then went on to lead America into the dangerous but also prosperous world of the Cold War. The book struck a nerve and soon was the number-one best-seller, being discussed on most of the network news programs and becoming the basis for a TV special.

In any case, in the midst of the most prodigious outburst of conspicuous consumption by ordinary Americans, a substantial portion of the population tried to remember how it all began. A generation of young men and women suffered through depression and war, and then went on to personal and economic successes, hoping to transmit the blessings that came with such accomplishments to their children, along with the ethic that made it all possible. In time, the baby boomers tried to do the same for their children. The GI generation did so in part with their profits from such stocks as Polaroid, Control Data, Thiokol, Ampex, and Fairchild Camera, which rose 20 to 30 percent in a year or so. Their children did so with the stocks of Intel, Digital Equipment, Apple, and a host of biochemical stocks that might double in a year. In the 1990s their grandchildren speculated in shares of America Online, Dell, Microsoft, Sun Microsystems, and a host of on-line companies whose stocks, by 1999, were tripling in price and more in their first day of trading.

There were differences beyond the relative performances of the stocks. While the grandparents might have celebrated a three-point advance in the price of Control Data with dinner at the nearby restaurant, their grandchildren marked a tripling in the price of eBay with a "look-see" at the Jaguar showroom. While the GI generation considered a stock advance of a few points in a day a windfall, their children celebrated a 10 percent move, and their grandchildren assumed a 100 point rise to be their birthright. At least for a while. But while the mania continued and thousands of novice investors made paper fortunes buying and selling on their home computers, others planned to make their fortunes by servicing them. New firms like Wit Capital and established ones that included Donaldson, Lufkin & Jenrette underwrote new Internet stocks. William Hambrecht, who earlier had been one of the founders of Hambrecht & Quist, which had been formed to capitalize on the boom of the 1960s, organized W. R. Hambrecht & Co. to cater to the desires of the new investors. Hambrecht would underwrite the new issue, placing most of the shares in accounts of "people who want to own the stock for the long run." The prices would be set though a "Dutch auction," in which bidders would indicate the maximum price they were prepared to pay. The offering would then be priced at the level geared to bring in the amount required to sell all of the shares. This would prevent the offering of shares at such low prices as to afford the initial purchasers huge profits, at the expense of the syndicate, which had been the experience of many initial public offerings in the late 1990s.

The unreal facet of the Internet market became more evident toward the end of the decade, when a new merger wave rippled through American—and indeed world—business. Ford acquired the automobile business of the Swedish firm Volvo, which had been very successful in selling its sedans, sports cars, station wagons, and vans in the North American market. The price was $6.5 billion, for a company whose 1998 revenues were $12.8 billion and that earned close to $320 million. At about the same time, the Internet company @Home paid $6.7 billion for Excite, an Internet favorite, which posted a loss of $37 million on 1998 revenues of $154 million, while

Yahoo! paid $4.6 billion for Geocities, which had 1998 revenues of $18.4 million and a loss of $20 million. None of this would have made sense to investors concerned with "value," or with the performance and even the "long-run" potential of all three companies. Volvo's customer base and reputation appeared secure, while the next blip in the technological landscape could spell the end for Excite and Geocities. In the long run, their prospects were questionable.

The trouble with this approach was that few of the initial purchasers thought in terms of the long run. But the appearance of new underwriters was yet another indication that the entrepreneurial juices that fueled previous manias were still flowing at the turn of the century. But whether such funds were appropriate for those World War II veterans contemplating retirement was another matter entirely.

A Matter of Trust

Lost in all of this was a matter of trust, something that had not been considered since the end of World War II. As the GI generation retired and the baby boomers prepared for their "days in the sun," the question of how retirement was to be financed was raised. The soldier who stormed the beaches at Normandy as a twenty-five-year-old reached the age of sixty-five in 1984, when one of the subjects of national debate was the future of Social Security and Medicare. As it turned out, that generation was safe. Social Security payments, adjusted for inflation, would continue to be made, and Medicare benefits would not be cut. In addition, many of the veterans had IRAs and Keoghs, as well as retirement packages from their employers along with savings, at a time when the stock markets were doing quite well. During the 1970s, newspaper stories appeared about old people, suffering from inflation, who were reduced to eating cat food. But not in the early 1990s. It appeared that the economy and their own good sense had made it possible for the veterans to enjoy their retirement years—and without having to rely upon their children and grandchildren to save them from cat-food diets. Even so, some of the statistics emanating from Washington in this period were disquieting. The pundits claimed that one-third of Americans had no savings at all, and the next third had less than $3,000 in savings. The claim was put forth that while the GI generation would do well in its last years, not so for many of the baby boomers, those born between 1946 and 1964. Unless changes were made in the tax laws, only 2 in 5 of them would be able to maintain their standards of living upon retirement.

One reason for this was a factor not discussed thus far: taxes. While tax rates and other parts of the law were adjusted regularly in the past, state and local taxes had increased in many parts of the country. Toward the end of the century, total tax burdens, when taking account of all taxes, were at the highest level since World War II. The median income for a two-earner family came to $55,000, and of this, $22,000 went for federal, state, and local taxes. Adjusted for inflation, this was 3 times the amount levied in 1955. Of course, these figures were for the median, and not presented for all levels. What of the top 10 percent, or even 25 percent—the ones whose homes and stock portfolios had risen sharply in value? Surely they did much better than that. In fact, as tax reform was debated in the last years of the century, the most excitement collected around discussions to cut back or eliminate estate taxes. The entire estate could pass down to the spouse without taxes, but when that person died, the taxes could be quite high. The first $600,000 was tax free, but then the bite became heavy. In addition, there was a provision that furnished large fees for estate attorneys. According to some tax reformers, this impacted unfavorably upon incentives to save and invest. Is the passing of large assets from generation to generation a wise policy? This question had been asked at other times in American history. But it had not been of major importance after World War II. To that generation, estates were concerns of the old rich, a classification that did not include them— and never would. They had hoped for decent, comfortable lives, for themselves and for their progeny. Had they been told in 1946 that estate taxes would be a significant issue for their children and grandchildren, they would have been amazed, and then reflected on what a wonderful country this was, and how successful they had been by taking advantage of the opportunities it presented.

Such thoughts would not have struck the baby boomers as many of them considered retirement. In the early 1990s, retirement at the age of sixty-two was becoming more popular. In 1995, babies born in 1946 were close to fifty years old, thinking of retirement, and at that point many took stock of what they had. The newspapers and television reports spoke of the viability of Social Security. Would it be there for them? At about this time, the booming stock market led some in and out of government to talk of investing part of the Social Security fund in common stocks. Such a thought probably never would have occurred to the New Dealers. In any case, independent polls indicated that a startling number of Americans trusted the stock market more than the government when it came to paying out earned benefits.

Ever since the advent of the Reagan Administration, it had been increasingly evident that trust in government was eroding while that in the free markets was increasing. The amazing performance of the Internet market in the late 1990s added to this sentiment. But perhaps even more important was the loss of the sense of community that had been engendered by the experiences of the Great Depression and World War II. Discussing this phenomenon, *New York Times* writer Kevin Sack opined, "One point agreed on by virtually all of the baby boomers interviewed was that they, unlike their parents, could not depend on Social Security to support their retirement." Of course, in its original form, Social Security payments were never intended to provide all the support for retirement, and the basic legislation was passed at a time when life expectancy was quite low by 1990s standards. In any case, by the late 1990s the general public had been made aware, through magazine articles and television programs, that the Social Security trust find was in trouble. Payments by workers into the fund were used to purchase special federal bonds, and the money obtained was spent for general purposes. In essence, the bonds remained in the fund, but when cashed the money would be used to pay benefits. What might happen if there were a shortfall? Clearly that would be made up by recourse to the general tax revenues. To fail to do so would be politically impossible, given the political and economic power of the older voters.

Even so, said one of those interviewed, something important was missing. "I think it's going to be every person for themselves," said Mr. Green, the lawyer. Then thirty-six years old with a successful Atlanta practice, he was the kind of person who did not have to worry unduly about his retirement. And yet he said, "I don't feel secure at all."

Toward the end of the twentieth century, a time when former World War II GIs were dying at the rate of 1,000 a day and the business and governmental worlds were being administered by their grandchildren, the shape of the future was, as always, in doubt. Americans, in the aggregate, had higher standards of living than they anticipated in 1945. But in the wake of the Clinton impeachment "crisis" the nation seemed troubled by the changes in the public morality that had taken place between the two generations. At one time it had been common to ridicule the puritanism of the older generation, complete with ideas of sexual fidelity and the importance of truthfulness. Now such matters were being reconsidered.

The Great Boom had taken place after the war, and had brought with it a high standard of living and greater expectations. That the baby boomers had benefited from this—always in the aggregate—was obvious. That they had succeeded in passing the torch to those of their offspring who wanted it was also apparent. By all such measures, it had been a successful half century.

And yet there were those who believed the nation— and the generation—either had failed in its mission, or had defined it without the required precision. Whatever the situation, America remained an unfinished country. It was that way in the beginning, and it remained so at the dawn of the new millennium.

The Sixtieth Anniversary Reunion

Whether any of these thoughts filtered through the minds of those who gathered at the Franklins' home in suburban Charleston on September 3, 2005, is not known. It was in a development known as Leisure Acres, complete with

brick walls enclosing the complex, limited entry, a clubhouse, two meals per day, low-cost cleaning service, and
boasting twenty-four-hour-a-day surveillance. Leisure
Acres had been designed with the elderly but ambulatory
in mind. There already were more than 100 of these
developments across the country, with more appearing at
a startling rate, and housing writers had condemned them
as sterile and architecturally impoverished. But for the
residents, Leisure Acres and its ilk were near-perfect. Most
were within walking distance of supermarkets, banks,
travel agencies, the community-supported library, the
swimming pool (for those who lacked their own private
ones), and all other amenities. The library and clubhouse
were meeting places for special interest groups, which
ranged from World War II studies to pottery. There was a
bus service that could deliver residents to any place in the
complex in less than an hour and to the local airport in
about the same time span. In the local newspaper, an article appeared by a reporter who noted that he was the
grandson of a major fault-finder with Levittown in the
early 1950s. "If you liked Levittown," the writer concluded, "you probably will like Leisure Acres."

No one thought to ask those people on that day, the
sixtieth anniversary of the formal surrender of the Japanese in World War II, which President Truman soon proclaimed to be "V-J Day," their thoughts on what the past
half century had meant to them. But, as might have been
expected, several questioners wanted to know how the
veterans felt on V-J Day. As on earlier anniversaries, the
newspapers noted that some 15.5 million Americans had
been in the armed services during the war, and 325,000 of
them had died. The alleged cost of the war varied from
newspaper to newspaper, but most settled somewhere in
the $330 billion area, with Lend-Lease adding another

$48 billion. It was thought that about 3 million veterans were still alive, but no one truly knew the exact or even approximate number, since deaths were occurring by the hour.

On every anniversary since the early 1950s, Bob and Jane Franklin had thrown such a party, to which they invited Bob's wartime buddies and their families, a few miscellaneous friends, and relatives. The practice had begun in Levittown, and continued as the Franklins moved from home to home, winding up, in Bob's retirement years, in Charleston. Their first party was attended by around 100 people. This one drew more than 400, from as far away as Long Island, Hawaii, and Texas, creating a major parking problem, which was alleviated when Bob notified the mayor's office which in turn asked the police department to help find parking places in the neighborhood.

There were three easily differentiated groups. Some of the attendees were above the age of eighty, and more than a few of them were in wheelchairs or used walkers or canes. Other than that, they seemed in good shape and were quite voluble, especially when discussing their accomplishments and those of their grandchildren (but not necessarily the accomplishments of their children). Their children, the baby boomers, mired in their fifties, were there, and their talk revolved around the stock market and their planned early retirements, with many noting that they could afford to stop working, but could not afford a home like the one enjoyed by the Franklins. The grandchildren, in their twenties and thirties, also discussed investments, but, in addition, were concerned with politics and the problems of finding proper schools for their children. Some of them, all below the age of ten, were at the party, but not many. Using baby-sitters was an easy option, which also gave the third generation the excuse to leave early, after making an appearance for the sake of their grandparents and parents, thereby demonstrating their respect.

The casual watcher might have noted that the grandparents and their cohort all were white, as were most of the children and their spouses, and there were black and Asian faces sprinkled among the grandchildren. Had those observers listened to the discussions, they would have realized that among the various families there were inevitable differences.

After the expected reminiscences about absent friends and wartime experiences they had survived, the usual anecdotes one expects at reunions of this type, many of the GIs turned to their thoughts about V-J Day. Virtually all of them had looked forward to their discharges, and all said they had plans for their civilian lives, from entering the family business to finding work in factories or offices near their homes. Most thought of families, marriage, buying a home and a car, and, of course, a civilian suit. Their hopes and dreams were not of the stuff from which fantasies are created. All seemed realizable. And, in fact, looking at them, one might easily assume all had been successful in their quests. America had experienced a major economic boom after World War II. As far as those veterans were concerned, they had been part of it.

Given their aspirations of 1945, they had been huge successes. A few had achieved wealth, which was signaled by their cars. Most of them had arrived in mid-level American and Japanese models, with Toyota Camrys and Chrysler Intrepids the predominant models, but there were some Chevrolets and Jaguars as well. Most were retired, but they did volunteer work in their communities. Their social and political attitudes were all over the map, and few of them seemed to take such matters with a great deal of seriousness, perhaps because they felt this was not the place for such discussions. In any event, they felt like the winners in the game of life, grateful for opportunities afforded them to achieve such status.

From time to time some of them would drag their sons and daughters over to meet one or more of their old friends. Whatever boasting took place had to do with the children's educational accomplishments, jobs, and status in their communities. There was little talk of wealth, except for the occasional mention of an Internet stock they had purchased at the initial public offering, or a home that had quadrupled in value. Few of the children appeared to have gone into politics or charitable work. Most were professionals, small businessmen, or executives in large corporations. But four were in state or the federal legislatures—three Republicans, one Democrat. In this regard, there were few surprises.

Now for the grandchildren. They were in their twenties and thirties, and, as might be expected, were able to talk more of their futures than of their pasts. One of the GI couples, after speaking with some of the grandchildren, retreated for their own moment of reflection. "How old do you think they are?" she asked him. He thought for a moment, and noted that his friend must be seventy-five, and that would make his daughter fifty or so, and her daughter twenty-five or thereabouts. That young woman had mentioned that she was an elementary school teacher, and then she had reflected on how her students were so much more socially aware than she had been when in her early teens. "What were the students' ambitions?" the old-timers had wanted to know. The answer came quickly: "To be decent human beings." It was not what they had expected. "Don't they want to do well professionally and financially?" they asked. "Of course. All of them will go to college," was the reply. "It was so different in our time," said the husband. "We looked upon those years as preparation for the 'real world.' They simply assume that if they go through the drill, success will be automatic."

So it went for the rest of the afternoon. After several hours of this, the GIs and their brides tended to look longingly at the children of those grandchildren. Maybe it will be different for them, they thought. One of the baby boomers pointed to his grandson and remarked, "He spends three hours a day on the Internet," as though that assured his success in the new millennium. Perhaps so. The youngster will live in a different kind of world than those who remember basic training at Fort Dix, landings on Omaha Beach, news of the atomic bomb, and most of all, returning home to a better life than they had expected.

The party started to break up around 5:00 P.M., but the last of the guests left five hours later. To no one's surprise, these were the GIs and their wives. They had the most memories to share and the most stories to tell. But the recollections of the baby boomers, and of the baby busters, and those who followed, were also important. Taken as a whole, they told one of the most extraordinary stories in all of American history. For had they invited their friends and business associates, the composition of the party might have been quite different. For one thing, the rise of a black middle and upper class might have been reflected, along with the wealth of Asians and the mixed nature of the Hispanic population. During the 1990s alone, the number of black households earning more than $100,000 annually rose from 220,000 to 415,000, and the general population became more aware of such matters.

In *Waking from the Dream: My Life in the Black Middle Class* (1996), Sam Fulwood reported tellingly on the existence of not only a black middle class, but of an upper class as well. A like situation exists in other racial and religious communities. The Great Boom has redounded to their benefit.

Such are the images of the Great Boom as seen from Charleston in 2005. All matters considered, it could have been much worse. But it wasn't, in large part because of those expectations of 1945 and beyond. Had the baby boomers been quizzed regarding their hopes, those who would have been asked to make projections would doubtless have been more hopeful than their parents, but, like them, they turned out to be overachievers. As for their hopes for their own children, it is too early to say much about that. It would appear, however, that the young people of the 1990s have reason for optimism. As before, if they learn the rules and follow them, the possibilities for success are boundless.

ACKNOWLEDGMENTS

It is with a mixture of gratitude and sadness that I acknowledge several individuals for their help with this book on behalf of my late husband, who died a few weeks after completing the final draft.

Mary Horn, Roberta Levin, and Barbara Sobel were tireless, patient, and precise manuscript typists. Beryl Brummer offered much of her time clarifying grammatical issues and verifying bibliographical citations. Alice Berridge was a relentless researcher, confirming many obscure references. These exceptional women offered their support and encouragement at all times. And, as they have done for decades during my husband's prolific career, the reference librarians at Hofstra University provided invaluable assistance.

I wish to give special thanks to Professor David Sicilia, a University of Maryland business historian and dear friend and colleague of Bob's, for graciously volunteering to help me edit the final version of the manuscript.

This team of very special people helped pull me through the bittersweet task of editing *The Great Boom*, which holds great meaning for me as the final project in my own forty-year career as Bob's associate.

—Carole Sobel
September 1999

SELECTED BIBLIOGRAPHY

Abrams, Charles. *The Future of Housing*. Harper & Brothers, 1946.

———. "Public Housing Myths." *New Leader*, Vol. 38 (30), July 25, 1955, p. 3.

Adams, F. G., and N. J. Glickman, eds. *Modeling the Multiregional Economic System: Prospectives for the Eighties*. Lexington Books, 1980.

Adams, Susan. "Build It and They Will Come." *Forbes*, Vol. 163, no. 7, April 5, 1999, p. 66.

Allen, Frederick Lewis. *The Big Change: America Transforms Itself, 1900–1950*. Harper, 1952.

———. *The Lord of Creation*. Harper, 1935.

Allen, Michael Patrick. *The Founding Fortunes: An Anatomy of Super-Rich Families in America*. Truman Talley Books/E. P. Dutton, 1987.

Andrews, Emily S. *The Changing Profile of Pensions in America*. EBRI, 1985.

Baker, George P., and George David Smith. *The New Financial Capitalists: Kohlberg Kravis Roberts and the Creation of Corporate Value*. Cambridge University Press. 1998.

Baldwin, James. *The Fire Next Time*. Dial Press, 1963.

Baritz, Loren. *The Good Life: The Meaning of Success for the American Middle Class*. Knopf, 1989.

Barlett, Donald L., and James B. Steele. *America: What Went Wrong?* Andrews and McMeel, 1992.

Battersby, Martin. *The Decorative Thirties*. Walker & Company, 1971.

Bell, Daniel. *The Cultural Contradiction of Capitalism*. Basic Books, 1976.

———. *The End of Ideology: On the Exhaustion of Political Ideas in the Fifties*. Free Press, 1960.

Bennett, Amanda. *The Death of the Organization Man*. William Morrow & Co., 1990.

Selected Bibliography

Bennett, Michael. *When Dreams Came True: The GI Bill and the Making of Modern America*. Brassey's, 1996.

Berman, Ronald. *America in the Sixties: An Intellectual History*. Free Press, 1968.

Bernstein, Jeremy. *The Analytical Engine: Computers—Past, Present, and Future*. William Morrow & Co., 1981.

Bernstein, Peter L. *Capital Ideas: The Improbable Origins of Modern Wall Street*. Macmillan, 1992.

Bina, Cyrus. *The Economics of the Oil Crisis: Theories of Oil Crisis, Oil Rent, and Internationalization of Capital in the Oil Industry*. St. Martin's Press, 1985.

Birch, David L. *Job Creation in America: How Our Smallest Companies Put the Most People to Work*. Free Press, 1987.

Bluestone, Barry, and Bennett Harrison. *The Deindustrialization of America: Plant Closings, Community Abandonment and the Dismantling of Basic Industry*. Basic Books, 1982.

Blum, John Morton. *Years of Discord: American Politics and Society, 1961–1974*. W. W. Norton, 1991.

Botkin, James W. "Route 128: Its History and Destiny," in Raymond W. Smilor, ed., et al. *Creating the Technopolis: Linking Technology, Commercialization and Economic Development*. Ballinger, 1988.

Boorstin, Daniel Joseph. *The Americans, The Democratic Experience*. Random House, 1973.

Bradbury, Katherine L. "The Shrinking Middle Class." *The New England Economic Review*, September/October, 1986, pp. 41–55.

Brauer, Carl M. *John F. Kennedy and the Second Reconstruction*. Columbia University Press, 1977.

Braun, Ernest, and Stuart MacDonald. *Revolution in Miniature: The History and Impact of Semiconductor Electronics Re-explored*. Cambridge University Press, 2nd ed., 1982.

Brett, Alistair, David Gibson, and Raymond Smilor, eds. *University Spin-off Companies: Economic Development, Faculty Entrepreneurs, and Technology Transfer*. Rowman & Littlefield, 1991.

British Medical Association. *Our Genetic Future: The Science and Ethics of Genetic Technology*. Oxford University Press, 1992.

Brogan, D. W. *American Themes*. H. Hamilton, 1948.

Bronner, Ethan. "In a Revolution of Rules, Campuses Go Full Circle." *The New York Times*, March 3, 1999, p. A1.

Brooks, John. *The Go-Go Years*. Weybright & Talley, 1973.

———. *The Great Leap: The Past Twenty-Five Years in America*. Harper & Row, 1966.

———. *Once in Golconda: A True Drama of Wall Street, 1920–1938*. Harper & Row, 1969.

Brown, Les. *Television: The Business Behind the Box*. Harcourt Brace Jovanovich, 1971.

Brownlee, W. Elliot. *Federal Taxation in America: A Short History*. Cambridge University Press, 1996.

Bruckberger, Raymond L. *Image of America*. Viking Press, 1959.

Budd, Edward C., ed. *Inequality and Poverty*. W. W. Norton, 1967.

Burness, Tad. *Cars of the Early Thirties*. Chilton Book Company, 1970.

Bylinsky, Gene. *The Innovation Millionaires: How They Succeed*. Scribner's, 1976.

Campbell, Arthur A. "Baby Boom to Birth Dearth and Beyond." *Annals of the American Academy of Political and Social Science*, Vol. 435, 1978, p. 40 ff.

Carey, James W., and John I. Quirk. "The Mythos of the Electronic Revolution." *American Scholar*, Vol. 39, no. 2, Spring 1970, pp. 219–241.

Carmichael, Stokely, and C. V. Hamilton Jr., *Black Power: The Politics of Liberation in America*. Random House, 1967.

Carnoy, Martin, and Derek Shearer. *Economic Democracy: Challenge of the 1980s*. M. E. Sharpe, 1980.

Cawelti, John G. *Apostles of the Self-Made Man*. University of Chicago Press, 1965.

Chafe. William. H. *The American Woman: Her Changing Social, Economic and Political Roles, 1920–1970*. Oxford University Press, 1972.

Chase, Alton. "Skipping through College." *The Atlantic Monthly*, Vol. 242, (3), September 1978, pp. 33–40.

Chenoweth, Lawrence. *The American Dream of Success: The Search for the Self in the Twentieth Century*. Duxbury, 1974.

Cleaver, Eldridge. *Soul on Ice*. McGraw-Hill, 1967.

Close, K. "Young Families in 1950." *Survey*, January 1950.

Coleman, John Royston, ed. *The Changing American Economy*. Basic Books, 1967.

Coles, Robert. *Privileged Ones: The Well-Off and the Rich in America*. Little, Brown, 1977.

Congdon, Don, ed. *The Thirties: A Time to Remember*. Simon & Schuster, 1962.

Congressional Quarterly. *Social Security and Retirement: Private Goals, Public Policy*. Congressional Quarterly, 1983.

Connell, Stephen, and Ian A. Galbraith. *Electronic Mail: A Revolution in Business Communication*. Knowledge Industry Publications, 1982.

Coontz, Stephanie. *The Way We Never Were: American Families and the Nostalgia Trap*. Basic Books, 1992.

Cornich, Edward, ed. *1999: The World of Tomorrow*. World Future Society, 1978.

Cray, Ed. *Chrome Colossus: General Motors and Its Times*. McGraw-Hill, 1980.

Critchlow, Donald. *Studebaker: The Life and Death of an American Corporation*. Indiana University Press, 1996.

Curti, Merle, Richard H. Shryock, Thomas C. Cochran, and Fred Harvey Harrington. *An American History*. Vol. 2. Harper, 1950.

Cusumano, Michael, and Richard Selby. *Microsoft Secrets*. The Free Press, 1995.

Daly, Peter. *The Biotechnology Business*. Rowman & Allanheld, 1985.

Danziger, Sheldon, and Peter Gottschalk. *America Unequal*. Harvard University Press, 1996.

Dicke, Thomas. *Franchising in America: The Development of a Business Method 1840–1980*. University of North Carolina Press, 1992.

Dickstein, Morris. *Gates of Eden: American Culture in the Sixties*. Basic Books, 1977.

Diggins, John. *The Proud Decades: America in War and Peace, 1941–1960*. W. W. Norton, 1988.

Dines, James. *The Invisible Crash: What It Is, Why It Happened, How to Protect Yourself Against It*. Random House, 1975.

Doane, Robert. *The Anatomy of American Wealth*. Harper, 1940.

Domhoff, G. William. *Who Rules America?* Prentice Hall, 1967.

———. *Who Rules America Now?* Prentice Hall, 1983.

Donaldson, Scott. *The Suburban Myth*. Columbia University Press, 1969.

Draper, Hal. *Berkeley: The New Student Revolt*. Grove Press, 1965.

Drucker, Peter F. *America's Next Twenty Years*. Harper & Brothers, 1957.

Duesenberry, James. *Income, Saving and the Theory of Consumer Behavior*. Harvard University Press, 1962.

Easterlin, Richard A. *The American Baby Boom in Historical Perspective*. National Bureau of Economic Research, 1962.

———. *Birth and Fortune: The Impact of Numbers on Personal Welfare*. 2nd ed. University of Chicago Press, 1987.

———. "Here Comes Another Baby Boom." *Wharton Magazine*, Summer 1979.

Edmundson, Mark. "Crashing the Academy." *The New York Times Magazine*, April 4, 1999.

Elder, Glen. *Children of the Great Depression: Social Change in Life Experience*. University of Chicago Press, 1974.

Elkington, John. *The Gene Factory: Inside the Genetic and Biotechnology Business*. Carroll & Graff, 1985.

Elliott, Michael. *The Day Before Yesterday: Reconsidering America's Past, Rediscovering the Present*. Simon & Schuster, 1996.

Emerson, Robert. *Fast Food: The Endless Shakeout*. Lebhar-Friedman, 1979.

Ernst, Morris. *Utopia, 1976*. Rinehart, 1955.

Evans, Christopher. *The Making of the Micro: A History of the Computer*. Van Nostrand Reinhold, 1981.

"Expense Accounts." *Harvard Business Review*, Vol. 38 (2), March–April 1960, p. 6.

Falk, Bennett. *The Internet Roadmap*. Sybex Inc., 1994.

Farr, J. Michael. *America's Top Jobs for People Without College Degrees*. 3rd ed. JIST Works, 1997.

Ferman, Louis, Joyce Kornbluh, and Alan Haber, eds. *Poverty in America: A Book of Readings*. University of Michigan Press, 1965.

Feuss, Claude M. "Perils of Conformity." *Saturday Review of Literature*, Vol. 35 (2), January 12, 1952, p. 7.

Florida, Richard, and Martin Kenney. "Silicon Valley and Routes 128 Won't Save Us." *California Management Review*, Vol. 33, no. 1, Fall 1990, pp. 68ff.

Forester, Tom, ed. *The Information Technology Revolution*. MIT Press, 1985.

Fortune, eds. "Preview of the Postwar Generation." *Fortune*, Vol. 27 (3), March 1943, p. 116.

———. "The Fortune Survey." Vol. 33 (4), April 1946, p. 266.

———. "Metropolitan Life Makes Housing Pay: How to Order a City." Vol. 33 (4), April 1946, p. 133.

———. "Where is Prefabrication?" Vol. 33 (4), April 1946, p. 127.

———. "Mr. Wyatt's Shortage." Vol. 33 (4), April 1946, p. 105.

———. "The Boom." Vol. 33 (6), June 1946, p. 97.

———. "American Youth: Its Outlook Is Changing the World." Vol. 79 (1). January 1969, special ed.

———. "The Egghead Millionaires." Vol. 62 (3), September 1960, p. 172.

———. *The Changing American Market*. Hanover House. 1955.

Foster, William, and Waddell Catchings. "The Dilemma of Thrift." *Atlantic Monthly*, Vol. 137 (4), April 1926, pp. 533–543.

Frank, Robert. *Luxury Fever: Why Money Fails to Satisfy in an Era of Excess*. The Free Press, 1999.

Frederikson, Norman, and William Schrader. *Adjustment to College: A Study of 10,000 Veteran and Nonveteran Students in Sixteen American Colleges*. Educational Testing Service, 1951.

Freedman, David H. "Net vs. Norm. Nothing but Homework." *Forbes ASAP*. February 22, 1999, pp. 31ff.

Friedan, Betty. *The Feminine Mystique*. W. W. Norton, 1963.

Fulwood, Sam. *Waking from the Dream: My Life in the Black Middle Class*. Anchor Books, 1996.

Galbraith, John K. *The Affluent Society*. Houghton Mifflin, 1958.

————. *American Capitalism*. Rev. ed. Houghton Mifflin, 1956.

————. *The New Industrial State*. Houghton Mifflin, 1967.

Galanoy, Terry. *Charge It: Inside the Credit Card Conspiracy*. G. P. Putnam's Sons, 1980.

Gans, Herbert. *The Levittowners: Ways of Life and Politics in a New Suburban Community*. Pantheon Books, 1982.

Garreau, Joel. *The Nine Nations of North America*. Houghton Mifflin, 1981.

Gibson, William. *Neuromancer*. Ace, 1984.

Gilder, George. *Wealth and Poverty*. Basic Books, 1981.

Gimbel, John. *The Origins of the Marshall Plan*. Stanford University Press, 1976.

Ginzberg, Eli, et al. *Life Styles of Educated Women*. Columbia University Press, 1966.

Gitlin, Todd. *The Sixties: Years of Hope, Days of Rage*. Bantam Books, 1987.

Goldman, Eric F. *The Crucial Decade: America 1945–1955*. Knopf, 1956.

Goldsmith, Raymond. *The National Wealth of the United States in the Postwar Period*. Princeton University Press, 1962.

Goodman, Jack, ed. *While You Were Gone: A Report on Wartime Life in the United States*. Simon & Schuster, 1946.

Goulden, Joseph C. *The Best Years: 1945–1950*. Atheneum, 1976.

Graham, Lawrence. *Our Kind of People: Inside America's Black Upper Class*. HarperCollins, 1999.

Grant, James. *Money of the Mind: Borrowing and Lending in America from the Civil War to Michael Milken*. Farrar Straus & Giroux, 1992.

Green, Timothy. *The World of Gold Today*. Walker & Company, 1973.

Gunderson, Gerald. *The Wealth Creators: An Entrepreneurial History of the United States*. E. P. Dutton & Co, 1989.

Gunther, John. *Inside U.S.A.* Harper, 1947.

Hacker, Andrew. *The End of the American Era*. Atheneum, 1970.

————. *Money: Who Has How Much and Why*. Scribner's, 1997.

Hafner, Katie, and Matthew Lyon. *Where Wizards Stay Up Late: The Origins of the Internet*. Simon & Schuster, 1996.

Hale, W. H. "Back to Nature With Two Cars: Exurbanites." *Reporter*. November 3, 1956.

Hall, John T., ed. *REITs: The First Decade: A Collection of Writings*. Mequon, 1974.

Handel, Samuel. *The Electronic Revolution*. Penguin, 1967.

Hanson, Dirk. *The New Alchemists: Silicon Valley and the Microelectrics Revolution*. Little, Brown, 1982.

Harrington, Michael. *The Other America; Poverty in the United States*. Macmillan, 1962.

Harris, Seymour. *The European Recovery Program*. Harvard University Press, 1948.

Hart, Jeffrey. *When the Going was Good! American Life in the Fifties*. Crown, 1982.

Hauben, Michael, and Ronda Hauben. *Netizens: On the History and Impact of Usenet and the Internet*. IEEE Computer Society Press, 1997.

Heilbroner, Robert. *Business Civilization in Decline*. W. W. Norton, 1976.

———. *The Quest for Wealth: A Study of Acquisitive Man*. Simon & Schuster, 1956.

Helitzer, Melvin, and Carl Heyel. *The Youth Market: Its Dimensions, Influence, and Opportunities for You*. Media Books, 1970.

Heller, L. G. *The Death of the American University: With Special Reference to the Collapse of the City College of New York*. Arlington House, 1973.

Heller, Robert. *The Age of the Common Millionaire*. Truman Talley Books/ E. P. Dutton, 1988.

Hertz, Louis. *The Toy Collector*. Funk & Wagnalls, 1969.

Hilsman, Roger. *To Move a Nation: The Politics of Foreign Policy in the Administration of John F. Kennedy*. Doubleday, 1967.

Hiltzik, Michael. *Dealers of Lightning: Xerox PARC and the Dawn of the Computer Age*. HarperBusiness, 1999.

Hochschild, Jennifer. *What's Fair: American Beliefs about Distributive Justice*. Harvard University Press, 1981.

Hodgson, Godfrey. *America in Our Time*. Doubleday, 1976.

Hofstadter, Richard. *The American Political Tradition and the Men Who Made It*. Knopf, 1948.

Selected Bibliography

Hogan, Michael. *The Marshall Plan: America, Britain and the Reconstruction of Western Europe, 1947–1952.* Cambridge University Press, 1987.

Horowitz, David, ed. *Corporations and the Cold War.* Monthly Review Press, 1970.

Horowitz, Irving Louis. *The Struggle Is the Message: The Organization and Ideology of the Anti-War Movement.* Glendessary Press, 1970.

Howard, Ted, and Jeremy Rifkin. *Who Should Play God: The Artificial Creation of Life and What It Means for the Future of the Human Race.* Dell Books, 1977.

Hunter, Floyd. *The Big Rich and the Little Rich.* Doubleday, 1965.

Institute for Econometric Research. *Mutual Fund Forecaster,* February 5, 1999.

Issel, William. *Social Change in the United States, 1945–1983.* Schocken, 1985.

Ivins, David. "Rampaging Rustics." *The New York Times,* February 25, 1999, p. A27.

Jakle, John, and Keith Sculle. *The Gas Station in America.* Johns Hopkins University Press, 1994.

Jakle, John A., et al. *The Motel in America.* Johns Hopkins University Press, 1996.

Jezer, Marty. *The Dark Ages: Life in the United States, 1945–1960.* South End Press, 1982.

Johnson, Warren. *The Future Is Not What It Used to Be: Returning to Traditional Values in an Age of Scarcity.* Dodd Mead, 1985.

Johnston, Moira. *Roller Coaster: The Bank of America and the Future of American Banking.* Ticknor & Fields, 1990.

Jones, Arthur. *The Decline of Capital.* Cromwell, 1976.

Jones, Constance, and the Philip Lief Group. *The 200 Best Franchises to Buy.* Rev. ed. Bantam Books, 1993.

Jones, Landon. *Great Expectations: America and the Baby Boom Generation.* Coward, McCann & Geoghegan, 1980.

Judson, Horace. *The Eighth Day of Creation: Makers of the Revolution in Biology.* Simon & Schuster, 1979.

Kahin, Brian, and James Keller, eds. *Public Access to the Internet*. MIT Press, 1995.

Kahn, Herman. *The Coming Boom: Economic, Political and Social*. Simon & Schuster, 1982.

Kearns, Doris. *Lyndon Johnson and the American Dream*. Harper & Row, 1976.

Keats, John. *The Crack in the Picture Window*. Houghton Mifflin, 1956.

———. *The Insolent Chariots*. Lippincott, 1958.

Kehrer, Daniel. *The Cautious Investor's Guide to Profits in Precious Metals*. Times Books, 1985.

Keniston, Kenneth. *Young Radicals: Notes on Committed Youth*. Harcourt, Brace & World, 1968.

Kennedy, David. *Freedom from Fear: The American People in Depression and War, 1929–1945*. Oxford University Press, 1998.

Kennedy, Edward D. *The Automobile Industry: The Coming Age of Capitalism's Favorite Child*. Reynal & Hitchcock, 1941.

Kenney, Martin. *Biotechnology: The University-Industrial Complex*. Yale University Press, 1986.

Kerouac, Jack. *The Dharma Bums*. Viking Press, 1958.

———. *On the Road*. Viking Press, 1957.

Kimmel, Lewis. *Share Ownership in the United States*. Brookings Institute, 1952.

Kolko, Gabriel. *Wealth and Power in America: An Analysis of Social Class and Income Distribution*. Praeger, 1962.

Kristof, Kathy. "Small Savings Can Bring Bigger Fortunes." *Newsday*, February 21, 1999, p. F17.

Kristol, Irving. "The 20th Century Began in 1945." *The New York Times Magazine*, May 2, 1965.

Kroc, Ray. *Grinding It Out: The Making of McDonald's*. St. Martin's Press, 1977.

Kroll, Ed, ed. *The Whole Internet: User's Guide and Catalog*. O'Reilly & Associates, 1992.

Krugman, Paul R. *The Age of Diminished Expectations: U.S. Economic Policy in the 1990s*. MIT Press, 1990.

Kuttner, Robert. "The Declining Middle Class." *The Atlantic Monthly*, Vol. 252, July 1983, pp. 60–64.

Lamott, Kenneth Church. *The Moneymakers: The Great Big New Rich in America*. Little, Brown, 1969.

Lampe, David, ed. *The Massachusetts Miracle: High Technology and Economic Revitalization*. MIT Press, 1988.

Lampman, Robert. "Changes in the Share of Wealth Held by Top Wealth-Holders, 1922–1956." *Review of Economics and Statistics*, Vol. 41 (4), November 1959, pp. 379–392.

———. *The Share of Top Wealth-Holders in National Wealth, 1922–1956*. Princeton University Press, 1962.

Lapham, Lewis H. *Money and Class in America: Notes and Observations on Our Civil Religion*. Weidenfeld & Nicholson, 1988.

LaQuey, Tracy, with Jeanne C. Ryer. *The Internet Companion: A Beginner's Guide to Global Networking*. Addison-Wesley, 1993.

Lasch, Christopher. *The Agony of the American Left*. Knopf, 1969.

———. *The Culture of Narcissism: American Life in an Age of Diminishing Expectations*. W. W. Norton, 1979.

Lasch, Robert. *Breaking the Building Blockade*. University of Chicago Press, 1946.

Leech, Kenneth. *Youthquake: The Growth of a Counter-Culture Through Two Decades*. Littlefield, Adams, 1977.

Leinberger, Paul, and Bruce Tucker. *The New Individualists: The Generation After the Organization Man*. HarperCollins, 1991.

Lerner, Max. *America as a Civilization*. Simon & Schuster, 1957.

Leuchtenberg, William. *A Troubled Feast: American Society Since 1945*. Little, Brown, 1983.

Levy, Frank. *Dollars and Dreams: The Changing American Income Distribution*. W. W. Norton, 1988.

Levy, Stephen. *Hackers: Heroes of the Computer Revolution*. Doubleday, 1984.

Lewis, Peter. *The Fifties*. Lippincott, 1978.

Light, Paul. *Baby Boomers*. W. W. Norton, 1988.

Linzmeyer, Owen. *Apple Confidential: The Real Story of Apple Computer, Inc.* No Starch Press, 1999.

Longman, Phillip. *Born to Pay: The New Politics of Aging in America.* Houghton Mifflin, 1987.

Lundberg, Ferdinand. *The Rich and the Super-Rich: A Study in the Power of Money.* Lyle Stuart, 1968.

Luttwak, Edward. *Turbo-Capitalism: Winners and Losers in the Global Economy.* HarperCollins, 1999.

Lyon, Cody. "Sprawl Spoils More than Beauty." *The New York Times,* February 25, 1999, p. 26.

MacLeish, Archibald. *Housing America by the Editors of* Fortune *Magazine.* Harcourt Brace, 1932.

McCreary, Edward A. *The Americanization of Europe: The Impact of Americans and American Business on the Uncommon Market.* Doubleday, 1964.

McLaughlin, Steven, et al. *The Changing Lives of American Women.* University of North Carolina Press, 1988.

McMenamin, Brigid. "The Tyranny of the Diploma." *Forbes,* Vol. 162, no. 14, December 28, 1998, pp. 104–109.

McQuaid, Kim. *Big Business and Presidential Power: From FDR to Reagan.* William Morrow & Co, 1982.

Maccoby, Michael. *The Gamesman: The New Corporate Leaders.* Simon & Schuster, 1976.

MacPherson, Myra. *Long Time Passing: Vietnam and the Haunted Generation.* New American Library, 1984.

Malabre, Alfred L. *Beyond Our Means: How America's Long Years of Debt, Deficits and Reckless Borrowing Now Threaten to Overwhelm Us.* Random House, 1987.

Malone, Michael. *Infinite Loop: How the World's Most Insanely Great Computer Company Went Insane.* Doubleday, 1999.

Mandell, Lewis. *The Credit Card Industry: A History.* Twayne Publishers, 1990.

Marcus, George. *Lives in Trust: The Fortunes of Dynastic Families in Late Twentieth Century America.* Westview Press, 1992.

Marglin, Stephen, and Juliet Schor, eds. *The Golden Age of Capitalism.* Clarendon Press, 1990.

Markoff, John. "Saying Goodbye, Good Riddance to Silicon Valley." *The New York Times,* January 17, 1999, Section 3, p. 1.

Matusow, Allen J. *Nixon's Economy: Booms, Busts, Dollars, and Votes*. University of Kansas Press, 1998.

————. *The Unraveling of America: A History of Liberalism in the 1960s*. Harper & Row, 1984.

Mayer, Martin. "The Theory of the Leisure Class." *Esquire*, Vol. 59, no. 3, March 1963, pp. 16–26.

Mebane, John. *Collecting Nostalgia: The First Guide to the Antiques of the 30s and 40s*. Popular Library, 1972.

————. *New Horizons in Collecting*. Barnes, 1964.

Medved, Michael, and David Wallenchinsky. *What Really Happened to the Class of 65*. Random House, 1976.

Miller, Herman. *Income of the American People*. John Wiley & Sons, 1955.

Mills, C. Wright. *The Power Elite*. Oxford University Press, 1956.

Mills, D. Quinn. *The New Competitors: A Report on American Managers from D. Quinn Mills of the Harvard Business School*. John Wiley & Sons, 1985.

Mintz, Morton, and Jerry Cohen. *America Inc.: Who Owes and Operates the United States*. Dial Press, 1971.

Moravec, Hans P. *Robot: Mere Machine to Transcendent Mind*. Oxford University Press, 1999.

Moynihan, Daniel Patrick. *Family and Nation*. Harcourt Brace Jovanovich, 1986.

Naisbitt, John. *Megatrends: Ten New Directions Transforming Our Lives*. Warner Books, 1982.

Nau, Henry R. *The Myth of America's Decline: Leading the World Economy into the 1990s*. Oxford University Press, 1990.

Newcomer, Mabel. *The Big Business Executive: The Factors That Made Him, 1900–1950*. Columbia University Press, 1955.

Niskanen, William A. *Reagonomics: An Insider's Account of the Policies and the People*. Oxford University Press, 1988.

Nocera, Joseph. *A Piece of the Action: How the Middle Class Joined the Money Class*. Simon & Schuster, 1994.

Oglesby, Carl, ed. *The New Left Reader*. Grove Press, 1969.

Olson, Keith. *The G.I. Bill, the Veterans and the Colleges*. University of Kentucky Press, 1974.

O'Neill, William. *American High: The Years of Confidence, 1945–1960*. Free Press, 1986.

———. *Coming Apart: An Informal History of America in the 1960s*. Quadrangle Books Press, 1971.

O'Rourke, P. J. *Eat the Rich*. Atlantic Monthly Press, 1998.

Orsenigo, Luigi. *The Emergence of Biotechnology*. St. Martin's Press, 1989.

Packard, Vance. *The Hidden Persuaders*. David McKay, 1957.

———. *The Ultra-Rich: How Much is Too Much?* Little, Brown, 1989.

Patterson, James. *Mr. Republican: A Biography of Robert A. Taft*. Houghton Mifflin, 1972.

Peal, David. *Access the Internet*. Sybex, 1994.

Peterson, Peter G. *Gray Dawn: How the Coming Age Wave Will Transform America—And the World*. Times Books, 1999.

Phillips, Kevin P. *The Politics of Rich and Poor: Wealth and the American Electorate in the Reagan Aftermath*. Random House, 1990.

Pines, Burton Yale. *Back to Basics: The Traditionalist Movement that is Sweeping Grass-roots America*. William Morrow & Co., 1982.

Postrel, Virginia. *The Future and Its Enemies: The Growing Conflict Over Creativity, Enterprise, and Progress*. Free Press, 1998.

Potter, David Morris. *People of Plenty: Economic Abundance and the American Character*. University of Chicago Press, 1954.

Preer, Robert W. *The Emergence of Technopolis: Knowledge-Intensive Technologies and Regional Development*. Praeger, 1992.

Randall, Neil. *The Soul of the Internet: Net Gods and the Wiring of the World*. International Thomson Computer Press, 1997.

Rees, Goronwy. *The Multimillionaires: Six Studies in Wealth*. Macmillan, 1961.

Reich, Charles. *The Greening of America*. Random House, 1970.

Reich, Robert. *The Next American Frontier*. Times Books, 1983.

Reid, Robert H. *Architects of the Web: 1,000 Days That Built the Future of Business*. John Wiley & Sons, 1997.

Riesman, David, with Reuel Denney and Nathan Glazer. *The Lonely Crowd*. Doubleday, 1953.

Reiter, Ester, and Richard Slye. *Making Fast Food*. McGill Queens University Press, 1991.

Selected Bibliography

Rheingold, Howard. *The Virtual Community: Homesteading on the Electronic Frontier*. Addison-Wesley, 1993.

Riordan, Michael, and Lillian Hoddeson. *Crystal Fire: The Birth of the Information Age*. W. W. Norton, 1997.

Rochlin, Gene I. *Trapped in the Net: The Unanticipated Consequences of Computerization*. Princeton University Press, 1997.

Rogers, Everett M., and Judith K. Larsen. *Silicon Valley Fever: Growth of High-Technology Culture*. Basic Books, 1984.

Rohatyn, Felix G. *The Twenty-Year Century: Essays on Economics and Public Finance*. Random House, 1983.

Rosegrant, Susan, and David Lampe. *Route 128: Lessons from Boston's High-Tech Community*. Basic Books, 1992.

Ross, Davis. *Preparing for Ulysses: Politics and Veterans During World War II*. Columbia University Press, 1969.

Roszak, Theodore. *The Making of a Counter Culture: Reflections on the Technocratic Society and Its Youthful Opposition*. Doubleday, 1969.

Rugg, Donald, and Norman Hale. *The Dow-Jones-Irwin Guide to Mutual Funds*. Dow-Jones-Irwin, 1983.

Russell, Louise. *The Baby Boom Generation and the Economy*. Brookings Institute, 1982.

Sargent, Lyman Tower. *New Left Thought: An Introduction*. Dorsey Press, 1972.

Sarnoff, Paul. *Trading in Gold: How to Buy, Sell, and Profit in the Gold Market*. Simon & Schuster, 1981.

Satin, Joseph. *The 1950s: America's "Placid" Decade*. Houghton Mifflin, 1960.

Saxenian, Annalee. *Regional Advantage: Culture and Competition in Silicon Valley and Route 128*. Harvard University Press, 1994.

Sayles, Leonard. *Individualism and Big Business*. McGraw-Hill, 1963.

Schervish, Paul G., Platon Coutsoukis and Ethan Lewis. *Gospels of Wealth: How the Rich Portray Their Lives*. Praeger, 1994.

Schlosstein, Steven. *The End of the American Century*. Congdon & Weed, 1989.

Schonfeld, Erick. "The Bizarre New World of Chips." *Fortune*. March 1, 1999.

Schor, Juliet. *The Overspent American: Upscaling, Downshifting, and the New Consumer*. Basic Books, 1998.

Schwarz, John E. *America's Hidden Success: A Reassessment of Public Policy From Kennedy to Reagan*. W. W. Norton, 1988.

Scott, Allen. *Technopolis: High-Technology Industry and Regional Development in Southern California*. University of California Press, 1993.

Seltzer, Mildred M., ed. *The Impact of Increased Life Expectancy: Beyond the Gray Horizon*. Springer, 1995.

Shilling, A. Gray, and Kiril Sokoloff. *Is Inflation Ending? Are You Ready?* McGraw-Hill, 1983.

Shook, Robert. *The Entrepreneurs: Twelve Who Took Risks and Succeeded*. Harper & Row, 1980.

Siegfried, André. *America at Midcentury*. Harcourt, Brace, 1955.

Smith, Adam. *The Roaring 80s*. Summit Books, 1988.

Smith, James, and Stephen Franklin. "The Concentration of Personal Wealth, 1922–1969." *American Economic Review*. Vol. 2 (2), May 1974, pp. 162–167.

Sobel, Robert. *Dangerous Dreamers: The Financial Innovators from Charles Merrill to Michael Milken*. Wiley & Sons, 1993.

———. *The Manipulators: America in the Media Age*. Doubleday, 1976.

———. *The Worldly Economists*. Free Press, 1980.

Spectorsky, A. C. *The Exurbanites*. Lippincott, 1955.

Spock, Benjamin. *The Common Sense Book of Baby and Child Care*. The 3rd ed. Duell, Sloan & Pearce, 1957.

Stern, Philip M. *The Great Treasury Raid*. Random House, 1964.

Stoll, Clifford. *Silicon Snake Oil: Second Thoughts on the Information Highway*. Doubleday, 1995.

Straus, Nathan. *Two-Thirds of a Nation: A Housing Program*. Knopf, 1951.

Strobel, Frederick R. *Upward Dreams, Downward Mobility: The Economic Decline of the American Middle Class*. Rowman & Littlefield, 1993.

Stross, Randall E. *The Microsoft Way: The Real Story of How the Company Outsmarts Its Competition*. Addison-Wesley, 1996.

Sutton, Francis X., et al. *The American Business Creed*. Harvard University Press, 1956.

Selected Bibliography

Sylvester, Edward J., and Lynn C. Klotz. *The Gene Age: Genetic Engineering and the Next Industrial Revolution*. Scribner's, 1983.

Teachout, Terry, ed. *Beyond the Boom: New Voices on American Life, Culture, and Politics*. Poseidon Press, 1990.

Teitelman, Robert. *Gene Dreams: Wall Street, Academia, and the Rise of Biotechnology*. Basic Books, 1989.

Thompson, Jacqueline. *Future Rich: The People, Companies, and Industries Creating America's Next Fortunes*. William Morrow & Co, 1985.

Thorndike, Joseph. *The Very Rich: A History of Wealth*. American Heritage, 1976.

Toffler, Alvin. *Future Shock*. Random House, 1970.

———. *The Third Wave*. William Morrow & Co., 1980.

Train, John. *The Money Masters*. Harper & Row, 1980.

Tuckman, Howard. *The Economics of the Rich*. Random House, 1973.

Ullman, John E., ed. *The Improvement of Productivity: Myths and Realities*. Praeger, 1980.

———. *The Prospects of American Industrial Recovery*. Quorum Books, 1985.

Unger, Irwin, and Debi Unger. *Turning Point: 1968*. Scribner's, 1988.

———. *The Movement: A History of the American New Left, 1959–1972*. Dodd, Mead, 1974.

Vatter, Harold, and John Walker, eds. *History of the U.S. Economy Since World War II*. Sharpe, 1996.

Vaughn, Charles. *Franchising: Its Nature, Scope, Advantages, and Development*. Lexington, 1979.

Wachter, Susan M., ed. *Social Security and Private Pensions: Providing for Retirement in the Twenty-First Century*. Lexington, 1988.

Wagner, Walter. *Money Talks: How Americans Get It, Use It, and Abuse It*. Bobbs-Merrill, 1978.

Warner, W. Lloyd, and James Abegglen. *Big Business Leaders in America*. Atheneum, 1963.

Warshofsky, Fred. *The Chip War: The Battle for the World of Tomorrow*. Scribner, 1989.

Watson, James D. *The Double Helix: A Personal Account of the Discovery of the Structure of DNA*. Atheneum, 1968.

Selected Bibliography

Wattenberg, Benjamin J., with Richard M. Scammon. *This U.S.A.: An Unexpected Family Portrait of 194,067,296 Americans Drawn from the Census*. Doubleday, 1965.

Wecter, Dixon. *When Johnny Comes Marching Home*. Houghton Mifflin, 1944.

Weiss, Michael. *The Clustering of America*. Harper & Row, 1988.

Weissman, Rudolph Leo. *The New Wall Street*. Arno Press, 1975.

Welch, Finis. "Effect and Cohort Size on Warnings: The Baby Boom Babies' Financial Bust." *Journal of Political Economy*, Vol. 87, no. 5, pt. 2, October 1979, pp. 565–597.

Whyte, William H. *The Organization Man*. Simon & Schuster, 1956.

Wilson, Sloan. *The Man in the Gray Flannel Suit*. Amereon House, 1955.

Wormser, Rene Albert. "How to Save Money by Giving It Away: Excerpts from Personal Estate Planning in a Changing World." *U.S. News & World Report*, Vol. 41, December 28, 1956, pp. 106–139.

Wriston, Walter. *Risk and Other Four-Letter Words*. Harper & Row, 1986.

Wyckoff, D. Daryl, and W. Earl Sasser. *The Chain-Restaurant Industry*. Lexington, 1978.

Wyllie, Irvin G. *The Self-Made Man in America; The Myth of Rags to Riches*. Rutgers University Press, 1954.

Yates, Gayle G. *What Women Want: The Ideas of the Movement*. Harvard University Press, 1975.

Young, Jeffrey. *Forbes Greatest Technology Stories: Inspiring Tales of the Entrepreneurs and Inventors Who Revolutionized Modern Business*. John Wiley, 1998.

INDEX

Index

Bankers, 163–64. *see also* Investment
   bankers
Banks, and credit cards, 192–93
Barron's, 182
Bartlett, Donald, 334
Bear Stearns, 329
Beatrice, 319
Beats, 19, 265–66, 275, 354
Beaumont, Texas, race riots, 64
Beckman Instruments, 212, 214
Bell, Daniel, 114
Bell Laboratories, 214
Belridge Oil, 321
Bendix, William, 124
Benham, James, 303
Bent, Bruce, 303
Berle, Adolf A., Jr., 24–25
Berners-Lee, Tim, 393–94
Best Years of Our Lives, The (film), 57, 60
Biller, Moe, 231–32, 238
Biogen, 387
Biotechnology, 383, 384–87
Birth rate, 26, 61, 116–17, 258–59
Black Power movement, 267
Blacks, 38; and brokerages, 158,
   168–69; and corporate jobs, 268;
   and education, 268, 364, 348; and
   franchise boom, 158; and home
   buying, 77, 94–96, 157–58; middle
   class, 417–18; postwar racism
   against, 63–67; rights of, 262; and
   suburbs, 363; unemployment, 63.
   See also Civil rights movement
Blue chip stocks, 179–80
Blue-collar families, 39; and automobile
   imports, 251–52; income and
   ambitions of postwar, 123–24; job
   loss, 261; and student movement of
   1960s, 273–74; TV shows about,
   132–33
Bonds, 131, 171
Bonfire of the Vanities, The (Wolfe), 135
Bradley, Gen. Omar, 47
Bristol Myers, 386
Brokaw, Tom, 406
Brokers, 159, 164, 167, 326; and blacks,
   158, 168–69; discount, 305; and
   Internet, 396–97; and new issues,
   184; revolutionized by Merrill
   Lynch, 166–69
Brooks, John, 133–34
Brown, Henry, 303
Brown, H. Rap, 267
Brown v. Board of Education, 266

Bruce, Ailsa, 134
Bruck, Connie, 329
Buchanan, Pat, 208
BUNCH, 198, 202
Bureau of Labor Statistics, 255, 334
Burger King, 146
Burroughs, 198
Burtless, Gary, 337
Bush, George (father), 55, 363
Bush, George W., 1
Bush, Vannevar, 20, 212
Bushnell, Nolan, 199, 205
Business-cycle theory, 32
Business Week, 173, 174–75
Byte Shop, 199–200

Calculators, 199
California, 45, 209, 218, 253
Cannon, Lou, 238
Cannon Couseling Group, 354
Capital gains, 172, 173
Capital investment, 46
Capitalism, 24, 59–60
Capital Preservation Fund, 303
Carmichael, Stokely, 267, 268
Carnegie, Andrew, 137, 399
Carr, Fred, 187
Carter, Jimmy, 55, 111, 306–7
"Case Against Home Ownership, The"
   (Chase), 86–87
Cash Campus Schools, 348
Castro, Fidel, 263
Catalog sales, 400–1
Catchings, Waddell, 114
Census Bureau, 12, 334, 353
Center for Integrated Systems, 214
Certificates of deposit, 304
Cetus Corp., 384, 386–87, 404
Chambers, Frank, 177
Chan, Savio, 366–67
Charles Schwab, 305
Charter schools, 346–47
Chase, Stuart, 53, 56, 86–87
Chevron, 322–23
Chicago Board of Trade, 292
Chicago Board Options Exchange, 305–6
Chicago Mercantile exchange, 306
Children, 110–11, 239
Christian Nationalist Party, 54
Chrysler, 45, 106, 108
CIA, 55, 269
Cisco Systems, 212, 394, 404
City College of New York, 38, 51
Civil Rights Acts, 266

Index

Index

Index

Index

Index

Index

Index

Index

Index

Index